ECONOMICS
FOR EVERYONE
SEVENTH EDITION

"Economics is the Study of Mankind in the Ordinary Business of Life" Alfred Marshall

"*The definition of insanity is doing the same thing over and over again and expecting different result.*"
Albert Einstein

RICHARD E. CARMICHAEL, PH.D.

Copyright © by Richard E. Carmichael - 2017

All rights reserved. No part of this book may be reproduced in any form or by any means, electronic or mechanical, including information storage and retrieval systems without permission in writing from the publisher. No liability is assumed with respect to the use of the information contained herein.

Printed in the United States of America

Library of Congress Cataloging-in Publication Data

Carmichael, Richard E.

Economics for Everyone Six Edition
Richard E. Carmichael
Includes biographical references and index.
Library of Congress Control Number: TX 6-454-782
ISBN: 978-1974672905

R. Carmichael Company
Conover, North Carolina
August, 2017

Economics for Everyone Seventh Edition is also, available for the Amazon Kindle, in PDF format.

ACKNOWLEDGMENT

I would like to thank my wife Kay for the numerous hours that they spent proofreading and making suggestions for improving the readability of this book. Kay has a degree in Languages and was instrumental in editing this book.

The Internet was used extensively to obtain the latest government data on domestic and international trade. The major sources of Data for the book were from the Bureau of Economic Analysis, The President's 2017 Budget and The Department of Labor. Many of the pictures of the classical economists were made available through the McMaster University Economic History database located in Hamilton, Ontario, Canada.

INTRODUCTION

In the twenty-first century, market niche competition will give way to head-to head competition among the industrial giants of the world. The key to competing in this environment will be the ability to create and sustain a competitive advantage over a company or country's economic rivals. Each country has a unique culture that determines how it approaches the marketplace. This will require that industrialized countries look to its history to determine its strengths and weaknesses, its opportunities and threats, relative to the competition.

The purpose of this book is to provide the reader with an easy to understand description of the basic theories of economics, including the latest data available on the United States economy. An additional purpose is to examine the evolution of economic thought and the historical events that affected the economic growth of the world's industrialized countries, with emphasis of the United States.

This is not a book about government, or industry. The major theories of micro and macroeconomics are discussed but the major emphasis is how these theories were developed and taught by those economists who invented them in the first place.

The book is available in both electronic and paperback formats. The electronic version is in both the Kindle and E-Nook Reader format. The paperback version is available through Amazon.com and Barnes and Noble. The book is published on a "print on demand" basis. This enables the book to be completely updated every year with the latest available economic data.

BRIEF TABLE OF CONTENTS

CP
NO   CHAPTER TITLES

Part I. – Introduction to Microeconomics
1. The Economic Way of Thinking
2. Demand, Supply and Elasticity
3. Production and Costs

Part II. – Classical Economics
4. The Foundations of Classical Economics
5. Finance and Banking (1800-1913)
6. The Evolution of Classical Economics
7. Neoclassical Economics

Part III. – Macroeconomics
8. Franklin Roosevelt and the New Deal
9. Keynesian Economics
10. National Income Accounting and Forecasting
11. Inflation and Monetarism
12. Ronald Reagan and the 1980's
13. National Debt and International Trade Deficits
14. Economics and Public Choice
15. Economic Growth and Employment

Part IV. – Money and Banking
16. Money and The Federal Reserve
17. Economics in the Twenty-First Century – The George W. Bush Administration.
18. Economics in the Twenty-First Century – Barack Obama And Donald Trump.

LIST OF TABLES AND FIGURES

Table:		Page
2-1	Prices and Quantity of Chicken	15
3-1	Production Possibilities for Rifles and Chicken	31
3-2	The Production Function and Total Cost of Ricardo's Pizza Store	34
3-3	Fixed and Variable Costs of Producing Bagels	36
3-4	Analysis of Profit	40
10-1	National Income Accounting Source and Use of Funds Statement 2016	123
11-1	Nominal and Real GDP	133
13-1	U.S. Asian Trade	159
13-2	Net Exports from 1990 through 2016	163
13-3	U.S. Balance of Payments for 2016	164
13-4	Federal Debt Outstanding 2006 – 2016	166
13-5	Gross National Debt Percent of GDP From 1990 through 2016	173
13-6	Change in Federal Debt	175
15-1	Calculation of the Unemployment Rate	195
15-2	Unemployment Rate by Group	196
15-3	Industry Payroll Employment	199
15-4	Trends in the Payroll and Household Survey	202
16-1	Money Stock Measures	208
16-2	Federal Reserve Balance Sheet 2016 vs. 2015	212
17.1	Treasury's Activity for the Troubled Asset Relief Program	237
17-2	Economic Stimulus Plan Distribution of Expenditures	239
17-3	Proposed Federal Budget for 2017	240
17-4	Real Gross Domestic Product for 2015	250

Figure:		Page
2-1	The Demand Curve for Whole Chickens	16
2-2	Supply Curve for Perdue Whole Chickens	18
2-3	Demand, Supply and Equilibrium	19
17-1	Gross Federal Debt Outstanding	166

LIST OF PHOTOGRAPHS

Photographs were provided by the McMaster University (Hamilton, Ontario Canada), Economic History Database. Additional photographs are from the Biographical File at the U.S. Library of Congress.

Description

1. John Maynard Keynes
2. Alfred Marshall
3. Joseph Schumpeter
4. Jean Baptiste Say
5. Adam Smith
6. Herbert Spencer
7. William G. Sumner
8. Karl Marx
9. Andrew Carnegie
10. Ronald Reagan
11. John D. Rockefeller
12. Franklin D. Roosevelt
13. Milton Friedman
14. David Ricardo
15. Thomas Malthus
16. Henry George
17. Thorstein Veblen
18. Jeremy Bentham
19. John Stewart Mills

RICHARD E. CARMICHAEL, Ph.D.

ABOUT THE AUTHOR

Richard Carmichael is a professor in the College of Business Degree Completion Program at Gardner-Webb University. He previously served as the Alex Lee Professor of Business at Lenoir-Rhyne College. He also served as a Visiting Professor of Finance at Washington College in Chestertown, MD and a Faculty Associate with the Johns Hopkins University Division of Business in Baltimore, MD. He has had teaching assignments in American Economic History, Strategic Management, Business Economics, International Business, Small Business Management and Financial Markets and Institutions.

In addition, Dr. Carmichael has over twenty years of business experience in the fields of Financial Management, Economic Forecasting and Marketing. He has held executive positions with First Interstate Bank of California as Vice President of Strategic Planning and Marketing, BankAmerica Corp., as Vice President of Market Planning and Research, Manufacturers Hanover Corp. as Financial Economists for the Bank's National Division. Also, he has over ten years' experience with the U.S. Government as Budget Manager for the U.S. Bankruptcy Court in Maryland and as Branch Chief for Credit Programs for the Small Business Administration in Washington, DC. He holds BS in Economics, an MBA in Financial Management and a Ph.D. in Business Administration

CHAPTER 1

THE ECONOMIC WAY OF THINKING

"Political Economy or Economics is a study of mankind in the ordinary business of life." --Alfred Marshall

WHAT IS ECONOMIC HISTORY

After World War II, the United States dominated the world in almost every aspect of global business. Mass marketing was effectively an American monopoly. American companies were superior in technology, their workers were better educated and more skilled, and American managers were the best educated and trained in the world. The United States was clearly the world leader in manufacturing in both new product and new process development. In the twentieth century, almost everything that plugged into an electrical outlet was invented in America and this country was the clear leader in determining what new products would be manufactured and how they would be made. However, America no longer dominates the world in the field of new process engineering. Japan's consumer electronics industry is now the most productive in the world and the three largest chemical companies in the world are in Germany. American Scholars invented one of today's most prevalent management theories "Total Quality Management," but its application was perfected in Japan.

America has lost its position of total world dominance in manufacturing. There is now a three-way race between the European Union, Japan, and the United States. The race is to determine who will be the leader of the industrial world in the twenty-first century. The question in the twenty-first century will not be who is perfect, but who is doing the best job, and who is creating the most value for its customers. In the nineteenth century, the American forte was not as the original inventor but as the innovators. American businessmen acquired technological processes from abroad and then experimented with them, often greatly improving on the original invention. The Europeans themselves were the first to recognize that the American approach was different. It was the Europeans, who coined the term the "American System." America is still in the best position to remain the industrial leader of the twenty-first century; however, there will be increased competition for world dominance from the European Union and Japan. America needs to look at the past, and to understand what made it the greatest county in the world. For it is only with an understanding of past events that a country can effectively plan for the future

The purpose of this book is to examine the evolution of economic thought and how historical events have affected the economic growth of the world's industrialized countries. The first step in this analysis is to examine the field of economics itself. First, the basic theory of modern day economics will be explored to give the reader some understanding of what economics is and what economic theory attempts to accomplish. The theories of many famous European and American economists are then described and placed in a historical context.

Economics has always been a reflection of historical events and has evolved as a field of study that proposes to explain current events. Therefore, the focus of this book is to trace the evolution of economics, referred to as Political Economics until 1776, and to examine how the evolution of economic belief explained the growth of the economies of the leading industrialized countries of the world. Our exploration of economic history will begin with ancient history, which traces political economics all the way back to the writings of Aristotle. However, the emphasis of the book is the United States, and its continuing debate as to the proper role of government in controlling economic activity. Still, this analysis will not arbitrarily end in the 1990's. In addition to attempting to explain the past, this book analyzes the strengths and weaknesses of the Industrial World's leading economies and provides a picture of what these countries might look like in the twenty-first century.

BASIC ECONOMIC TERMS AND THEORY

Economics can be defined as the social science that seeks to examine and understand the choices people make in using scarce resources to meet their demands. Economic history is the subject that deals with the ways in which man has used his limited resources to satisfy his wants and with the institutions he has developed to organize economic activity.

"Political Economy or Economics," according to Alfred Marshall, "is a study of mankind in the ordinary business of life".[1] However, for practical purposes, the scope of this book is limited to the analysis of the questions that are most commonly asked by economists and other interested persons. Central to the study of economics is the question of what determines prices, how proceeds of economic activity are distributed and what determines the share of income that goes to wages, profits, interest and rents.

In every economy, certain basic choices have to be made. Among these choices, the most important are what goods will be produced, how they will be produced, who will do which jobs and for whom the results of economic activity will be made available. Each of these choices is made necessary because of scarcity, and each can be used to introduce key elements of the historical as well as the current economic way of analyzing a situation. To define the economic way of thinking, exploring the key elements of economic analysis, is useful.

Deciding What to Produce

In any economy, the number of goods and services that could be provided is immense. The impossibility of producing as much of everything as people want reflects a scarcity of the productive resources that are used to make all goods. Many scarce productive resources must be combined to make even the simplest product or to produce a simple service. These productive resources are referred to by economists as the factors of production and are usually grouped by labor, capital and natural resources. Labor can be defined as the contribution to production made by people working with their minds and muscles. Labor can further be divided into those persons who organize the factors of production, i.e., the business owners, and those who actually perform the physical tasks required to produce a product, the workers.

Capital is the means of production that are created by people, including structures, machines, tools and systems. In economics, capital is defined as goods that are produced and used for the purpose of increasing the quantity of future goods. Natural Resources is anything that can be used as a productive input in its natural state, such as farmland, residential and commercial building sites, forests, fossil fuel and mineral deposits.

Deciding How to Produce

There is more than one way to produce almost any product. As a nation's economy advances, new methods of production are continually being developed. Business owners operate to make a profit. In order to make a profit, they have to find a way to allocate the factors of production efficiently. The owners of a business usually organize their company in an attempt to operate efficiently. Efficiency means producing a product with a minimum expense, effort and waste. However, over time, production potential can only be expanded by accumulating more of the factors of production and finding new technology to make the factors more productive. The act of increasing the economy's supply of production inputs made by people is known as capital investment. Investment is the act of increasing the economy's stock of capital. To accumulate capital, individuals have to save some of their income.[2]

Deciding Who Will Do the Work

The question of who will do the work, who will organize the tasks, who will develop the systems and who will do the physical work is a matter of organizing the social division of labor. Will everyone do everything independently, or will people cooperate? Economists answer these questions by pointing out that it is more efficient to cooperate. Three things make cooperation effective; they are, teamwork, learning by doing and comparative advantage. Teamwork requires that people work together to accomplish a task more efficiently than if they work independently. Learning by doing implies that people get better at some jobs by doing the work repeatedly. Comparative advantage is the ability to produce goods or services at a relatively lower opportunity cost than someone else.[3]

Deciding for Whom Goods and Services Will be Produced

In any economy, a decision has to be made about who will receive the benefits of production. Are goods and services to be distributed equally to everyone? Or are they to be sold to those willing and able to pay. If the goods produced are distributed only to those persons that are willing to pay, people with higher incomes will enjoy more and better products than people with lower incomes.

Distribution of purchasing power is never perfectly equal because some people have the financial resources to enjoy great quantities of goods and services. Other people, even in a nation as wealthy as the United States, live in poverty. No society has yet discovered how to provide equally for the demands of everyone, and at the same time, to provide the incentives that encourages high quality production and continued technological innovation.[4]

The question of distribution of output, among members of society, has implications in terms of both efficiency and fairness. Efficiency is the part of economics that is concerned with facts and the relationships among them. This is referred to as positive economics. However, a great portion of economic analysis is based on the fairness of distribution. This part of the analysis is called normative economics which is the area of economics that is devoted to judgments about which conditions and policies are good or bad.[5]

Additional Questions that Concern Economists

Another question that concerns many economists is what variables depress or stimulate total economic growth and what are the causes of the uneven levels of severity of business cycles? Also, emerging as a ponderable question is why it is so difficult in the modern economy to find useful employment for people that are willing and able to work.

In addition to these questions, the role of institutions such as business enterprises, banks and central banks, and government policies must be considered. All these questions, the solutions past, present, and the courses of action that are taken are the subject of economic history.

SCOPE OF THE BOOK

The study of economics is a study of change, from the merchant capitalism that preceded the American revolution, to the industrial revolution and the productivity revolution, through the Great Depression of the 1930's, two world wars, and culminating with the head to head competition of the modern day global economy.

Economics does not consist of one theory; it consists of many theories that have evolved throughout the history of the modern world. While examining every economic theory in the context of one book, is not possible, the objective of this work is to analyze historical events using the most prevalent economic theory and the most noted economist of the time under evaluation.

Modern history has often presented a stage for the debate of the role of government in the economy. In 1576, Jean Bodin defined the role of the leaders of the new "Nation-State," as maintaining the climate for economic growth, keeping taxes low, and defending the realm. In the mid-eighteenth century, a group of French Philosophers called the Physiocrates created the idea of an economic system as an interconnected and interdependent structure. Their system contained a controlling natural law of economic behavior, and a guiding rule of laissez faire, or a hands-off policy by government in the affairs of trade. In 1776, Adam Smith wrote "The Wealth of Nations," where he defined the role of government as a source of calculable law, a defender of the nation and a promoter of the freedom of internal and international trade.

In the nineteenth century, economists such as David Ricardo, John Stuart Mill, and Karl Marx, continued the debate which by that time was centered on the fairness of the distribution of profit between the workers and the capitalists. Alfred Marshall took the theories of the classical economists and developed economics as a separate field apart from politics, history and moral issues. Classical economics or neoclassical economics, as it was now called, supported the basic theory that there was a self-adjusting mechanism that prevented an economy from entering into a long and severe depression. Since, by theory, depression could not be sustained, it was not necessary for government to take an active role in controlling the economy.

During the Great Depression that started in 1929, the leading economists of the day urged their governments to do nothing to improve their economic situation. However, by 1933, the newly elected American president Franklin D. Roosevelt found an economy with 25 percent of its employable workers not able to find jobs. Roosevelt's solution was to put people to work in jobs provided by the federal government and the Federal Emergency Relief Administration was created for this purpose. By 1937, eight million Americans were employed by their government.

In 1936, a new economic theory was created by John Maynard Keynes in his book, "The General Theory of Employment, Interest, and Money." According to Keynes, it is not necessary to wait for the economy to self adjust to a depression. The government should take steps to overcome a shortage of total demand. In a depression, the desire of the federal government to balance their budget must give way to the need to stimulate economic growth. The great depression and the theories of Keynes started the transition of the United States and most of Europe, from the national state to the fiscal state. The depression gave rise to the belief that the national government should control its country's economic environment.

Joseph Schumpeter, a contemporary of Keynes, pointed out that as long as revenues were considered as a constraint, it was difficult for the government to act as either a social or economic agent. Following World War II, most developed countries adopted the theories of Keynesian economics. Keynes assumed that a wise and efficient government would apply sound fiscal policy. However, in the hands of modern day politicians, government has become the master of the individual in society.

In 1964 President Johnson passed the tax reduction plan that was proposed by John F. Kennedy. The result of the tax reductions was a decrease in the unemployment rate to 4 percent. In addition, in 1965 with the economy already running at nearly full capacity, Johnson instituted his "Great Society" social welfare program. At the same time America had begun a military involvement in South Vietnam which greatly increased defense spending. The combination of reduced taxes and increased spending led to the inflation of the 1970s.

In 1975, President Ford called into conference some of the country's better-known economists to prescribe a remedy for inflation, as there was a 13.5 percent increase in the consumer price index that year. The entire group agreed on only one remedy: government should remove any impediments to market competition. For practical effect this was no better than Ford's own prescription, which was wearing of buttons with the insignia (WIN – Whip Inflation Now). The Keynes system of using fiscal policy was proven in practice to be of limited value in fighting inflation. Keynes had assumed a benevolent government, however; Congress was not going to vote to increase taxes or to reduce expenditures to decrease inflation especially during elections. Consequently, there remained only one viable course of action to use monetary policy to control inflation.

In 1981 President Reagan's advisors urged him implement a program of supply-side economics. The basic premise of supply-side economics is that it places supply over demand in the hierarchy of economics and therefore deals with enhancing economic production, efficiency, and growth within the context of the marketplace. This change in economic policy became known as Reaganomics and consisted of four key elements designed to reverse the high-inflation, slow growth economy of the 1970s. The key elements were as follows: (1) A restrictive monetary policy engineered through the Federal Reserve; (2) the economic recovery Tax Act of 1981 including a 25 percent across the board tax cut; (3) A promise to balance the budget through domestic spending restraint; (4) A program to roll back many restrictive government regulations. During the 1980s the American economy produced 17 million new jobs. When Reagan left office in 1989, the unemployment rate had fallen to 5.5 percent, the inflation rate had fallen to 4.1 percent, the Dow Jones Industrial Index had doubled in value and America had reaffirmed its position as the world's preeminent economy. However, the economic progress came at a cost as the federal government accumulated over $2 trillion in debt during the Reagan administration.

Schumpeter warned in 1918, that the fiscal state would in the end undermine government's ability to govern. Eighteen years later, Keynes hailed the fiscal state as the great liberator of a depressed economy. Keynes argued that government, no longer limited by restraints on expenditures, could effectively control economic growth by manipulating government spending and taxation. However, in the 1990's many economists and politicians believe that Schumpeter might have been right. By 1996, most of the governments of the industrialized world had run up such large federal deficits that fiscal policy became almost useless in fighting either recession or inflation. In 1997 and 1998 the U.S. economy continued to grow at historically high rates, which resulted in higher tax revenue for the federal government. In 1998 federal government tax revenues exceeded expenses resulting in a budget surplus for the first time in almost 50 years. A saying attributed to both John F. Kennedy and Ronald Reagan can be used to explain the government surplus: "A Rising Tide Lifts All Boats."

The debate continued into the 2000 American presidential campaign where both the Republican and Democratic parties have attempted to define their positions based on the perceived role of government. The Republicans led by Texas Governor George W. Bush defined their position as one of a reduced tax burden on its citizens, along with a smaller, and less intrusive role of the federal government. Their position is similar to the theories of Alfred Marshall and Neoclassical economics. The Democrats under, Vice President Al Gore, defined their position more along the lines of Keynesian economic theory, calling for a larger role of government in controlling the economy.

The election of 2000 was one of the closest votes in American history. The election came down to who would be awarded the 25 Electoral College votes from Florida. It took more than a month and a Supreme Court decision to decide the issue. On December 12th 2000 George W. Bush was officially declared to be the new president of the

United States. George W. Bush won the election with an Electoral College vote of 271 to Al Gore's 266 but lost the popular vote by 541 thousand. However, Bush was not the only president to lose the popular vote and win the election, two other presidents were elected by receiving a majority of the electoral votes and losing the popular vote. The other two presidents were Rutherford Hayes in 1876 and Benjamin Harrison in 1888.

The 2008 presidential elections were held on November 4th. After a long primary campaign, Republican's choose John McCain a long-time Senator from Arizona and a Viet Nam War Hero and Democrats choose Barack Obama a young senator from Illinois. Young and charismatic but with little experience on the national level, Obama smashed through racial barriers and easily defeated John McCain to become the first African-American destined to sit in the Oval Office as America's 44th president.

As president, Obama faces daunting problems. How to fix a financial system no one seems to fully understand. How to defeat terrorist enemies sheltered in the territory of our putative ally Pakistan. How to live up to the high expectations so visible in the cheering faces of his followers.

The Business Cycle Dating Committee of the National Bureau of Economic Research met by conference call on Friday, November 28, 2008. The committee maintains a chronology of the beginning and ending dates (months and quarters) of U.S. recessions. The committee determined that the economy was in a recession that started in December 2007. Getting the economy growing again is one of President Obama's priorities in 2009 and beyond. The American Recovery and Reinvestment Act of 2009 passed Congress with no Republican votes in the House and only 3 in the Senate. The plan called for a fiscal stimulus package in the amount of $797 billion. Many Republicans criticized the bill for not providing enough tax relief. Only 36 percent of the stimulus was for tax reductions. Some Democrats argued that the amount of stimulus was not large enough to end the recession.

As for the current generation of Americans and Western Europeans, we may never completely settle the question of the proper role of government in the economy. However, the actions of the Obama administration including the 2017 budget proposal and the 2009 stimulus package will most likely lead to an increased roll of government in business over the next coming years. The debate about the role of government will continue into 2017 when President Obama's term ends. The leading Republican candidates are advocating a smaller more efficient government while the Democrat contenders prefer a much larger role for government. The voters in November of 2016 chose Republican and business man Donald Trump over the Democrat candidate Hillary Clinton with the hope of smaller government and reduced federal spending.

Business by its nature requires change, however, in life there is only one certainty, for as John Maynard Keynes once wrote: "In the long run we are all dead." Therefore, the main purpose of this book may, be summarized as follows:

- To see economics as a reflection of the world in which specific economic ideas have developed over time.
- To isolate and emphasize the most lasting concepts of the leading economists of their time.
- To examine the economic policies of past and present U. S. Government administrations.
- To explain the basis theories of economics in easy to understand terms.
- To use the lessons from the past so that we can avoid repeating our mistakes in the future.

NOTES:

Chapter 1
The Economic Way of Thinking

1.   Marshall, Alfred, <u>Principles of Economics, 9th Edition</u>, London, England, Macmillan, 1920, p. 1.

2. Dolan, Edward S. & Lindsey, David E., <u>Economics, Seventh Edition</u>, The Dryden Press, Orlando, FL, 1994, p. 9.
3. Dolan and Lindsey, p. 10.
4. Hyman, David N., <u>Economics, Third Edition</u>, Boston, MA, Irwin, 1994, p.10.
5. Dolan and Lindsey, p. 14

CHAPTER 2

DEMAND, SUPPLY AND ELASTICITY

"If all economists were laid end to end, they would not reach a conclusion." – George Bernard Shaw

THE LAW OF SUPPLY AND DEMAND

Economics can be defined as the social science that seeks to understand the choices people make in using scarce resources to meet their wants. In economics, we want to know how each of the four basic types of choices (Deciding what to produce, deciding how to produce, deciding who will do which work, and deciding for whom goods will be produced) are related to the context in which they are made, and how outcomes are related to these choices. A representative of the way in which facts are related is often referred to as a theory or a model. Economists tend to use the term theory to refer to more general statements about economic relationships and the term model to refer to more specific statements, especially those that take the form of graphs or mathematical equations.

This chapter outlines a model of price determination in a market economy, the supply-and-demand model. Demand refers to buyers' willingness and ability to purchase goods while supply refers to sellers' willingness and ability to produce goods and services for sale in a market. The law of demand states that in any market, other things being equal, an inverse relationship exists between the price of a good and the quantity of the good that buyer's demand. We expect this to happen for two reasons. First, if the price of one good falls while the prices of other goods that satisfy the same consumer need stay the same, people are likely to substitute the cheaper good. Second, when the price of one good falls while incomes and other prices stay the same, people feel a little richer. They often use their additional buying power to increase the quantity of the good they already buy.

The Demand Curve

Economists' use the term "Other things being equal" to analyze the relationships between two variables. When drawing a single demand curve for a good all other conditions that affect demand are assumed to be fixed or constant under this clause. As long as the clause is in force, the only two variables at work are quantity demanded and price. Table 2.1 represents this one-to-one relationship between single producers of a product. Perdue Farms Incorporated. Perdue Farms is a leading food and agricultural products company with sales in excess of $2.7 billion. Their retail division markets their branded chicken and turkey products to retail supermarkets, grocery stores and butcher shops from Maine to Florida and as far west as Chicago and St. Louis. The Perdue brand is featured on whole chickens, chicken parts, Oven Stuffer roasters, and turkeys and Cornish hens. Table 2.1 uses Perdue whole chickens for analysis purposes. The numbers are for illustration purposes and do not represent the actual production and sales of Perdue Farms Incorporated which is a privately held company. The table shows the demand relationship for one of their products, whole chicken, in two different ways. The first row of Table 2.1 shows that when the price of whole chicken is $ 1.20 a pound, the quantity demanded per year is 600 million pounds. Reading down the table, you see that as the price falls, the quantity demanded rises. At $ .80 per pound, buyers purchase 1.0 billion pounds; and so on. Figure 2.1 shows the same information in graphical form. The graph is called a demand curve for Perdue whole chicken. The demand curve can be used to determine what quantity of chicken will be demanded at a price of $.80 per pound. The quantity of chicken is plotted on the vertical axis and the price per pound is plotted on the horizontal axis. Starting at the $.80 on the vertical axis, move across until you reach the demand curve. Then drop down to the horizontal axis. Reading from the scale on the axis you see that the quantity demanded at a price of $ .80 per pound is 1.0 billion pounds per year. That point on the demand curve corresponds to the quantity demanded at a price of $.80 per pound. The effect of a change in the price of whole chicken that is shown from one point to another along the demand curve for chicken is referred to as a movement along the demand curve. Because of the inverse relationship between price and quantity demanded, the demand curve has a negative slope. Economists' refer to a movement along a demand curve as a change in quantity demanded. Such a movement represents buyers' reaction to a change in the price of the consumer good in question.

Shifts in the Demand Curve

The demand curve in Figure 2.1 represents a relationship between two variables' the price of whole chicken and the quantity of chicken demanded. However, other things do not usually remain unchanged. Changes in other variables can also affect people's purchases of Perdue and other brands of chicken. In the case of chicken, the prices of beef and pork could also affect demand. Economists call such pairs of goods substitutes. This is because when the price of chicken goes up the quantity demanded of beef also goes up as consumers substitute beef for chicken. Consumers may react differently to price changes when two goods tend to be used together. For example, when the price of gasoline goes up, people tend to drive less; therefore, they require fewer oil changes even if there is no change in the price of oil.

Consumer incomes are a second variable that can affect demand. When incomes rise, people tend to buy larger quantities of many goods, assuming that the prices of those goods do not change. Also, with higher incomes, people become choosier about what they eat and demand higher quality. They do not just want calories; they want high-quality calories from foods that are tasty, healthful and convenient. These considerations have made chicken increasingly popular as consumer's incomes have risen. The major producers of chicken have responded to changing market demands by developing products in addition to whole birds such as chicken parts including breasts thighs and legs, Oven Stuffer roasters and precooked chicken.

Basic Economics

Table 2.1 Price and Quantity of Chicken

Price per Pound (in Dollars)	Quantity Demanded (Billions of Pounds)	Quantity Supplied (Billions of Pounds)
1.5	0.3	1.5
1.4	0.4	1.4
1.3	0.5	1.3
1.2	0.6	1.2
1.1	0.7	1.1
1.0	0.8	1.0
0.9	0.9	0.9
0.8	1.0	0.8
0.7	1.1	0.7
0.6	1.2	0.6
0.5	1.3	0.5
0.4	1.4	0.4
0.3	1.5	0.3

  Changes in consumer expectations about the future are a third way that can shift the demand curves. If people expect something other than price increase to raise the opportunity cost of acquiring products, they will step up their rate of purchase before the change takes place. An example is an increase in home sales when consumers expect the interest rate on mortgages to go up.

  Changes in consumer tastes, such as an increasing preference for foods with low saturated-fat content, are a fourth way that demand for chicken consumption can change. For example, in recent years' consumers have been more health conscious than they were in the past. The result has been reduced demand for unhealthy products such as cigarettes and high-cholesterol foods, along with increased demand for fish and chicken.

Figure 2.1: The Demand Curve for Perdue Whole Chicken

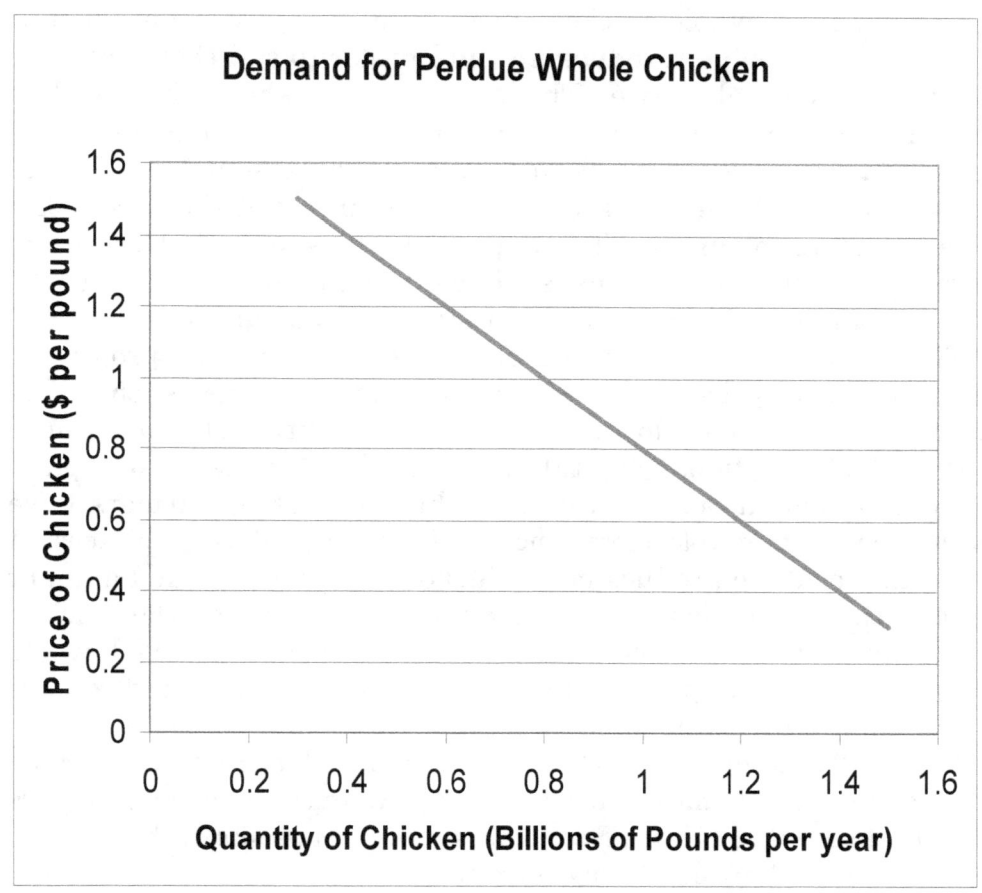

When you look beyond the "other things being equal" clause and find that there is a change in a variable that is not represented on one of the axis, the effect is explained as a shift in the demand curve. When the demand curve shifts, in its new position the demand curve still represents a two-variable price-quantity relationship, but it is a different relationship than before because one of the other variables has changed.[1]

The Supply Curve

Consumers of whole chickens would prefer to buy the product at the lowest price possible. Producers would prefer to sell their products at the highest possible price. The supply curve shows how sellers change their plans in response to a change in the price of whole chickens. The supply curve is a graphical representation of the relationship of the price of a good and the quantity of that good that sellers are willing to supply. The supply curve assumes that there are no changes in other conditions such as the prices of other goods, production techniques, input prices, and future expectations.

The supply curve is positively sloped because of producers' response to market price incentives, or increasing expense such as the rising cost of producing additional output in facilities of a fixed size, and the cost of additional capital that may be necessary to expand production. When the market price of chicken goes up farmers have increased incentive to devote more time and effort to producing chickens. A farmer could decide to produce more chickens, but with a fixed amount of facilities the production of chickens would diminish, as the chicken coupes became more crowded. Eventually, the farmer would have to increase his facilities to produce more chickens and that would require additional capital investment.

Figure 2-3 shows the supply and demand curves for Perdue whole chicken. The demand curve shows how many chickens' buyers plan to purchase at a given price. The supply curve shows how much producers such as Perdue Farms plan to sell at a given price. At only one price, $ .90 per pound, do buyers and sellers' plans exactly match?

That is the equilibrium price. A higher price causes a surplus as farmers produce more whole chicken than buyers wish to buy and this puts downward pressure on the price. A lower price causes shortages and puts upward pressure on price. When quantity demanded exceeds quantity supplied, because the low price keeps some producers out of the market, the difference is called excess in quantity demanded or a shortage.

Figure 2.2: Supply Curve for Perdue Whole Chickens

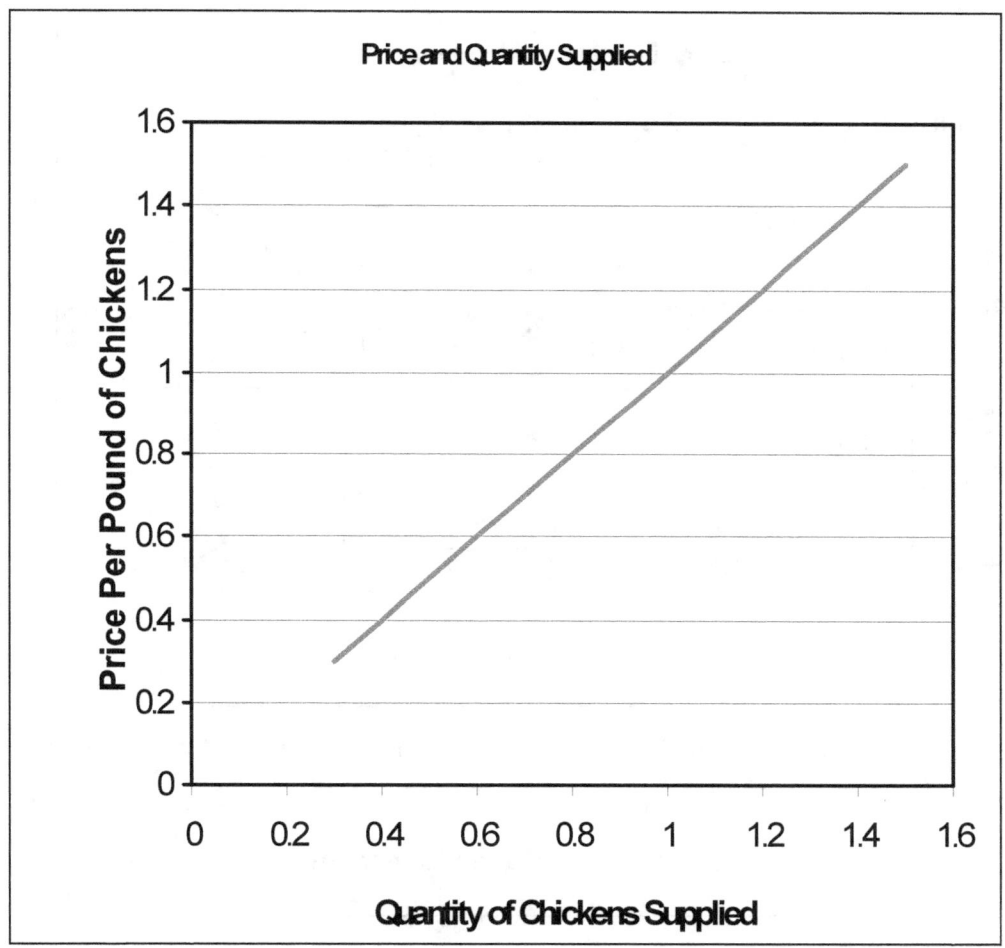

Figure 2.3: Demand, Supply and Equilibrium:

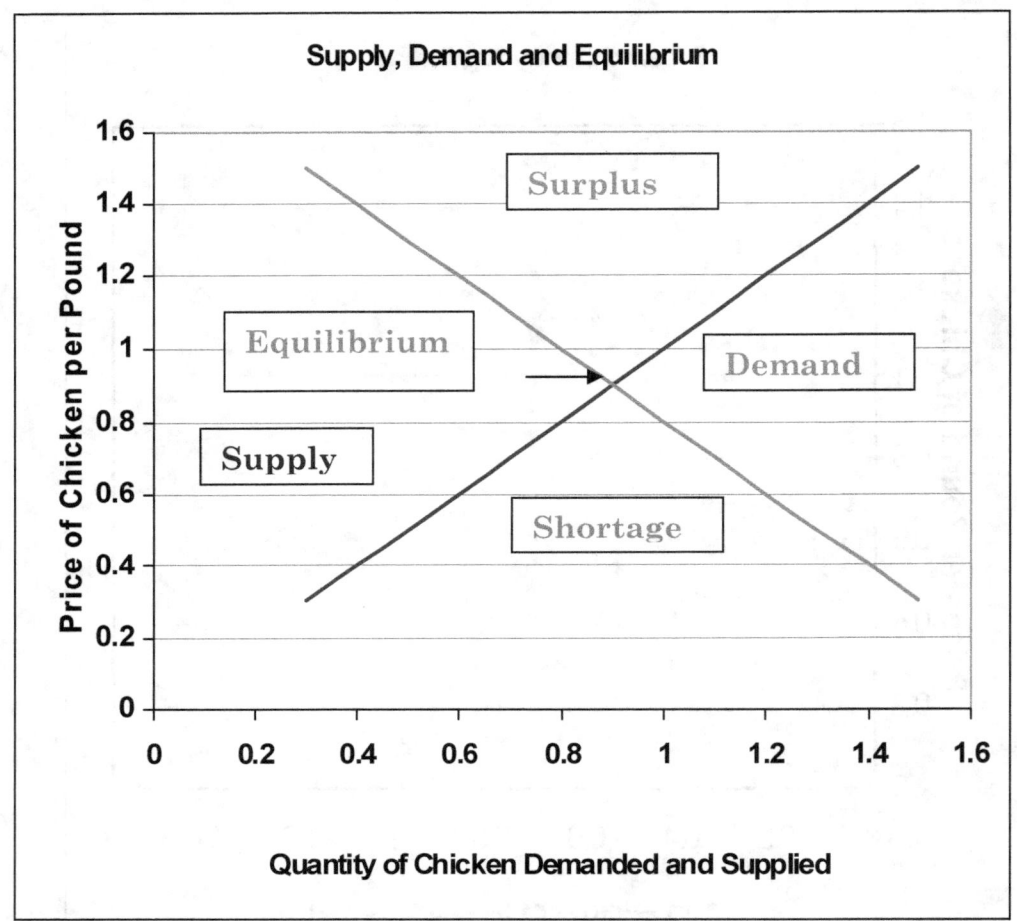

In most markets the first sign of a shortage is a drop-in inventory, or in the stock of the good that is being analyzed. Inventory in this example is a stock of finished goods that is waiting to be sold. When sellers see their inventory dropping below planned levels, they change plans and often try to rebuild their inventory by increasing production. Some sellers may take advantage of the strong demand for their product to raise prices, knowing that buyers will be willing to pay

Economics for Everyone

more. If the sellers do not take the initiative, buyers will, as they will offer to pay more if sellers will supply more. The result of this adjustment to increased demand will be and upward movement along the supply curves as both the price and quantity demanded will increase.

Alfred Marshall who is the main subject of a later chapter described the relationship between supply and demand in his 1890 publication "The Principles of Economics." According to Marshall, "In spite of a great variety in detail, nearly all the chief problems of economics agree in that they have a kernel of the same kind. This kernel is an inquiry as to the balancing of two opposed classes of motives: the one consisting of desires to acquire certain new goods, and thus satisfy wants; while the other consists of desires to avoid certain efforts or retain certain immediate enjoyment. In other words, it is an inquiry into the balancing of the forces of demand and supply."

Shifts in the Supply Curve

Economists' refer of a movement along a supply curve as a change in quantity supplied. Such a movement represents sellers' reaction to a change in the price that consumers are willing to pay for the good in question. A change in a condition other than the price of chicken is shown on the supply curve as a shift in the supply curve. There are four sources of a change in supply that are worth noting. They are changes in technology, changes in input prices, changes in the prices of other goods and changes in expectations. Each is related to the theory that the supply curve reflects the opportunity costs of producing the good in question.

First, when entrepreneurs are able to reduce the costs of production by introducing new technology, they can either increase their profit margin by selling the good at the same price of they can increase the sales and their market share by lowering their price below that of the competition. In addition, if an increase in the input prices reduces the profit margin of the good, producers may decide to reduce the quantity of that good. Also, changes in the prices of other goods that could be produced using the same factors of production can produce a shift in the supply curve for whole chicken. An example of this could be if the price of corn rises while the market price of whole chickens stays the same. The rise in the price of corn gives some farmers who would otherwise have produced chickens an incentive to shift the use of their labor, land and capital to the production of corn. Finally, changes in expectation can cause supply curves to shift in much the same way that they cause demand curves to shift. Using the example of corn and chickens, the incentive to increase the production of corn will be stronger if the price of corn is expected to remain high in the future.

Market Equilibrium

If buyers and sellers plans come together when they meet in the marketplace, no buyers or sellers need to change their plans. Under these conditions, the market is said to be in equilibrium. Figure 2.3 shows the plans of buyers and sellers on the same graph. If the quantity of planned sales of Perdue whole chicken at each price is compared with the quantity of planned purchases at that price, it can be seen that there is only one price at which the two sets of plans mesh. That price, of $.90 per pound, is the equilibrium price. If all buyers and sellers make their plans with the expectation of a price of $.90 per pound, no one will be surprised and no plans will have to be changed.

ELASTICITY

We have seen that the quantity of a good that is demanded and subsequently purchased is influenced by its price. However, this is not always a one to one relationship. For example, former President Clinton recently underwent coronary bypass surgery in New York Presbyterian Hospital. Clinton had a team of highly qualified heart surgeons perform the operation. His decision to have the operation at Presbyterian and performed by top rated doctors was not based on price, it was based on the probability that he would and consequently did survive the operation. This service performed on Clinton provides a good example of price elasticity or in this case the lack of it. Elasticity is the measure of the response of one variable to a change in another stated as a ratio of the percentage change in one variable to the associated percentage change in another variable. Price elasticity of demand is the ratio of the percentage change in the quantity demanded to a given percentage change in its price, other things being equal.

Elasticity of Demand

Elasticity of demand can take three forms, elastic demand, inelastic demand, and unit elastic demand. The amount of change in demand can be measured by the change in corresponding revenue. Revenue is defined as the unit price of a good times its sales volume. For example, if the price of a good is $100 and the amount sold is 100 than the revenue would be $10,000. If demand were elastic than the quantity demanded would change by a larger percentage than price, so that total revenue would increase as price decreases. For example, if the price of a good were lowered from $100 to $75 and the quantity demanded increased from 100 to 150, the total revenue would increase to $11,250 ($75 x 150). Inelastic demand is a situation in which quantity demanded changes by a smaller percentage than the price, so that total revenue decreases as price decreases. If in the above example, demand increased to only 125 units, total revenue would be reduced to $9,000. Former President Clinton's operation would be an example of perfectly inelastic demand, since a lower price by a less experienced surgeon would have not influenced his decision as to where to have his operation. Unit elastic demand is a situation in which price and quantity demanded change by the same percentage, so that total revenue remains unchanged as price changes.

Price elasticity of demand can also be calculated with statistics using the midpoint formula for elasticity. With P1 and Q1 representing price and quantity before a change and P2 and Q2, representing price and quantity after the change, the midpoint formula for elasticity is:

$$\frac{\% \text{ change in quantity demanded}}{\% \text{ change in price}} = \frac{(Q2-Q1)/(Q1+Q2)}{(P2-P1)/(P1+P2)}$$

Where: P1 = Price before change = $100
               P2 = Price after change =   75

$$Q1 = \text{Quantity before change} = 100$$
$$Q2 = \text{Quantity after change} = 150$$

$$\text{Elasticity} = \frac{(150-100)/(150+100)}{(75-100)/(75+100)} = \frac{50/250}{-25/175}$$

$$\text{Elasticity} = \frac{.2}{.142} = -1.4$$

Elasticity in this example is -1.4. Because demand curves have negative slopes, this formula yields a negative value for elasticity. The reason is that quantity demanded changes in the direction opposite to that of the price change. If the percentage is equal to 1 or above then the change in quantity demanded based on the reduction in price is elastic and should lead to an increase in revenue. In this example an elasticity of -1.4 means that the quantity demanded will increase by 1.4 percent for each 1 percent change in price. Each of the terms elastic, inelastic and unit elastic corresponds to a numerical value or range of values of elasticity. A perfectly inelastic demand curve has a numerical value of 0 since any change in price produces no change in quantity demanded. The term inelastic demand applies to numerical values from 0 up to but not including 1. Unit elasticity means a numerical value of exactly 1 and elastic demand means any value for elasticity that is greater than one.[2]

Elasticity of Supply

The concept of elasticity can also be used to describe the response of the quantity supplied to a change in price. The price elasticity of supply of a good such as whole chickens is defined as the percentage change in the quantity of the good supplied divided by the percentage change in its price. The midpoint formula can be used to calculate the elasticity of supply by substituting quantity supplied for quantity demanded in the elasticity of demand formula. Because price and quantity supplied change in the same direction along a positively sloped supply curve, the formula gives a positive value for the elasticity of supply. As in demand elasticity, a result of greater than 1 indicates that supply is elastic, of less than one indicates that supply is inelastic and a result of 1 indicates unit elasticity.

There are several reasons why supply is or is not elastic. Two of the more important reasons are the mobility of the factors of production and the greater the time available to make the necessary changes to increase supply. Mobility means the ease with which the factors of production can be attracted away from some other use as well as the ease with which they can be converted from their current use. For example, if the price of corn increased relative to the price of tomatoes, farmers could shift their production to tomatoes using the same land and equipment. However, if the price of gasoline increases it is much more difficult to find new sources of oil and to manufacture more drilling rigs to immediately take advantage of the increased price.

A second determinant of elasticity of supply is time. Price elasticity of supply tends to be greater in the long run than in the short run. In the short-run supply can often be increased by adding more workers. At some level of production the adding of more workers becomes less efficient. This is referred to by economists as the law of diminishing returns. This law states that as more and more workers are added to the same amount of capital, their efficiency is decreased and the product unit cost is increased. If a firm expects market conditions to warrant an increase in supply in the long run, it may decide to invest in additional amounts of capital equipment, which could result in a lowering of the unit cost of the product. The theory of elasticity has many real-world applications. For example, the marketing research department of a consumer product's company such as Proctor & Gamble would find elasticity useful in determining the reactions to their customers to a change in the price of one of their leading detergent products. Also, a government agency might wish to determine reaction of both renters and landlords to a price ceiling on rental properties.

MARKETS, CONSUMERS AND UTILITY

When all of the demand for a product such as whole chickens is added up this equates to the market demand for the product. In actual practice sellers do not add up individual demand but estimate the total market demand for their products. The total demand curve for a product then becomes smooth and slopes downward. This is based on two reasons: At lower prices, existing demanders tend to purchase more and at lower prices, new demanders will enter the market. Sellers are also interested in market supply. Sellers such as Perdue Farms pay particular attention to the strategies of other suppliers of chicken. For example, let's say that the market supply for chicken is made up of 4 producers, Perdue Farms, Tyson Inc., Foster Farms and producers of super market store brands. If each producer supplies one fourth of the market and the total supply of whole chickens is 10 billion pounds per year, than each producer supplies 2.5 billion pounds and their market share is 25 percent. The concept of market share is important to producers because if one firm dominates the market that firm often gets to determine the pricing structure of their products.

Consumers and Utility

One of the major functions performed by markets is to enable consumers to choose the products and services that will give them the most satisfaction. Economists use the term utility to describe the level of consumer satisfaction and say that consumers usually attempt to maximize their utility. When you go into a yogurt store such as TCBY, you do not order the entire amount of yogurt even if you could afford to do so. Eating the yogurt obeys the law of diminishing returns. You do not spend more than a few dollars on a yogurt cone, because the additional yogurt is not worth as much to you as the first scoop or two. Economists believe that consumers make these sorts of decisions instinctively. For each product or service in the economy, every consumer will act as if they increased their purchase of the good or service until the dollar value of the utility from the next unit no longer exceeds the price. Economists use the term utility function to describe how purchase decisions are made. Using this concept, we might say that consumer utility is a function of the amount of candy they eat, the amount of hours spend each week on country dancing, the reliability of their car or the look of their clothes. Each good or service that they buy goes into the utility function as the consumer equates his or her marginal utility or the satisfaction they get out of the next purchase to the price of the good or service. If the consumer, given the price of a product determines that the marginal utility is greater than the marginal cost, they will most likely to make a purchase.

THE THEORY OF MARKET STRUCTURE

The structure of a market is a term that refers to the conditions under which firms compete in it. The key traits of a market include the number and size of firms, the nature of the products, the ease of entry and exit from the market, and the information available to the competing companies.

Monopoly is a market structure in which there is a single supplier of a product. A monopolistic firm is the only supplier of a particular product. In addition, a monopoly firm must sell a product for which there are no close substitutes. The company sets the price of the product. A monopoly is a price maker in the marketplace. An electric and gas utility is an example of a monopolistic firm.

Perfect competition is characterized by a large number of small firms, none with a significant share of the market; a product that is standardized, little or no barriers to either entry or exit from the business, and that all buyers and sellers have complete information about the price of the products, the inputs used to produce them and equal knowledge about industry production technology. A Company in a purely competitive industry takes the price that the market establishes. Purely competitively firms are price takers. Agricultural products are a good example of pure competition.

An oligopoly is a market structure with a few firms, at least some of which are large in relation to the size of the market. The product may be either standardized or differentiated; there may or may not be significant barriers to entry, and buyers and sellers do not have equal access to available information. The industry consists of both price makers and price takers as the firm with the largest market share often takes the lead in product pricing while the other companies follow the dominant firm. The automobile industry is an example of an oligopoly.

Monopolistic (differentiated) competition resembles perfect competition in that there are many small firms with easy entry and exit, but under this market structure, the various firms' products are differentiated from one another. Firms in this market structure invest additional amounts of money into expanding the features of their products to add value for their customers. Also, these companies usually spend large amounts on advertising to create a favorable image of their products with potential distributors and retail customers. Companies that can successfully differentiate their products in the eyes of the consumers are price makers as they can usually charge a premium for their output. The restaurant industry is an example of monopolistic competition.

STRATEGIC MARKET MANAGEMENT

Strategic Market Management is a system designed to help management make strategic business decisions. Strategic market management is concerned with both an internal and external analysis of a company. One of the major parts of strategic market analysis is a study of the firm's customers. Customer analysis involves identifying the organization's customer segments and each segment's motivations and unmet needs. Segment identification defines alternative product markets and thus structures what investment levels to assign to each market. The analysis of customer motivations provides information needed to decide why a customer chooses to buy a particular product. An unmet need is a need not currently being met by existing products.

An example of a company offering different services to different customer groups is the luxury hotel industry. One segmentation scheme could distinguish customers between tourists, convention attendees, and business travelers. Each type of traveler has a very different set of motivations. The tourist is concerned with price and their purchase decision would be motivated by value. The conventioneer would be more motivated with the facilities for presentations and the business traveler would be more motivated by comfort and Internet access.[3]

Strategic marketing managers often use the economic theories of demand, supply and elasticity in order understand the purchase motivations of their customers and to design product offerings to satisfy the unmet needs of those customers. Large firms develop multimillion-dollar advertising budgets designed to inform customers of the value of their products. Some customers make purchases based substantially on price such as vacationers selecting an inexpensive hotel and others based their purchase on their perception of quality such as buyers of BMW automobiles, which are advertised as the "Ultimate Driving Machine." Customer orientated companies' study the reason consumers make purchases and design products based on the information they obtain. For as Walter Wriston, the former CEO of Citicorp, Inc. once said, "The purpose of a business is to create a customer."

NOTES:

Chapter 2
Demand, Supply and Elasticity

1. Dolan, Edward S. & Lindsey David E., <u>Economics, Seventh Edition</u>, The Dryden Press, Orlando, FL, 1994. p. 45
2. Dolan and Lindsey, p. 71
3. Aaker, David, <u>Strategic Market Management</u>, John Wiley & Sons, Inc., Hoboken, NJ, 2005, P. 21.

CHAPTER 3

PRODUCTION AND COSTS

"An economist is a man who states the obvious in terms of the incomprehensible" – Alfred Knoph

TOTAL REVENUE, TOTAL COSTS AND PROFIT

In Chapter 2 the supply curve was used to summarize a firm's decision on what to produce and at what quantity. According to the law of supply, firms are willing to produce and sell a greater quantity of a good when the price of the good is high. This response by sellers leads to a supply curve that slopes upward. This chapter will examine the behavior of a firm in determining the price, costs and expected profit from producing a product or service. The study is about how firms' production decisions regarding price and quantity depend on the market conditions they face.

We can begin the study of costs with an example company, Ricardo's Pizza Restaurant. Ricardo, the owner of the firm buys flour, tomato paste, cheese and other toppings for his pizza. He also buys the mixers and ovens and hires workers to mix the dough and to bake the pizzas. The owner must also find a place where the product will be produced such as retail store, or a factory depending on the type of business. Ricardo will most likely start his pizza restaurant in a retail store and hopes that the business will make a profit. The amount that a firm receives from the sale of its output is called revenue. Total revenue is based on the price of a single unit, in this example, 1 pizza times the number of units sold. The amount that Ricardo pays to buy product inputs such as flour and tomato paste, the costs of workers and in this example rent for the store are his total costs. We can therefore define profit as a firm's total revenue minus its total costs or:

Profit = Total Revenue − Total Costs.

Ricardo's objective is to operate his restaurant in a manor that will generate the most profit.

The Production Possibility Table

The choices that society must take are often presented in terms of a production possibility table. The production possibility table is related to the concept of opportunity costs. In economic terms opportunity cost is the cost of a good or service measured in terms of the foregone opportunity to pursue the best possible alternative activity with the same resources and time. Opportunity costs can be shown numerically with a production possibility table that summarizes the alternative outputs that can be achieved with a fixed amount of inputs. Where output is a result of activity and input is what you put into the production process to achieve an output.

The production possibility table demonstrates that:

1. There is a limit to what you can achieve, given the existing institutions, resources and technology available in an economy.

2. Every choice has an opportunity cost. You can get more of something else only by giving up something else.

Table 3.1 contains the information on the trade-off between the production of rifles and pounds of chicken. As you move along the production possibility table from A to F, trading chickens for rifles results in fewer rifles for each pound of chicken given up. That is the opportunity cost of choosing rifles over chickens' increases as the production of rifles increases. This concept is called the principle of increasing marginal opportunity cost. The phenomenon occurs because some resources are better suited for the production of chickens than for the production of rifles. The production possibility table assumes that the factors of production land, natural resources, labor, capital and

Basic Economics

technology remain constant. Even if all available resources are devoted to rifles there is a limit to the number of rifles that can be produced in one year. The extreme possibility of producing 100 million rifles and no chickens is shown in row F and of producing 15 million pounds of chicken and no rifles in row A of the table.

Table 3.1: Production Possibility Table for Rifles and Chicken

Percent of Resources Devoted to the Production of Rifles	Number of Rifles (in millions)	Percent of Resources Devoted to Producing Chickens	Number of Chickens in (million of Pounds)	Row
0	0	100	15	A
20	4	80	14	B
40	7	60	12	C
60	9	40	9	D
80	11	20	5	E
100	12	0	0	F

Notice that as you go down the table, there is not a constant trade-off between the production of rifles and chickens. For example, in row B the farmer has only to give up 1 million pounds of chicken to enable the economy to product 4 million rifles. In column C, the farmer has to give up 2 extra million pounds of chicken to produce 3 million additional rifles. Therefore, the amount of chicken production that has to be forgone to increase the number of rifles increases as you move further down the table from row A through row F. This demonstrates the economic theory of increasing marginal opportunity costs that was just introduced.

The production possibility table demonstrates the trade-off that an economy has to make when deciding what goods and services to produce. If production is along the parameters of the table then an economy is assumed to be operating at its full potential. If the economy is operating for example in row C and was producing only 6 million rifles and 11 million pounds of chicken it would be operating below its potential and may be in a recession. However, given the assumed amount of resources, the economy can not produce beyond the levels shown in the table, (the 7 million riffles and 12 million pounds of chicken shown in row C). The production possibility table presents a picture of a static economy that can only produce within the amounts shown in the table. If the economy is to grow than one or more of the factors of production must increase, that is there must be an increase in the amount and the productivity of at least one or more of the factors of production. This would increase the productivity of labor and capital. Productivity is a measure of the amount of output produced for a given level of input. Some ways that productivity could be increased is listed below:

Factors of Production: Ways to Increase Productivity

Land	Develop more land for useful purposes
Natural Resources	Explore and produce more resources
Labor	Increase the size and skill of labor
Capital	Increase the amount of capital equipment
Technology	Increase the productivity of labor and capital

The Production Function

Continuing with the example of Ricardo's pizza store, Ricardo has certain things that he can manage. The factors of production in Ricardo's example include land (the retail store), resources (flour and tomato paste), capital equipment (the pizza stoves) and technology (computers). In this example the size of Ricardo's pizza store is fixed and that he can vary the quantity of pizzas produced only by changing the number workers. Table 3.2 shows how the quantity of pizzas Ricardo's store produces per day depends on the number of workers. If there are no workers in the store no pizzas are produced. When there are just 1 worker 50 pizzas are produced. When there are 2 workers, 90 pizzas are produced. This increase comes about because the workers can specialize in making the pizzas. For example, one worker could roll the dough and the next worker could put on the toppings and put the pizza in the oven and the third worker could run the front counter and take customer orders. This relationship between the quantity of inputs (workers) and the quantity of output (pizzas) is called the production function. This idea of outputs related to inputs is the key to understanding how firms decide how many workers to hire and how much output to produce.

    The third column of table 3.2 shows the marginal product of each worker. The marginal product of any input into production is the increase in the quantity of output from an additional unit of input. When the number of workers goes from 1 to 2, the pizza production goes from 50 to 90. When the number of workers goes from 2 to 3, pizza production goes from 90 to 120, so the marginal product contributed to the third worker is 30 pizzas. Notice that as the number of workers increases, the marginal product declines. The second worker has a marginal product of 40 pizzas, the third worker has a marginal product of 30 pizzas, and the fourth worker has a marginal product of 20 pizzas.

This property is called the diminishing marginal product. At first, when only a few workers are hired, they have plenty of room to get around and use the kitchen equipment. As the number of workers increases, additional workers have to share equipment and work in more crowded conditions as the store's kitchen is fixed in size. Hence as more workers are hired they contribute less and less to the increased production of pizzas. This happens because the increase in workers is greater than the increase in capital equipment. If Ricardo purchased another pizza over and hired one worker for each oven, then the marginal product of each work might not be reduced when adding the additional worker.

Table 3-2: The Production Function and Total Costs of Ricardo's Pizza Store

Number of Workers	Output – quantity of pizzas per day	Marginal product of labor	Cost of store (fixed costs)	Cost of workers (variable costs)	Total Costs of inputs
0	0		$30	$0	$30
1	50	50	$30	$10	$40
2	90	40	$30	$20	$50
3	120	30	$30	$30	$60
4	140	20	$30	$40	$70

Fixed, Variable and Total Costs

From the data on a firm's total cost, several related measures of costs can be developed. An example of how the different measures of costs can be developed is displayed in table 3-3. This table presents the costs of Ricardo's neighbor Bob's Bagel Shop. Bob's total cost can be divided into two types. Some costs are fixed and do not vary with the quantity of output produced. Bob's fixed costs include rent because this cost is the same regardless of how many bagels Bob produces. Also, Bob's salary is a fixed cost because he pays himself regardless of the level of production.

In addition to the payment of rent and Bob's salary, the firm incurs other costs that are directly related to the production of bagels. These are called variable costs as they change with the level of production. Bob can determine the fixed costs of his bagel store on an hourly basis as follows:

Basic Economics   35

Monthly Costs:
    Rent on the Store: $500
    Cost of Ovens $100
    Bob's Salary $400

Total Fixed Cost $1,000

Bob plans to operate his bagel store for 50 hours each week or 200 hours per month. His fixed cost per hour can therefore be determined by dividing his total monthly fixed cost by the number of hours his store is open each month.

    Total fixed cost/Total operating hours = Fixed cost per hour

    Fixed cost per hour of operation = $1,000/200 = $5 per hour

Bob's variable costs include the cost of flour, butter and sugar. The more bagels Bob makes, the more flour, butter and sugar he needs to buy. Similarly, if Bob needs to hire someone to operate the front counter and take orders for bagels, the salary of this worker is a fixed cost in the short run. The fourth column of table 3-3 shows Bob's variable costs per hour. The variable cost per hour is the cost per bagel of $.25 times the number of bagels produced and sold per hour. The variable costs are $0 if he produces nothing, $2.50 if he produces 10 bagels, $5.00 if he produces 20 bagels, and so on. A firm's total costs are the sum of fixed and variable costs, which is shown in column 2 of the table. For example,

The total cost of producing 20 bagels

    Variable costs per hour $ 5.00
    Fixed cost per hour $ 5.00

    Total Cost per hour $10.00

Table 3-3: Fixed and Variable Costs of Producing Bagels

Quantity of Bagels Per hour	Total Cost	Fixed Cost Per Hour	Var. Cost Per Hour	Avg. Fixed Cost Per Bagel	Avg. Var. Cost Per Bagel	Avg. Total Cost Per Bagel	Marg. Cost Per Bagel
0	$5.0	$5.0	$0.0	—	—	—	
10	7.50	5.00	2.5	$.50	$.25	$.75	$.75
20	10.0	5.00	5.0	0.25	0.25	0.50	.25
30	12.5	5.00	7.5	0.17	0.25	0.42	.08
40	15.0	5.00	10.0	0.13	0.25	0.38	.04
50	17.5	5.00	12.5	0.10	0.25	0.35	.03
60	26.0	11.0	15.0	0.18	0.25	0.43	.08
70	28.5	11.0	17.5	0.18	$.25	0.40	.03
80	31.0	11.0	20.0	0.14	$.25	0.38	.02

Bob decides to charge $.50 per bagel which equates to $20 of revenue at a sales level of 20 bagels per hour. At the sales level of 20 bagels per hour, Bob's profit will be zero (Revenue of $20 minus total costs of $20 equals a profit of $0).

The Relationship between Marginal Cost and Average Cost

Average costs are determined by dividing the fixed costs, variable costs and total costs by the total volume of production. For example, at a quantity of 20 bagels per hour:

Average Fixed Costs = Total fixed cost/Total bagels per hour
　　　　AFC = $5.0/20 = $.25

Basic Economics   37

Average variable costs = Total variable cost/Total bagels per hour
  AVC = $5.0/20 = $.25
Average total cost = (Average fixed cost + Average variable cost)
  ATC = ($.25 + $.25) = $.50 per bagel

Although average total costs tell us the cost of the typical unit, it does not tell us how much total costs will change as the firm alters its level of production. The last column of table 3-3 shows the amount that total cost rises when the firm increases production by one unit of output. This number is called the marginal costs. For example, if Bob increases production from 20 to 30 bagels, total costs rises from $10.00 to $12.50, so the marginal cost per bagel of the 10 additional bagels is ($12.50 - $10.00)/10 or $.25. If the variable cost continues at $.25 per bagel, then the marginal cost will steadily decline as the sales of bagels increase and the average fixed cost decreases. For example, at sales of 30 bagels per hour marginal costs per bagel are $.08 and average cost is $.42, at 40 bagels marginal costs are $.04 and the average cost is $.38 per bagel and so on. Therefore, as long as marginal cost is below average cost the average cost per bagel will decrease as sales volume increases.

However, at some level of production and sales of bagels, Bob will have to hire an additional worker. The additional worker's salary will be a fixed cost in the short run as it will not vary with the production of bagels. Bob calculates that he will need to hire a worker for the front counter when his sales volume reaches 60 bagels per hour. The additional worker will cost him $840 per month or $6.00 per hour. This will increase the fixed cost of selling 60 bagels to $11.00 per hour. At sales of 60 bagels per hour total cost will increase to $26 per hour and average total cost to $.43 per bagel. The increase in average total cost per bagel is still below the price Bob charges per bagel, so the increased cost will still result in a profit of $4.20 for sales of 60 bagels

Average fixed cost =	$.18
Average variable cost	$.25

Average total cost	$.43
Unit Price	$.50

38 Economics for Everyone

Profit Margin	$.07

Profit margin $.07 times volume 60 = profit $4.20

At bagel sales of 70 and per hour the marginal cost decreases to $.03 average total cost decreases to $.40 per bagel profit margin increases to $.10 and profit increases to $7.00.

Marginal analysis can be used in many other ways. For example, marginal analysis can be used to demonstrate the effect on a student's grade point average by taking one additional college course. Let's assume that as a junior in college you have previously taken and passed 16 courses. For the courses taken you earned 48 credit hours, and your grade point average is 3.0 or an average letter grade of B. If you take a course in economics, your grade point average can either decrease, increase or stay the same. If you receive a B for the course your grade point average will not change. If you receive an A (4.0 grade points) for the course your grade point average will increase and if you receive a C (2.0 grade points) for the course your grade point average will decrease. The grades of A, B, and C are your marginal or additional grade for this course. As long as your marginal grade is higher than the grade point average your grade point average will increase. The calculations of the grade point average are shown below:

Grade Points Awarded

A = 4.0 C = 20
B = 3.0 D = 10

Total grade points awarded = 16 courses taken times an average grade of 3.0 equals total grade points previously awarded of 48.

Grade for Economics Course	Marginal Points	New GPA
A	4.0	3.05
B	3.0	3.00
C	2.0	2.94
D	1.0	2.88

The moral to this story is that you should study hard and get a grade of B or better for the economics course to maintain or increase your GPA.

BREAK EVEN ANALYSIS

Table 3-4 shows average fixed costs, variable costs, marginal costs and profit per hour of Bob's Bagel Shop. At a sales level of 20 bagels per hour Bob's profit is $0.0. This is his break-even point. The break-even point can also, be calculated using the following formula:

$$\text{Break Even Volume} = \frac{\text{Average Fixed Cost}}{(\text{Unit Price} - \text{Variable Cost})}$$

$$\text{Break Even Volume} = \frac{5.00 \text{ Per Hour}}{(\$.50 - \$.25)} = 20 \text{ Bagels per hour}$$

Bob decides to hire an additional worker when his sales reach 60 bagels per hour. This will increase his fixed cost in the short run from $5.00 per hour to $11.00 hour. Notice that at sales of 60 bagels per hour the marginal cost increases from $.03 to $.08 and the average cost increases from $.35 per bagel to $.43 per bagel. This illustrates that when marginal cost or the cost of the next bagel increases the average cost per bagel also increases.

Figure 3.4: Analysis of Profit (Unit Price = $.50 Per Bagel)

Quantity of Bagels Per hour	Total Cost	Avg. Fixed Cost Per Bagel	Avg. Variable Cost Per Bagel	Avg. Total Cost Per Bagel	Marginal Cost Per Bagel	Profit per hour
0	$5.00	—	—	—	—	$- 5.00
10	7.50	$.50	$.25	$.75		-.2.50
					$.25	
20	10.00	0.25	0.25	0.50		0.00
					.08	
30	12.50	0.17	0.25	0.42		2.50
					.04	
40	15.00	0.13	0.25	0.38		5.00
					.03	
50	17.50	0.10	0.25	0.35		7.50
					.03	
60	26.00	0.18	0.25	0.43		4.00
					.08	
70	28.50	0.18	0.25	0.40		6.50
					.03	
80	31.00	0.14	0.25	0.38		9.00
					.02	

MARKETS, SPECIALIZATION AND GROWTH

If we examine the growth of the world economy over the last two millennia, it shows that for the first 1,700 years the world economy grew very slowly. Then at the end of the 18th century with the introduction of markets and the spread of democracy, the world economy has grown at increasing rates. Markets allow specialization and trade. As individuals compete and specialize they learn by doing, gaining efficiency at what they do. Markets also foster competition, which pushes individuals to find better ways of doing things. An industrialized economy also develops new technology and finds better ways to educate its workers. A market economy also, provides opportunity for entrepreneurs who are willing to take risks to produce new products or better ways to produce existing ones. The factors of production have to be managed and industrialized economies provide education and training to develop the future managers of their country. All of this taken together leads to economic growth and an increased standard of living for everyone engaged in the production process.

The new millennium is offering new ways for individuals to specialize and compete. More and more businesses are trading on the Internet a worldwide network of computers that is just a little more than a decade old. For example, college students now have a choice of where to buy their textbooks. They can still purchase them at the college bookstore or they can buy online at Amazon.com and BarnesandNoble.com. As Internet technology becomes built into our economy, we can expect more specialization, more division of labor, and the economic growth that follows.[4]

NOTES:
Chapter 3

Production and Costs

1. Dolan, Edward S. & Lindsey David E., <u>Economics, Seventh Edition</u>, The Dryden Press, Orlando, FL, 1994. p. 45
2. Dolan and Lindsey, p. 71
3. Aaker, David, <u>Strategic Market Management</u>, John Wiley & Sons, Inc., Hoboken, NJ, 2005, P. 21.
4. Colander, David C., <u>Macroeconomics, Fifth Edition</u>, McGraw-Hill Irwin, New York, NY, 2004, p. 30.

CHAPTER 4

THE FOUNDATIONS OF CLASSICAL ECONOMICS

"It is not its silver or gold that measures a nation's wealth. It is the annual labour of every nation that is the fund which originally supplies it with all the necessaries and conveniences of life." —Adam Smith

ADAM SMITH (1723-1790)

Adam Smith

The industrial revolution, which came to England and Southern Europe in the last third of the eighteenth century, brought workers to the factories and the factory towns. These workers previously produced goods in their cottages or food and wool on their farms. The capital that merchants had invested in raw materials and sent to the villages to be made into cloth was now being invested in factories. However, to operate these new factories a much larger investment was needed in the factors of production, i.e., land, labor, and natural resources. The dominant figure in this change was the industrialist whose purpose was the increased production of goods. The industrial revolution profoundly shaped the development of economics and from it emerged one of the most celebrated figures in the history of the subject. Adam Smith was the prophet of the industrial revolutions achievements and the original source of its explanation.

Adam Smith is considered to have been the founder of economics as a distinct field of study, although he wrote only one book on the subject "An Inquiry into the Nature and Causes of the Wealth of Nations," published in 1776. Smith was 53 years old at the time. His friend David Hume found the book such hard reading that he doubted that many people would read it. However, Hume's prophecy was wrong. People have been reading The Wealth of Nations, for more than 200 years.

Adam Smith wrote that the wealth of a nation was not a result of accumulating gold and silver, as the mercantilists believed. The wealth of a nation is measured by the outcome of the activities of ordinary people working and trading in free markets. To Smith, the remarkable thing about the wealth produced by a market economy, is that it is not a result of any organized plan but the unintended outcome of the actions of many people, each of whom is independently pursuing the incentives the market offers with his or her own interests in mind. Smith writes that: "It is not from the benevolence of the butcher, the brewer, or the baker that we expect our dinner, but from their regard to their own interest. Every individual is continually exerting himself to find out the most advantageous employment for whatever capital he can command. By directing that industry in such a manner as its produce may be of the greatest value, he intends only his own gain, and he is in this, as in many other cases, led by an invisible hand to promote an end which was no part of his intention."[1]

Much of the discipline of economics as it has developed over the past two centuries consists of elaborations on ideas found in Smith's work. The idea of the "invisible hand" of market incentives that channels people's efforts in directions that are beneficial to their neighbors remains the most durable of Smith's contributions to economics.

In his book, Smith describes the work of a pin factory, but one that was far from characteristic of the industrial plants of later decades. What captured Adam Smith's attention was not the machinery that characterized the industrial revolution but the way the job was divided so that each worker became an expert on his minuscule part of the task. The great efficiencies of contemporary enterprise, combined with man's natural propensity to truck, barter, and exchange one thing for another came from this specialization, this division of labor.

Smith's Lasting Contributions to Economics

Adam Smith's contributions to economics were many. There are, however, four critical areas that provide a starting point. These are his views on economic motivation, the distribution of revenue that was earned from the sale of goods, how prices are determined and the role of government in business and international trade. These issues still survive in today's college textbooks as the study of microeconomics.

Economic Motivation: This for Smith centers on the role of self-interest. The private and competitive pursuit of things that are in ones best interest is the source of the greatest benefit to the public. Smith adds, an invisible hand leads the individual to promote and end which was not part of his original intention. The person concerned with self-enrichment had previously been and object of doubt, suspicion and mistrust, feelings that went back through the middle ages to biblical times. Now, because of his self-interest, he had become the driving force behind the industrial revolution's propensity to produce a whole spectrum of new products.

The Distribution of Revenue: Prices and who gets the proceeds, were the second of the basic issues of economics that Smith addressed. In this regard, Smith analyzed the reasons for the distribution of revenue among the workers, the landlords and the owners. As workers were assembled in the factories, what determined their pay became highly relevant. As the capitalists assumed control of production, the question arose concerning a fair distribution of income to the workers and to the owner of the business.

The wage's that were paid to workers, Smith regarded generally as the price of attracting labor and the cost of sustaining them on the job. Profit, according to Smith is the appropriation of a surplus value that the worker creates over and above what the capitalist pays them. The capitalist, according to Smith, has a seemingly rightful claim. The question here was not if the capitalist deserved a return on the capital that they invested, but how much that return should be. In many circumstances, the amount of return that went to the capitalist was a result of the power that they held over the workers and not their contribution to the value of the goods sold.

The compensation paid to landlords as rent, entered into the composition of the price of commodities, in a different way from wages and profit. High or low wages and profit are the causes of high or low price; high or low rent is the effect of it. "The rent increases in proportion to the goodness of the pasture."[2]

How Prices are Determined: The interesting and disturbing circumstance that many of the best or most nearly essential things in life are virtually free, puzzled Smith. For example, water which was highly useful was very cheap while diamonds which were then, as now, expensive, were not really very useful. From this analysis came the troubling difference between value in use and value in exchange.

Smith resolved the problem in his time by simply setting value in use aside and asserting a value in exchange. This was a version of what came to be known as the "labor theory of value." According to Smith, the value of labor measures the worth of any possession and ultimately the amount for which it can be exchanged.[3]

Government's Role in Business and International Trade: Adam Smith's strongest recommendation as to public policy urges the freedom of internal and international trade. Many of Smith's recommendations come from his observation of the pin factory. According to Smith, only if there is freedom to barter and trade, can some workers specialize on pins. Also, others can devote their efforts to additional tasks, so that these efforts will come together for the exchange that satisfies several individual needs. If freedom of trade does not exist, each worker must concentrate incompetently on making his own pins; the economies from specialization are gone. From this analysis, Smith concludes that the wider the trading area, the greater the opportunity for specialization; for the division of labor, and the greater the productivity of labor.

Smith's case for free trade extends to a direct assault on the mercantilist view of gold and silver as the foundation of national wealth and to the belief that trade restrictions can enhance the stock of precious metals. In the opening words of The Wealth of Nations, Smith proclaims that it is not its silver or gold that measures a nation's wealth. It is "the annual labour of every nation that is the fund which originally supplies it with all the necessaries and conveniences of life." Wealth, Smith held, is enhanced by "the skill, dexterity, and judgment with which its labour is generally applied, and, secondly, by the proportion between the numbers of those who are employed in useful labour, and that of those who are not so employed."[4]

According to Smith the matters of labor and production are the most important ones to address. If they are managed successfully, prices will be low, and supplies of marketable products will be plentiful. Gold and silver will come in from abroad to purchase the products, and the supply of specie will take care of itself. Other countries cannot prevent their people from exchanging their gold and silver for useful products. Smith observes that, "All sanguinary laws of Spain and Portugal are not able to keep their gold and silver at home." Smith adds, "It is not by the importation of gold and silver, that the discovery of America has enriched Europe. By the abundance of the American mines, those metals have become cheaper."[5]

Smith was not totally rigid on the matter of free trade. He would allow tariffs for industries essential for defense and possibly in retaliation for tariff abuse abroad. Also, he would be tolerant of protecting new enterprises from competition abroad and recommend a gradual withdrawal of tariffs as these enterprises became capable of competing on an international level. Alexander Hamilton who recommended tariff protection for new and developing enterprises in America after the revolution, took this argument up later.

Smith's Laws of Accumulation and Population

Smith attempted to answer the question of what pushes a society toward the pursuit of wealth. Smith thought that part of the answer is the workings of the market system itself. The competitive force of the marketplace encourages businessmen to invent, innovate, to take risks, and to expand. Smith identified two basic laws of behavior that propel the market system toward increasing levels of productivity.

The first is the Law of Accumulation. The industrial revolution in its early stages provided many opportunities to obtain wealth for those who were industrious enough and smart enough to take advantage of the situation. The basic objective of most of the early industrialists was to accumulate their savings. Prior to the Civil War in America, bank loans were usually made for purchasing land and investment banking had not yet been developed in this country. Therefore, the money to build manufacturing facilities essentially came from the profit of the enterprise or the accumulated savings of the capitalist.

Smith believed that the accumulation of capital was a great benefit to society. For it was the capital that society invested in new facilities and machinery that provided the division of labor necessary to increase the workers' productivity. However, Smith identified a potential problem as he feared that accumulation could lead to market saturation. This was because accumulation would mean more machinery, and this would increase the demand for workers. The increased demand for workers would lead to higher and higher wages until profits would disappear.[6]

They would surmount this hurdle to economic growth, according to Smith, by the second great behavioral law, "The Law of Population." Smith believed that if wages were high, then the population would increase because families with higher incomes could afford more children and the infant mortality rate would decrease. Therefore, if the first effect of accumulation was to raise the wages of the working class, the second effect would be to encourage the increase in the number of workers. This meant that accumulation might continue for long periods. The increase in population controls the supply of workers and their ability to command higher wages. The growth in population limits the cost of labor which is the major obstacle to increased profits.

Through the laws of accumulation and population, Smith constructed for society an endless chain of increased productivity. The mechanism of the market and the price system first serves to equalize the distribution of income to labor and capital, sees to it that the products demanded are produced in the proper quantities, and further encourages competition that drives prices down to where they are equal to the cost of production. Smith believed that the new industrial society was dynamic, that accumulation of wealth would continue, and that accumulation would result in increased facilities for production and in a greater division of labor.[7]

Smith was the economist of preindustrial capitalism. He saw an evolution for society, but he did not see a revolution. His system presupposes that eighteenth-century England will remain unchanged forever. The system would grow only in quantity, more people, more products and more wealth, but its quality would stay the same. Smith's system is a static one that grows but one that never matures.

Adam Smith emphasized the commitment to competition as a prerequisite to all capitalists' societies. Smith assumed that competition in a capitalist system, would ensure optimal industrial performance. Adam Smith addressed an audience that was ready to receive his message and with his message the remnants of the out-of-date regime of merchant capitalism ended.

For one hundred years after Smith's death, economists would attempt to amend and sharpen his conclusions, and struggle to resolve his ambiguities. In the years following Adam Smith's death, three great figures one French and two British emerged. The main emphasis of their writing was to refine and extend Adam Smith's economic theories. All three witnessed the industrial revolution in full flower, and, improving on Smith, they sought to bring economics abreast of this enormous change. In addition, there was the beginning of economic commentary from America.

JEAN BAPTISTE SAY (1767-1832)

Jean Baptiste Say's business background led him to observe the distinctive role of the entrepreneur; the man who conceives or takes charge of an enterprise; sees and exploits opportunity, and is the motivating force for economic change and improvement. Say later in life was a professor ending his career at the College de France.

However, Say's major, and for a full 130 years, his lasting and most influential contribution to economic theory was his Law of Markets. To this day, economic textbooks continue to refer to Say's

Jean Baptiste Say

law. Say's Law held that out of the production of goods came an effective aggregate of demand sufficient to purchase the total supply of goods.[8]

Put in more modern terms, from the price of every product sold comes a return in wages, interest, profit or rent, sufficient to purchase that product. There can never be a shortage of demand. It is, indeed, possible that some people will save from the proceeds of the sale. However, the amount saved by consumers will be invested by companies in new production facilities. In other words, businesses would spend the saved income of consumers. Even if they hoard the receipts, this does not change the situation; prices adjust themselves downward and adjust to the lesser flow of income. There can still be no general excess of goods, no general shortage of purchasing power.

THOMAS ROBERT MALTHUS (1776-1834)

Thomas Malthus

Thomas Malthus was a British clergyman whom the British East Indian Company employed. Malthus wrote two books on classical economics and the industrial revolution, "An Essay on the Principle of Population" and "Principles of Political Economy." These works cover a wide range of subjects, but to the history of economics he contributed two theories.

Malthus' most noted contribution was the law he saw controlling the growth of population, and on how increased population affected the allocation of wages to the workers. From Thomas Malthus' observations came his basic conclusion:

- The mean of subsistence will limit population growth.

- Population increases when the mean of subsistence allows, and does so geometrically, while the best hope for increase in the food supply is arithmetic.

- This asymmetry will persist, so that the food supply will hold the population in check unless prior checks on its increase are operative. The possible prior checks are moral restraint, vice and misery.[9]

Using data from the United States, supplied by Benjamin Franklin, Malthus asserted that population tends to double every twenty-five years. Franklin also reported that some villages in the new country doubled in only fifteen years. Although Franklin did not provide any information on the food supply, Malthus concluded that output could never keep pace with population. Unchecked population grows at a geometric ratio, Malthus held, whereas food increases at merely an arithmetic ratio.

A geometric ratio means that a number continually multiplies itself by a constant, for example, a perpetual doubling. An arithmetic ratio simply adds a constant. Malthus provided a good example of his theory: where humans would increase by 1,2,4,8,16,32,64,128,256, while food would grow by 1,2,3,4,5,6,7,8,9. In this case if each person had one basket of food at the beginning of a period, two hundred years later, 256 people would have to share just nine baskets of food.

Malthus did not present a pleasant prospect for humanity. He did provide a powerful case against public or private charity and a greatly serviceable support to those who found it convenient to forgo help to the unfortunate.

Malthus' other claim to fame was his doubt about Say's Law. Malthus held that supply would not create its own demand, given the poverty of the workers. The workers have reduced themselves to the lowest levels of sustainable wages by their propensity to reproduce. There would be a tendency for more goods to be produced than could be bought and consumed by these workers. Also, at this time, banks did not make loans to business firms. Therefore, the only way that business owners could obtain capital, was by deferring consumption. This would result in increased savings at the expense of current consumption demand.

DAVID RICARDO (1772-1823)

David Ricardo

David Ricardo rescued Say's law from Malthus' attack. According to Ricardo, the flow of income from the production of goods did indeed create its own sufficient demand. Ricardo's writing was not similar to the method used by Adam Smith. Ricardo's work is grim and difficult. Ricardo offered an influential change of method. Ricardo was theoretical and inductive; proceeding from some empirical evidence, he continued by abstract reasoning to the plausible, or perhaps inevitable conclusion.

Ricardo's writing used a method that, in the future, would greatly appeal to economists. His method of writing reduced the research that is necessary to analyze a theory. It served Ricardo well. His method and his conclusions would lead the later defenders of capitalism, and its most passionate opponents, equally to firm conclusions.

One of Ricardo's most lasting contributions to economic theory was his Law of Comparative Advantage. During Ricardo's time, wealthy English landowners attempted to persuade Parliament to impose tariffs on the import of grain. The price of grain had soared during the Napoleonic Wars, partly because of Napoleon's embargo, and the landowners feared that a drop of prices would take place. On the other side of the argument were the new businessmen of the Industrial Revolution who preferred to see lower prices for food. The reason that businessmen preferred low prices is that the price of food affects their major cost, the wages paid to the workers. The landowners won the battle of influence, and in 1815 Parliament passed an act that prohibited imports of grain below a certain price, virtually granting

English farmers a monopoly. British dictionaries define "corn" as grain such as oats, rye, wheat and barley. Thus, they called the acts "Corn Laws."

Ricardo thought that Britain had two choices as to their position in international trade: as a projectionist island or as an extroverted trader. Ricardo recommended a free trade policy for Britain. Ricardo developed his theory to show that countries should specialize in whatever leads them to give up the least opportunity. This is their "comparative advantage." In addition, the sacrifice they make by not producing a product, is their "opportunity cost." Thus, according to Ricardo, specialization is determined by whoever has the lower opportunity cost.

For Ricardo, free trade makes it possible for households to consume more goods regardless of whether trading partners are more or less economically advanced. Ricardo's position on the "Corn Laws" was that if the French farmers are willing to feed us for less than it would cost to feed ourselves, Englishmen would be better off by eating French food and spending their time doing something else. In spite of his constant argument on this topic, Ricardo could not persuade Parliament to repeal these laws and they remained in effect until 1846. Ricardo did, however, provide a powerful argument for subsequent generations of economists. Ricardo's argument is that protection is usually bad for an economy as a whole, though sometimes good for a particular group of people. This debate continues today though in another form, between those who support managed trade and those who still believe that totally free trade is possible.

Ricardo follows Smith in identifying the main concerns of economics. Of the factors determining the value of price (value in exchange) of a product, Ricardo believed that the first must be utility. "If a commodity were in no way useful, in other words, if it could in no way contribute to our gratification, it would be destitute of exchangeable value."[8] Here emerges, in early form, the other side of the modern view of price making, the interaction of supply and demand. After establishing the need for "exchangeable products," Ricardo then saw the value of exchangeable products resulting from scarcity or from the quantity of labor required to obtain them. It is

Ricardo's commitment to a firm labor theory of value in exchange that is central to the influence he exercised in the years to come.

Next Ricardo addressed the return to landlords of rent, which he defined as, "That portion of the produce of the earth, which is paid to the landlord for the use of the original and indestructible powers of the soil." From the possession of the better land the landlord would receive a surplus over the cost or rent. The owner of good land was thus the beneficiary not only of his own good fortune but also of the increasing misery or poor fortune of all others. Rent did not force up prices; it was a residual accruing passively from the increase in population and the general progress of the society. The rise of rent is always the effect of the increasing wealth of the country, and of the difficulty of providing for its augmented population.[10]

Returning to wages, Ricardo said, "That wages are the price that is necessary to enable the laborers to subsist and to perpetuate their race, without either increase or reduction." This theory, "The Iron Law of Wages," was to enter history extending far beyond formal economics. The law established that those who worked were meant to be poor and were not to be rescued from their poverty by a compassionate state or employer or through trade unions or by other actions of their own. This, as we shall see was a very fortunate conclusion for the capitalist who received a seemingly excess value for their investment.

The Iron Law was the natural or equilibrium price of labor, the level to which, all else equal, wages tend to settle. However, Ricardo concluded that not only workers' necessities but also conveniences that were essential to them based on previous habit, should be considered. Taken together, these are what economists would now call the workers' accustomed standard of living. Also, the market price of labor in an improving society could be above the market rate in the short run. This could result when the demand for labor was greater than the current supply of labor. However, since higher wages encourage increases in population and as the number of laborers is increased, wages again fall to their natural price and sometimes fall below it. In modern terms, if the demand for labor is greater than the supply of labor, wages will increase. However, when living standards increase, families tend to have more children. This increases the supply of labor and reduces wages to a natural or equilibrium level.

It was for his controlling law of wages that Ricardo was to be remembered. From this controlling law came his commitment to the inevitable misery of those who live under capitalism and to the uselessness of any corrective action by government or by the workers themselves. This action Ricardo specifically condemned as he wrote; "Like all other contracts, wages should be left to the fair and free competition of the marketplace, and should never be controlled by the interference of the legislature." [11]

In the years to come there would be an increasingly angry division between those who spoke for the system and those who spoke for the masses who were perceived as the victims of the industrial revolution. From Malthus and especially from Ricardo came ideas that would serve both sides of the debate.

HENRY CHARLES CAREY (1793-1879)

Until the civil war and even after, what distinguished the American scene was a spacious abundance, a prospect of income and opportunity for farmer and worker, as well as businessman and capitalist, unimaginable in England. The leading American economic scholar of this time was Henry Charles Carey.

In his early work, Carey was a follower of the British classical theory. However, as he sought to apply classical theory to his American surroundings, he came to have his doubts. David Ricardo had seen increasing population and limited land resources pressing labor to an even lower marginal return. Carey saw the same processes leading labor to an ever-higher return as it became more productive.

In the new world settlement, had begun on the hilltops, where forests were less dense and resistant. Since property on a hilltop usually represented the most prestige to those of noble European heritage, settlers tended to assign the most value to these locations. In America, when the pioneers moved, it was often to more fertile, more productive valleys, thus achieving not a diminishing but an expanding return. The same was true when attention turned to the frontier and the great unexplored resources there.

This tendency rejected the views of Ricardo, and it destroyed those of Malthus. An increasing population was not dividing a stagnant or decreasing food supply, but one that was rapidly increasing. Henry Carey was not averse to the thought that on some distant day there might be too many people. However, he was content to believe that this evil was sufficient unto its own time. God had said "Be fruitful and multiply."[12]

NOTES:

Chapter 4
The Foundations of Classical Economics

1. Smith, Adam, <u>An Inquiry into the Nature and Causes of The Wealth of Nations</u>, R.H. Campbell, A.S. Skinner and W. B. Todd, Editors, Oxford, England, Clarendon Press, 1977 [1776], Introduction.
2. Smith, Book I, Chapter 2.
3. Smith, Book I, Chapter 5.
4. Smith, Introduction.
5. Smith, Book 4, Chapter 1.
6. Gailbraith, John Kenneth, <u>Economics in Perspective</u>, Boston, MA, Houghton Mifflin Company, 1987, p. 75.
7. Heilbroner, Robert L., <u>The Worldly Philosophers</u>, New York, Simon & Schuster, Inc., 1986, p. 65.
8. Heilbroner, p. 66.
9. Malthus, Thomas A., <u>An Essay on the Principle of Population, 6th Addition</u>, London, England, Ward Lock, 1890, p. 15.
10. Sraffa, Piero, <u>The Works and Correspondents of David Ricardo</u>, Cambridge, England, Cambridge University Press, 1951, p. 11.
11. Ricardo, p. 77.
12. Gailbraith, pp. 100-101.

CHAPTER 5

FINANCE AND BANKING
(1800-1913)

"The whole community derives benefit from a bank. It facilitates the commerce of the country. It quickens the means of purchasing and paying for country produce and hastens on the exportation of it." -- Thomas Paine

THE ROLE OF COMMERCIAL BANKS

Financial intermediaries play an important role in industrialized countries. The major function of a commercial bank is to gather the savings of many individuals and convert these funds into mortgage and business loans. Companies invest dollars in new plant and equipment and additions to inventory in order to increase the output of goods or services or to reduce the unit cost of producing these products. In modern times, many of these investment dollars come from the savings of individuals. Banks collect these dollars in demand and time deposits and in turn make loans to corporations. In addition, individuals may choose to invest their dollars directly in corporations by buying their stocks and bonds through a stockbroker.

The key to a bank's profitability is making loans to individuals and firms at a rate of interest that is higher than the interest that they give savers on their deposits. Also, the interest rate charged must be sufficient to cover administrative costs and provide a margin of profit. This in banking is called the interest rate spread. Also, prudent banks try to match the maturities of their deposit liabilities with lending assets. For example, if the bulk of a bank's savings and demand deposits mature on an average of six months, the bank should limit the maturities of their lending portfolio to between six months and one year.

When a bank mismatches its maturities, that is has the bulk of its liabilities maturing in six months or less and the bulk of its assets maturing at one year or greater, it runs the risk of becoming illiquid. If depositors become worried that they may not be able to convert their deposits into currency, a run on the bank may occur. This would cause the bank to become insolvent and probably would force the bank to stop doing business. Therefore, a bank must practice prudent and sound lending practices if it wishes to increase the probability that it will stay in business in the long-run.

BIMETALLIC MONEY

In 1792 Congress chose the dollar as the official United States currency. Congress defined the dollar as containing either 371.25 grains of silver or 24.75 grains of gold or a relationship between the two metals of fifteen silver to one gold. The government offered to buy and sell unlimited amounts of gold and silver at the fifteen to one ratio. These purchases could be in either coin of bullion. As long as this relationship held in the bullion markets, the system worked well. However, if the relative values of gold and silver as bullion differed from the fifteen to one ratio, people would exchange the overvalued metal for that which the U.S. mint undervalued.

Early in the nineteenth century, gold could be exchanged for sixteen times its weight in silver in the bullion markets. The result of this difference in the valuation of gold and silver as bullion versus the valuation of these metals as a medium of exchange was that U.S. gold coins disappeared from circulation. In 1834 Congress changed the mint relationship to sixteen silvers to one gold, but by this time the ratio overvalued gold. As a result of the changed relationship, silver coins became extremely scarce. The discovery of gold in California in 1848 only made the situation worse.[1]

When the United States defined the dollar as containing a specific amount of gold or silver, it determined the exchange rate between the dollar and foreign currencies, whose metallic content was also fixed. Dollars would exchange for British pound sterling in

58   Economics for Everyone

proportion to the rate that each currency could be exchanged for gold. Since gold could move freely between nations, there was only a limited extent to which the United States could both control its own monetary affairs and maintain fixed exchange rates.

BANKING BEFORE THE CIVIL WAR

Gold and silver coins were only part of the United States money supply. Most of the money that circulated was created by commercial banks. Prior to the Civil War, the use of bank checking accounts had become widespread, particularly in the Northeast and Mid- Atlantic states. In addition to checking deposits, banks could print notes that they could lend to customers. Today, in comparison, only Federal Reserve notes can circulate as U.S. currency. During the fifty years after 1800, the number of banks grew much faster than the rate of population, and bank assets, notes in circulation, and deposits grew even faster.

Since money's value depends on its scarcity, there are limits to a bank's ability to increase the money supply. Bank money has limited value if it is not convertible into legal tender. In the nineteenth century, legal tender meant gold or silver. Banks had to be able to exchange their notes and checking deposits for legal tender on demand from their customers. Under normal circumstances, only a small fraction of an individual bank's outstanding liabilities, would be presented for conversion to specie, on any given day. Thus, banks only had to retain about 10 to 30 percent of their notes or deposits in the form of gold or silver. The remaining deposits could be used to fund loans or to purchase securities.

If a bank's ability to convert its own money into specie was in doubt their notes would be accepted in trade at less than face value or at a discount. The discount would vary with the degree of uncertainty about the issuing bank's ability to redeem its obligations in full on demand. Information about the stability of banks generally became more difficult to obtain, when the issuing bank was located a great distance from the bank receiving the note. Therefore, most banks' notes were discounted at rates increasing with the distance from their point of origin.

ATTEMPTS TO REGULATE BANKS

Various attempts were made prior to the Civil War to regulate the state banking system. States often contributed to a bank's capital and did gain some control as stockholders. In general, banking laws specified the amount of capital that had to be subscribed by the bank's owners, limited the number of notes that it could issue, and made some provision for inspections to insure compliance with these regulations. The extent of regulations and its enforcement was inconsistent, stricter where merchant communities were well established, and very lax in the rural areas. Often the regulation of banks was left up to the institutions themselves. Some self- regulation did occur in the eastern states but very little in the western states. An example of self-regulation was the Suffolk Banking system that attempted to regulate banks in the New England region of the country.

In 1820, the newly established Suffolk Bank in Boston offered to accept the notes of any rural bank in New England that would keep a permanent deposit of $5,000 over the funds required by the state clearinghouse. The Suffolk Bank also allowed rural banks to redeem their notes at the same rate of discount for which Suffolk had accepted them. Rural banks, that did not cooperate, found that the Suffolk bank would accumulate large quantities of their notes and present them, without notice, to the rural bank for redemption for specie. The Suffolk system caused the notes of all New England banks to circulate within the region at their face value, therefore eliminating the need to discount bank notes within the region. This made bank money a better medium of exchange and made trade run smoother within the system.[2]

New York State attempted to alleviate the propensity of small local banks to fail and therefore cause large losses to their depositors, through an institution similar to the modern Federal Deposit Insurance Corporation. In 1828, the state required that all banks in New York contribute 1.5 percent of their capital annually, up to a maximum of 3 percent, to a fund that would be able to make good the notes of failed banks whose assets were not sufficient to cover their outstanding notes. Banks were required to join the system as a condition for renewal of their corporate charters. Although the safety fund created by this legislature apparently was capable of protecting investors against the occasional failures of individual banks, it proved insufficient to deal with the bank collapses of the latter part of the 1830's.

Left to regulate themselves, most state banking systems had serious weaknesses. Regulation varied greatly between states. This resulted in the instability of the entire United States banking system because there was no source of additional reserves available for the entire system. If enough people began to fear that their bank notes or demand deposits could not be converted into gold or silver, a run on the bank took place.[3]

ATTEMPTS TO ESTABLISH A CENTRAL BANK

The major function of a central bank in industrialized countries is to regulate the nation's money supply. Ideally, central banks attempt to prevent rapid changes in the money supply. Their major tool for this purpose is the control over private bank reserves. Also, central banks serve as government depositories and disbursing agencies performing clearinghouse functions for the settlement of inter-bank debts. In the first half of the nineteenth century, no country had fully developed the central bank, but the United States had two banks that exhibited some central bank characteristics.

The First Bank of the United States

During the first half of the nineteenth century two United States banks were established by Congress. In 1791, Congress granted a federal charter to the First Bank of the United States. The Bank had branches and did business throughout the country and served as the government's depository. This structure enabled the Bank to return its deposits of the notes of other banks for prompt collection. This practice aggravated the smaller banks as it tended to restrict their lending or as we might say in modern times, it required the smaller banks to follow more prudent bank lending practices. The practice of restricting the lending of smaller banks was a continuous point of argument between Alexander Hamilton and Thomas Jefferson; Hamilton on the side of safe banking. The charter of the First Bank of the United States expired in 1811, and a bill to extend its charter for twenty more years was defeated in Congress by only one vote.[4]

The Second Bank of the United States

In 1816, Congress granted a new charter, to the Second Bank of the United States. The Bank was headquartered in Philadelphia, then the country's financial center, and like the First Bank of the United States, had branches throughout the country. The Bank served as the federal government's depository, receiving all payments to the government. The Bank also accepted deposits and made loans in the same manner as the country's other commercial banks. The first two presidents of the Bank were not strong leaders and as a consequence the Bank was not very well run. In 1823, Nicholas Biddle became president of the Bank. Under Biddle's leadership, the Bank assumed some of the roles that are characteristic of a central bank. For example, the Bank began to use its position as a net creditor to the state banks to control the amount of their note issues. Because of this policy, the state banks were forced to limit their note issues to the growth of their reserves. This practice while good for the safety of the banking system, served to reduce the potential profit available to the state banks.

In addition to its other operations, the Bank could function as a lender of last resort. On occasion, the Bank made some loans of specie to state banks that were experiencing short term financial difficulty. Still, the Bank was first and foremost a profit-making institution. Because of its profit motive, the Bank made loans with the priority given to its own reserve position and its own profit potential. In addition, it occasionally increased its own reserves to meet a crisis by selling bonds to the public. This action when implemented by a central bank serves to reduce the money supply and therefore reduces business expansion. However, neither the First nor Second Bank of the United States could expand the money supply since they could not control the amount of reserves held by state banks.[5]

In 1832, President Andrew Jackson vetoed a bill passed by Congress to extend the Bank's charter for twenty more years. The

Bank did obtain a state charter from Pennsylvania, and continued in operation until 1841. However, after 1841, federal deposits were withdrawn from the Bank. These deposits were then placed in banks owned by Jackson's political allies. Finally, after the financial panic of 1837, in which the government lost large amounts of dollars that were deposited in these state banks, the government's deposits were kept in an independent treasury system. The era of a federal bank came to an end in 1832, and the country from then on, operated under a state chartered banking system until the Federal Reserve System was created in 1913.

THE STATE BANKING SYSTEM

In 1838, Michigan and New York passed laws that greatly eased the previous banking restrictions. These banks were no longer required to obtain individual charters from the state legislature. Instead they could enter the banking business by depositing approved securities with the states' banking officials and by observing a few basic rules. Other states instituted their own rules, which became known as "Free Banking" laws. As a result of the reduction of bank regulations in many states, the number of state banks increased from 691 in 1843, to 1,520 in 1860.[6]

Although the history of banking is full of colorful tails about irresponsible practices, by 1860 it was commonly agreed between bankers and regulators that banks should keep reserves against all liabilities. The enforcement of state regulations began to improve, and some states even provided for periodic examinations. Therefore, it does not appear, based on modern studies, that free banking resulted in any serious damage and did not retard the economic growth in the new country from 1800 through 1860.[7]

THE ERA OF DUAL BANKING

Prior to the Civil War, there were many controversies over money and banking. These controversies usually revolved around the quantity theory of money and the operation of the state banking system. Many people still held the conviction that capital could be created and prices could be increased by expanding the money supply. During the war, the union government could no longer make payments of money in the form of silver or gold. The Union government had to choose between increasing taxes to pay for the war or to begin printing money. Congress, unwilling to increase taxes to pay for the war, authorized the issue of $450 million in paper money. This authorization was in the form of United States Notes. These notes, commonly called "Greenbacks" were declared by Congress to be "Legal Tender" that could be used for payment of all debts.

In 1863, Congress passed the National Banking Act to provide a uniform currency to eliminate the oversupply of state bank notes, and to create a market for government bonds. One of the major provisions of the Act was to establish a bond-secured national currency. The Act created the national bank structure under the supervision of the Comptroller of the Currency. To obtain a national charter, groups of businessmen were required to deposit a specific amount of United States bonds with the Comptroller. These bonds could then be used as collateral that allowed the national chartered banks to issue national bank notes. National banks were also required to maintain reserves against their deposits, originally set at 25 percent for city banks and 15 percent for country banks.

After the Civil War, Congress amended the National Banking Act by imposing a 10 percent tax against state bank notes. The result of this tax was to drive state bank notes out of existence effectively creating a system of national currency. In addition, the National Banking System changed the philosophy of commercial banking by emphasizing the "Real Bills Doctrine." This doctrine confirmed that commercial banks should make only short term self-liquidating loans to businesses. Under the National Banking System, loans were made against commercial paper (short term unsecured liabilities of businesses) and were theoretically self-liquidating. This practice helped banks to better match the maturities of their assets and liabilities. This practice tends to increase the liquidity of the banking system by providing the ability to weather any crisis caused by a withdrawal of deposits. When the maturities of a bank's assets and liabilities are matched, it enables the institution to liquidate their loan and securities portfolios in order to accommodate any run on the bank's deposits.

While the National Banking System brought about many improvements in commercial banking, it also had some major weaknesses. The banking system allowed the practice of pyramiding bank reserves in New York City. Pyramiding of reserves occurred as out-of-town banks piled up deposits in New York. When additional funds were needed in rural areas, these country banks rapidly drew down their deposits forcing the New York banks to call in their short-term loans to brokers. This practice set in motion a chain reaction as brokers called in their margin loans to customers. The result was the reduction of the money supply during business contractions and the aggravation of financial panics.

Another weakness of the National Banking System was that it relied heavily on the real-bills doctrine, with its emphasis on commercial loans. This reliance on the real-bills doctrine, intensified tendencies toward boom and bust economic conditions. To add to this weakness, there was no central bank that could assist individual banks when they got into financial difficulty. In addition, there was no institution that could step in to stabilize the economy by discouraging speculative expansion during prosperity and softening the impact of deflation during panic and depression. Also, there was no national clearinghouse which continued the inefficient way in which check payments were made between different regions of the country.

In summary, the National Banking System made banking safer for national bank note holders and depositors; however, it made the currency less elastic (the supply of money does not expand or contract with the rise and fall of business activity) and capital funds less mobile. These weaknesses continued until the establishment of the Federal Reserve System in 1913.

JOHN PIERPONT MORGAN (1873-1913)

John Pierpont Morgan

John Pierpont Morgan was born on April 17th 1837 in Hartford Connecticut. His grandfather Joseph was an extremely successful businessman who left his son Julius (J.P. Morgan's father) more than $1 million when he died.

In 1854 Julius Morgan formed a partnership with prominent American banker George Peabody and moved to London. At the time, London was the center of the financial world. The partnership would eventually establish Julius as one of Europe's most prominent investment bankers. Pierpont, as he was often called, attended the University at Grottingen Germany, however; he spent much of his time in the German beer halls consuming large quantities of brew.

Alarmed by his son's behavior, Julius sent young Pierpont to work at Duncan, Sherman a merchant-banking firm in New York City. Morgan's apprenticeship at Duncan, Sherman lasted four years. He then persuaded his father for support in opening his own firm J.P. Morgan and Co. Julius supported Pierpont's request with the intention that the firm was to execute trades and represent Peabody and Co., at his father's direction. Pierpont had other ideas such as expanding the scope of the company into an investment-banking firm.

Banking in the latter half of the nineteenth century had a different set of rules than today. Lending money to a company usually meant also taking a board seat so that the investor could protect their interests. This was necessary then, for Wall Street was full of unscrupulous manipulators who regularly fleeced investors. By 1870 Dabney, Morgan & Co. was thriving. In 1871, when Dabney retired, Julius arranged for Morgan to form a new partnership with a prestigious banking firm in Philadelphia called Drexel and Co. The new firm was named Drexel, Morgan and Co.

Morgan was optimistic about America in the 1870's and always alert for promising new industries. In a bold move, he agreed to finance a young inventor named Thomas Edison and his experiments with an electric light bulb. The success of this and other ventures eventually lead to the formation of the General Electric Company which remains today as one of America's largest and most respected companies.

America slipped into a steep industrial decline in 1893. More than 15,000 businesses and 600 banks failed and clashes were commonplace between owners and workers. Railroads were particularly hard hit, since they were burdened with heavy debt. English investors who owned a large portion of the railroad debt urged Morgan to help them. His solution was the voting trust. Morgan developed a reorganization plan, often referred to as "Morganization," that offered relief to shareholders of a bankrupt company if they would transfer their shares to the voting trust in exchange for non-voting trust certificates. Morgan then engineered a restructuring of the company's finances, becoming not only the trustee for the voting trust but also the banker for the entire company. By the end of his career, Morgan had reorganized approximately 33,000 miles of railroad track, about one-sixth of all the nation's tracks.

By 1895, Morgan was in total control of his firm. The Drexel's retired from the company and Morgan reorganized the bank renaming it J.P. Morgan and Co., the firm that survives today. Recognizing the benefits from increasing market share through mergers, other corporations followed Morganization techniques with business-friendly states such as New Jersey offering liberal rules for forming trusts. Such changes enabled Morgan to even further consolidate his control over America's finances.

However, with all his other ventures, J.P. Morgan is probably most famous for rescuing the stock market during the financial panic of 1907. On October 24, 1907, Ransom Thomas, president of the New York Stock Exchange, rushed from his office to 23 Wall Street across the street where J.P. Morgan, the most powerful banker in America was located. The United States was in the grip of a financial panic and numerous banks had failed. As a result, Thomas faced the probable failure of 50 brokerage firms and even the New York Stock Exchange itself.

At two that afternoon, Morgan held a meeting in his office with several of the city's most important bank presidents. He persuaded them to pledge $24 million at 10 percent interest. At 2:16 p.m., an announcement of the $24 million in available broker call money was made on the floor of the stock exchange. A cheer immediately erupted as the relieved traders were giving the mighty financier an ovation for rescuing them from near financial disaster. In 1987 a similar situation emerged which was referred to as a liquidity crisis, and the Federal Reserve provided the necessary funds for the market to recover. However; in 1907 the Federal Reserve System was still six years away.

Morgan's accomplishments were many, not only did he save the New York Stock Exchange in 1907, he also rescued the U.S. government from bankruptcy 12 years earlier. He created the General Electric Company and U.S. Steel, at that time the world's largest company. At one point, he controlled more railroads than anyone in the United States did. His investment banking firm, J.P. Morgan & Co. remains today as one of the most influential firms of its kind in the world and with its recent merger with Chase Bank is now the second largest banking firm in America.[8]

NOTES:

Chapter 5
Finance and Banking (1800-1913)

1. Puth, Robert, C. American Economic History, Orlando, FL, The Dryden Press, 1993.
2. Esterlin, L. Davis, American Economic Growth: An Economists History of the United States, New York, N.Y., Harper and Row, 1971.
3. Calomiris, C., Is Deposit Insurance Necessary? A Historical Perspective, Journal of Economic History, June 1990.
4. Lee, S. and Passell, P., A New Economic View of American History, New York, N.Y., Norton, 1979, pp. 112-113.
5. Puth, p. 240.

6. Bureau of the Census, <u>Historical Statistics</u>, 1:1020.
7. Fogel and Engerman, <u>The Reinterpretation of American Economic History</u>, New York, N.Y. Harper and Row, 1971.
8. Gillen, Thomas F., <u>Cigar Aficionado</u>, New York, N.Y., p. 82-102 Note: The primary source of information for this article was taken from Ron Chernow's book, <u>The House of Morgan</u>.

CHAPTER 6

THE EVOLUTION OF CLASSICAL ECONOMICS

"Those organizations which are best fitted to their environment, or which change to fit themselves to their environment, will survive. The least fit will die out, leaving the strongest and best." —Herbert Spencer

THE THEORY OF MARGINAL UTILTIY

The primary concern of economics, throughout the nineteenth century, was with how prices, wages, rent, interest and profits, are determined. Ricardo had anchored the value of price of any manufactured product firmly on cost; the cost, in turn, was that of the labor going into the output under the least satisfactory circumstances of production. The price of the labor was only the cost of sustaining the laborer. The wages paid to labor were in equilibrium at the level sufficient to maintain their life. The difference, between the price of labor and the cost of labor, then accrued as rent to the landlord or as profit to the owners of the business.

This analysis was proper when the distribution was viewed from the point of positive economics. However, far too often, it was observed that profit was handsomely in excess of the outlays for wages. The distribution of profit to the owner was approved of if it was a result of their entrepreneurial ability. However, it was argued, that the unequal distribution of profit was due to the monopoly power that was held by the
Capitalist, not the ability to manage the factors of production.

Another earlier flaw in the classical system was corrected as the century passed. During the second half of the nineteenth century economic analysis shifted from cost to supply as a determinant of price, and to demand as a determinant not only of price but also, of the factors of production. For example, there were attempts by economists to explain why some workers could command greater wages than others. The demand for workers was based on the supply of workers that had the particular skills that were necessary to operate the factories and machine tools available at the time. This development grew out of the efforts to solve the old and seemingly stubborn problem of why the most useful things like water, has a small price and why things with little practical use like diamonds commanded a far greater price.

During the last part of the nineteenth century, economists became preoccupied with solving the problem of value in use and value in exchange. In 1871 there was a breakthrough in explaining the question of value. In that year, William Stanley Jevons (1835-1882) in England and Karl Menger (1840-1921) in Austria, followed a few years later by John Bates Clark (1847-1938) in the United States (professors respectively at London, Vienna and Columbia Universities), recognized the role of marginal utility in determining price. Marginal utility was first explained as the proposition that the utility of any good or service diminishes, all else equal, with increasing availability. These economists held that it is the utility of the last and least wanted; the utility of the marginal unit, that sets the value of all goods and services.[1]

In fact, the marginal utility of a good was merely the first step to a further and final formulation of theory. The concept of marginality could be applied not only to demand but also for supply. Goods are produced at different levels of costs. Accordingly, in industry as in agriculture, there is an omnipotent law of diminishing returns, or increasing cost at greater levels of production.

Because of the diminishing marginal utility to buyers, there is a collective reduction, on their part, to pay the listed price. In order for the producer to sell the remaining inventory of a product that had reached the level of diminishing marginal utility, the price of the product would have to be reduced. The result of this analysis was the downward sloping demand curve that stated that as marginal utility decreased, lowering prices to clear ever larger supplies from the market, would be necessary. Also, the cost of producing a product would increase as the productivity of the factors of production decreased. From the rising marginal costs of less efficient uses of the factors of production came the rising costs of additional supplies. The more of a good or service that is demanded, relative to the supply, the more that must be paid to producers to encourage them to produce that product. The determination that ever-higher prices are needed to cover marginal costs and attract increased supplies to the market led to the discovery of the upward ascending supply curve. Thus, the law of supply and demand was proposed with its supreme achievement at the intersection of the two curves; the price.

Also, there now appeared and was recognized as a major exception in the system, the monopoly. The monopolist extended production to where his more rapidly falling marginal return just covered the added costs. That was where profits were maximized. Production was at a theoretically smaller output than the competitive equilibrium. The monopolist could increase his profit by controlling supply and therefore keep prices artificially high. Accordingly, it was agreed that although the classical system generally was benign, monopoly was not. Monopoly established itself as the single great flaw in an otherwise thought to be perfect system.

UTILITARIANISM AND JEREMY BENTHAM (1784-1832)

Jeremy Bentham

One of the early defenses of the classical system came from outside the central current of economics. This was the Utilitarianism defense, which identified happiness or utility with that characteristic in any object that tends to produce benefit, advantage, pleasure, good, happiness or similarly prevents mischief, pain, evil or unhappiness. In early nineteenth century England, nearly every intellectual wanted to follow the direction of the great physicist, Sir Isaac Newton, and attempt to discover precise answers to the basic economic, political and moral questions of the time. Smith, Ricardo, and Malthus wanted to be the Isaac Newton of economics, by discovering the laws of nature. Jeremy Bentham, the acknowledged leader of the Utilitarianism movement, sought to be the Isaac Newton of the moral universe.

According to Bentham's gospel, nature has two masters, pain and pleasure.[2] Since all human beings like pleasure and hate pain, they choose to do that which gives them pleasure. Bentham continues by stating that when choices affect others, people should choose the alternative that maximizes the total pleasure of all. "The greatest happiness for the greatest number," was the leading emphasis of the Utilitarian movement. Bentham even devised a method of quantifying the amount of pleasure and pain in a situation, called the "Felicific Calculus." In his system, any single experience could be measured by four basic factors: (1) intensity, (2) duration, (3) certainty, and (4) proximity.

Utilitarian theory as it applies to economics held that the maximization of pleasure or happiness could and indeed did come from the maximization of the production of goods, which was the unchallenged achievement of the industrial revolution. What encouraged production was useful or beneficial whether it resulted in incidental suffering for the lesser number or not; the basic rule was the provision of, "The greatest happiness for the greatest number." The unhappiness, even if acute, of the lesser number must be accepted as a matter of practical policy.

Bentham was also involved in politics. He and his followers carried on the battle for free speech and democracy. They fought the Stamp Act, which taxed periodicals, and opposed various restrictions on the right of assembly, and the Corn Laws. Bentham also denounced the barbaric English prison system, arguing that punishment should be used to deter crime, not to wreak vengeance on those convicted of a crime and sent to prison.

JOHN STUART MILL (1806-1873)

Among the visible problems of the classical system there was first, the appalling difference between the wages and resulting living standard of the workers and those of the employers or capitalist. Next

John Stuart Mill

there was the unequal distribution of power inherent in the system. The worker, adult or child, was subject to the discipline that came from dependence on the job, and many times for the next meal. These necessities the employer could give or withhold at will, and he often did. The unequal distribution of power was an obvious flaw in the classical system, a flaw that required a defense.

John Stuart Mill's writing and political career reflect an enlightened and expanded version of Utilitarianism. Mill held that the greatest happiness depends upon more than just pleasure. His publications enhanced Utilitarianism by invoking Platonic virtues of honor, dignity and self-development. This is the reason that Mill became an ardent advocate of public education.

In one of his earliest books, "On Logic," Mill developed a distinction between positive and normative economics. Positive economics, according to Mill, describes and predicts what actually takes place in the world. Normative economics advocates what should take place based on one's moral philosophy. This distinction was carried onto many other of Mill's later works.

In 1848, John Stuart Mill published his most famous work in economics that was entitled "Principles of Political Economy." For decades, this work dominated the economics textbook market and was the principle textbook used in the major universities in England until 1919. In "Principles of Political Economy," Mill developed a comprehensive review of accepted economic doctrine and he added numerous improvements to existing theory. He wrote about the management of a firm; supply and demand as an equation rather than a ratio, and demand as a major factor in Ricardo's law of comparative advantage.[3] Mill firmly attributed the poverty of the working man to the immutable physical law of diminishing returns to labor and the relentless desire of the masses to reproduce themselves. The law of diminishing returns to labor states that as more and more workers are added to a fixed amount of capital there will come a point where the productivity of labor declines. Mill continues by writing that, "Little improvement can be expected in morality until the producing families are regarded with the same feelings as drunkenness or any other physical excess."

Mill also examined the value of providing relief to the poor. Mill wondered how society could give relief to the poor without dissuading them from obtaining work. Mill distinguished the able-bodied from the disabled, elderly, and the very young. Mill did not believe that society should cut its relief efforts for the disabled. However, he was not as lenient with those who were physically fit. He proposed that recipients of aid from the state, exchange their labor for welfare payments. Mill feared that if welfare was too easily doled out, generations of poor people would be born into families weaned of the work ethnic. In addition, Mill thought that higher welfare payments would only promote higher birth rates. Thus, Mill rejected socialist proposals for increasing relief benefits or wages for the masses.[4]

Ricardo, Malthus, and John Stuart Mill, still have a large amount of influence in the attitudes towards the problems of our large inner cities. Also, the critics of the welfare state can find a lot of ammunition in their theories. Requiring physically fit persons to perform work in return for welfare payments is in 1994, still a critical topic of concern for the American Congress.

Thus, in summary, John Stuart Mill both advertised dramatically the hardship that the Utilitarians accepted as necessary to progress and, as would many who followed him, appealed for patience and hope to withstand it. This remedy, like the knowledge that one was being sacrificed to the larger good, was never wholly satisfactory to those afflicted.

KARL MARX (1818-1883) AND THE GRAND ASSAULT

It is widely believed that Communism was born in the mind of Karl Marx in the middle of the nineteenth century. Also, it is believed that Communism received its first definitive expression in 1848, when Marx and Frederick Engles published, "The Communist Manifesto."

Karl Marx

In 1848 there were no communist states in the world and no revolutionary governments of any sort. A few countries of Northeast Europe and the United States were industrializing rapidly, but there was no city in the world with a population greater than two million people, and no state; even Great Britain, in which a majority of the people did not live in the country and farmed for a living. While the skilled workers in the industrialized countries were beginning to form a middle class, over 90 percent of the World's population lived in poverty.

Into this world, Karl Marx was born in 1818, in the Western German city of Treves. Treves was then a part of Prussia, the second most powerful of the independent German States. The Marx family was originally Jewish as both parents were descendants of rabbis. However, when Marx was six, his family was baptized as Lutherans, in order to save his father's career, in what was officially Lutheran Prussia.[5]

Marx's father wanted his son to become a lawyer like himself, and sent him through the best schools in Treves. In 1835, Marx was sent to the University of Bonn, and then in 1841 to the University of Berlin to study law.

In his years at the University of Berlin, some of Karl Marx's philosophy began to evolve. He came to believe that all the various sciences and philosophies were part of one over-arching system, which when completed would give a true and total picture of the universe and man. The romantic philosophers of the time had transformed this faith, which they had inherited from their scientific predecessors. Marx believed that the core of such a science and philosophy was the growth, development, progress, and evolution of the world, human society, and the individual. He believed that nature and men evolve according to certain inexorable scientific laws, whose working can be embodied but not opposed by even the greatest of leaders.

Marx found the most thorough statement of these views in the works of the recently deceased philosopher, George Frederick Hegel. However, unlike Hegel, Marx came to believe that there was no God.[6] Marx became convinced that Europe was on the edge of reaction and revolution and that most of mankind was unhappy, held down by society, and cut off from its own true nature. Such convictions were a variety of radical Romanticism that the Germans called "Left Hegelianism."[7]

Having become a radical, Marx decided to give up his pursuit of the law and became a journalist in 1842, when he joined the staff of the "Rheinische Zeitung," a liberal newspaper in Cologne. However, the paper was closed in 1843 by the Prussian police due to its radical editorials, mostly written by Marx.

During 1843 and 1844, Marx was acquiring yet another set of convictions. He read the works of Malthus, Ricardo and other British economists of the time. Marx accepted much of the classical economic analysis, but disagreed with their pessimism and their political judgments of the workingmen. Instead, Marx picked the industrial workingmen (for whom he adopted a term out of ancient Roman history, the Proletarian) as the key to the future development of society.

By the end of 1844, Marx had established his lifelong friendship with Frederick Engels. Engels was born of a Calvinist father in 1820 in Barmen, Prussia, which was south of the Ruhr. Young Engels had become converted to radicalism, in 1841, at the University of Berlin. During the middle of the 1840's, Marx and Engels produced a number of works where they depicted the ghastly condition of the growing working class. Also, they began to set forth their own version of a new social theory that they called "Communism," in the 1840's. Thus, since 1850, Communism has been considered to be a revolutionary form of Socialism.

Marx and Engels were atheist Socialists, who being far different from those who wanted to reform society by peaceful means, urged violent revolution to be followed by a brief dictatorship of the proletariat. In 1847, Marx and Engels were commissioned by the Communist League in London. The commission was to develop a theoretical and practical platform for the new Communist party. The result of this commission was the writing of the Communist Manifesto, which was published in February of 1848 in London. To this day, the Communist Manifesto has survived as the first definitive statement of the Communist variety of Socialism and has become one of the most widely read and influential pamphlets in the history of the world.

The first chapter of the Communist Manifesto, pictured Europe as being in the middle of a tremendous struggle for control between the rising bourgeoisie and the developing proletariat. Marx defined the bourgeoisie as the people in the class of modern capitalists, owners of the means of social production and employers of wage labor.[8]

Chapter one begins by stating that "The history of all hither to existing society is the history of class struggles." Marx continues by stating that, "Society as a whole is more and more splitting up into two hostile camps; into two great classes directly facing each other, the bourgeoisie and proletariat. We see, therefore, how the modern bourgeoisie is itself the product of a long course of development, a series of revolutions in the modes of production and of exchange." According to Marx, "The bourgeoisie has at last, since the establishment of modern industry and of the world market, conquered for itself, in the modern representative state, exclusive political sway." Marx continues by saying, "The executive of the modern state is but a committee for managing the common affairs of the whole bourgeoisie."[9]

Marx did not question the productive achievements of the industrial system. What Marx did question was the vulnerable points in the capitalist system which he interpreted as the distribution of power, the highly unequal distribution of income, susceptibility to depression, and monopoly.

The Distribution of Power

The power in capitalism, according to Marx, resides with the capitalist; it is the natural attribute of the productive property he owns. The payments proceeding there from command the obedience and submission of people, who have no property and thus no alternative income. Nor is the power of the capitalist confined to the enterprise. He extends this power to the society and the State.

The Highly Unequal Distribution of Income.

The worker at the margin receives payment in wages reflecting his added contribution to the total revenue of the enterprise. That contribution diminishes as workers are added and the marginal wage sets the wage for all. However, those back from the margin, though paid the marginal wage, contribute more to earnings than their wage. They are in the infra-marginal, more fruitful stages of diminishing return. This is surplus value they create, and this surplus value accrues not to those who earn it but to the capitalist. It rightly belongs to the worker, but the Capitalist intervenes to appropriate it, i.e., steals the surplus value.

The Susceptibility of an Economy to Depression

The productive power of capitalism would press its goods relentlessly on markets, and as the labor supply became fully employed, wages would inevitably rise. The result would be a falling rate of profits, a loss and retrenching by the producing firms, and imbalance in the productive process. Balance would be restored only as diminished production, unemployment and falling wages allowed production to be profitable again. It was an important point for Marx that the system is stable only when wages are held down by a reserve of unemployed workers.

Monopoly

A flaw conceded by the Classical tradition. To the Classicists, monopoly was the exception to the competitive rule, and it presented no threat to the system as a whole. For Marx, monopoly was much more than a flaw; the increasing concentration of economic activity in the hands of ever fewer capitalists was an organic tendency of capitalism, one that proceeded with irresistible force.[10]

Thus, per Marx, the economic system celebrated by the classical tradition would come to an end brought about by characteristics, some of the most important of which had already been identified by the Classical Economists themselves. However, capitalism is not dead yet for it has produced a middle class that indirectly owns some of the means of production through the stock markets. Some of Marx's defenders point to the growth of government in capitalist nations as the surprising savior of capitalism. Social welfare spending protects the capitalists from deeper depressions and revolution. Marx's defenders are probably right. However, we must remember, that Marx predicted that the political system would stay static, resistant to change and that inflexibility would destroy the entire system. In this respect as well as others, Marx will go down in history as a false prophet.

HERBERT SPENCER AND INDIVIDUALISM (1820-1903)

Herbert Spencer

The rise of socialism and its cry for social justice required still another defense from the supporters of classical economics. Because Karl Marx's criticism of capitalism was based on Ricardo's labor theory of value, a theoretical defense of the system was needed.

One answer to Marx and capitalism was the nineteenth century philosophy of individualism, which developed as the ideology of the capitalist enterprise in the years after the Civil War, and endured until 1914. The basis for this new theory was a reinforced version of laissez faire, which defended the interest of the successful capitalist.

An English philosopher and economist Herbert Spencer, and an American sociologist, William Graham Sumner (1840-1910), were the leaders in the development of the philosophy of individualism. Spencer was an evolutionist even before Charles Darwin. In 1850, Spencer published "Social Statistics," where he argued that all social systems develop and change by a natural process those results in a maximization of individual welfare. This process of natural development stems from competition among individuals. Spencer held that any interference on the part of the government prevents full achievement of society's ideal goal.[11]

Spencer's early writings were followed by a ten-volume work entitled "Synthetic Philosophy," that sought to show that evolutionary progress occurred in all phenomena, in the biological world, in the human mind, in society, and in ethics. Where Darwin explained evolution in the terms of "Natural Selection," it was Herbert Spencer who coined the deathless phrase "Survival of the Fittest," as the source of economic and social progress. Spencer held that institutions conducted their business in such a way as to benefit the organization involved. "Those organizations which are best fitted to their environment, or which change to fit themselves to their environment, will survive. The least fit will die out, leaving the strongest and best."[12] According to Spencer the weakest individuals and the least useful social institutions gradually are eliminated. Since the individual member of society is the decision maker, the social organization that emerges from the process of change is more closely adapted to meeting the needs of the individual.

The ideas of Spencer led to a description of the ideal society, conceived as a static equilibrium between people and their surroundings, brought about by the full exercise of individual rights. The role of government was therefore limited to the protection of people and property and the enforcement of private contracts, nothing else.

One cannot avoid admiration for the comprehensive way in which Spencer and Social Darwinism served the defense of the system. Inequality and hardship were made socially benign and the mitigation of hardship was made socially acceptable. The fortunate and the affluent could have no sense of guilt, for they were the natural beneficiaries of their excellence, and nature had selected them as part of a relentless progress to an improved world.[13] Spencer's books sold hundreds of thousands of copies; his visit to New York in 1882 had some of the aspects of the coming of Saint Paul. A generation of American scholars echoed his thoughts.

William Graham Sumner

Spencer's greatest follower in America was William Graham Sumner, an Episcopalian minister and economist at Yale University.

William G. Sumner

Sumner's major work in the field of sociology was "Folk Ways," published in 1907. In this book, Sumner examined social mores, which he defined as institutions and conventions that developed and continually change by process of adaptation to individual needs. If such institutions, according to Sumner, do not contribute to welfare and survival, they are gradually replaced by more effective methods, and the social system evolves into a higher and better form.

Sumner goes on to say that within the social system, individuals are also rising and falling. The person with ability, intelligence, and drive will rise to prominence by competing with all others. The lazy, ignorant, and weak will fall out of sight. The emergence of leading individuals brings progress, because these are the ones who innovate, who think, and who develop new ideas.

In a series of essays, most notably "The Concentration of Wealth: Its Economic Justification," Sumner applied his theory of society to questions of contemporary political and economic policy. Concentrated wealth, Sumner held, was justified because it was used to produce for others. The economic elite rose to the top only because they expanded activity and provided the goods and services that society demanded. In fact, Sumner proclaimed that "The millionaires are a product of natural selection. They get high wages and live in luxury, but the bargain is a good one for society."

Individualism was the evolutionary philosophy applied to the social system. It justified the wealth of the owners of production, on the ground that only social good could come from competition. It justified the unequal distribution of income because wealth existed only because it served others. It justified lack of social responsibility because anyone destroyed by competition could be considered "unfit," not capable of making a large enough contribution to the social order to survive.[12]

Rugged Individualism was a rigorous philosophy that associated success with right and failure with wrong, wealth with public service and poverty with uselessness. Thus, the stage is now set for our understanding of the mind set of the industrial capitalist of the period and also, of the response of the workers and the less fortunate, who needless to say, never completely bought into this philosophy.

NOTES:

Chapter 6
The Evolution of Classical Economics

1. Galbraith, John Kenneth, <u>Economics in Perspective</u>, Boston, MA, Houghton Mifflin Co., 1987, p. 108.
2. Bentham, Jeremy, <u>Introduction to the Principles of Moralsand Legislation</u>, New York, NY, Haffner, 1948, p. 1.
3. Buchholz, Todd G., <u>New Ideas From Dead Economists</u>, New York, NY, Penguin Books, 1989, p. 99.
4. Buchholz, p. 102.
5. Marx, Karl and Engels, Friedrich, <u>The Communist Manifesto, Edited by Francis B. Randall</u>, New York, N.Y., Simon & Schuster, 1964. p 11.
6. Marx, p. 16.
7. Marx, p. 16.
8. Marx, p. 57.
9. Marx, p. 61.
10. Galbraith, p. 133
11. Fusfeld, Daniel R., <u>the Age of the Economists, Fifth Edition</u>, Glenview, IL, Scott Foresman and Co., 1986, p. 72
12. Fusfeld, p. 72.

CHAPTER 7

NEOCLASSICAL ECONOMICS

"The institution of a leisure class is found in its best development at the higher stages of the barbarian culture. And the tribal rites of the latter have their counterpart in the dinners, dances and other entertainments at the great houses in New York and Newport." —Thorstein Veblen.

ALFRED MARSHALL (1842-1924)

Alfred Marshall

William Stanley Jevons contributed many important ideas about marginal utility, but it was Alfred Marshall who developed the idea of Marginalism into a practical economic theory. Alfred Marshall was born in 1842 in Bermondsey England. Marshall's father wanted him to attend Oxford University, where he could study Latin and prepare for the ministry. However, to his father's disappointment, Marshall did not hear a voice from God. Instead of a voice from God, Marshall heard cries of the poor, urging him to study economics. Up until the nineteenth century three educational disciplines reigned in English Universities: Theology, aimed at spiritual perfection; Law aimed at justice; and Medicine, aimed at physical soundness. Marshall offered a fourth great vocation, the study of economics. Throughout his life, Marshall fought for economics as a separate field apart from politics, history and moral issues. In 1885, Marshall was appointed as the Chair in Political Economy, but it wasn't until 1903 that Cambridge University decided to establish a separate economics course.

In 1890 Marshall published his most famous work, "Principles of Economics," where in the beginning of his book he describes his basic belief "Natura Non Facit Saltum," Nature makes no sudden leaps. Whereas classical economists followed a Newtonian Scientific approach searching for laws of nature, Marshall emphasized a more evolutionary approach. For Marshall, the theories of Charles Darwin and biology were more important than the physics of Isaac Newton. In this regard, Alfred Marshall's concepts about Marginalism, are like the theory of evolution, if this theory was applied to economics. According to Marshall, the businessman and the consumer make no great leaps, but gradually attempt to improve their situations. Individuals, companies, and governments all conform to changing situations and changing prices. In the long run, only those firms that can adapt to change, only those firms that are the fittest, survive.[1]

Marshall realized that like biological time, economic time, was not a constant. Marshall's way of dealing with time constraints was to create an ingenious system of analysis. While he was looking at one factor, he set aside all other into a "pound." He called the pound "Ceteris Paribus," meaning "other things being equal." Prior economists had already devised a ceteris paribus assumption, but Marshall derived an explicit method and constructed rigorous theories according to it. Today, microeconomics textbooks are still based on Marshall's method of analysis.

According to Marshall, economic events must be analyzed in conjunction with the time that is necessary for both consumers and producers to make adjustments. Marshall's analysis broke time into three different areas. First there was the very short run. This is the time of just one day where only demand can fluctuate. This is because producers generally cannot adjust supply in such a short period. Next there was the short run. In the short run, according to Marshall, producers can supply more of a product by hiring more labor and purchasing additional amounts of raw material. However, the short run does not last long enough to increase the capacity of existing equipment or to build additional manufacturing capacity. The third period Marshall called the long run. This was a period when producers

Basic Economics 85

have enough time to build new machinery and new factories, as well as to vary labor and materials. Also, in the long run, new producers could enter the industry; old and less efficient companies would be forced to leave and the surviving firms would earn profit margins that were normal for the industry. This analysis has a key implication for the long run growth of any economy. Government intervention can serve to increase or reduce economic activity in the short run, but in the long run the output of any economy can only increase through increases in productivity, i.e., output per man hour of work.

Marshall on Supply and Demand

Marshall did not agree with Ricardo's claim that the value of a product reflects the amount of labor it took to produce it. He thought that the supply and demand for a product were equally important. Based on the marginalist theory, economists had previously developed the downward-sloping demand curves, but Marshall developed the "Law of Demand," which stated that the greater the amount of products to be offered for sale, the smaller must be the price of those products. "The amount of a product demanded increases with a fall in the price, and diminishes with a rise in price."[2]

Marshall's analysis was based on the principle of "all other things being equal," but he knew that factors other than price entered into the analysis of demand. The most important of these factors were, consumer taste and preferences, customers' disposable income, and the price of substitute goods. In modern terms, a change in quantity due to a change in price is depicted as a movement along a demand curve, whereas a change in factors other than price would be represented as a shift in the demand curve.

Marshall developed a similar framework for suppliers. As producers supply more of a product, the total costs of production will rise. Therefore, supply will rise only if the price paid to the producer increases. The producer will compare the additional cost of producing one more unit to the price he can obtain when selling that output. This, according to Marshall, is the reason that the supply curve slopes upward, whereas the demand curve slopes downward.[3]

Marshall held that, in the same way that the consumer compares the marginal utility of spending on various products, producers constantly compare the potential returns from spending. In this case, the producer is comparing the potential returns from investing in capital equipment versus labor. The business owner to be successful must engage in a constant balancing act among capital, labor and natural resources, i.e., between new and used equipment and between skilled and unskilled labor. For this reason, Marshall came out strongly against unions that supported make-work projects and featherbedding, as their lack of productivity would only serve to reduce profits and in the long run hurt their members.

Marshall on Social Concerns

While Marshall's "Principle of Economics" tended to be theoretical, he insisted that economics must also be practical. Marshall frequently served on royal commissions and testified before parliament. He supported public education and a moderate redistribution of wealth, because it would heighten productivity and social welfare. However, he was not by any means a socialist and at one point called this philosophy the "greatest present danger." Just like philosophers and economists as far back as Aristotle, Marshall feared that collective ownership would "deaden the energies of mankind, and arrest economic progress; unless before its introduction the whole people had acquired an unselfish devotion to public good."

Marshall thought that the classical pessimists and the romantic Marxists were both wrong. The stationary state had not arrived. Population did not outstrip food as Malthus had predicted. Landlords did not reign. Although poverty still degraded a portion of the people, Marshall held that the "hope and poverty and ignorance may gradually be extinguished and this philosophy was supported by the steady progress of the working class during the nineteenth century. The steam-engine had relieved them of much of their exhausting and degrading toil; wages had increased; education had been improved and the railway and the printing press had enabled members of the same trade in different parts of the country to communicate easily with one another.[4]

Alfred Marshall remained a professor at Cambridge until he was over eighty years old. John Maynard Keynes, who was his pupil, once praised the "old professor of Cambridge" as he wrote, "The master economist must, like Marshall, be a mathematician, historian, statesman and philosopher to some degree. He must study the present in light of the past for purposes of the future."[5]

AMERICAN CONTRIBUTIONS TO ECONOMIC THEORY

In the nineteenth century, the United States was a world of improving land, life and well being. During that time the U.S. was a country of owner-operated farms. In the Southern states until the Civil War, wages were excluded from consideration because slavery, as in Aristotle's time, greatly focused attention on such ethical and moral issues as emancipation rather than on economic ones.

In the U.S., the discussion of economics was based on practical economic topics. These included the tariff, monopoly, the social behavior and defense of the very rich, and the diverse questions pertaining to banks and money. The American Economic Association, formed in 1885, was initially a protest against the highly conservative support accorded industrial capitalism by the accepted classical theory and the companion commitment to laissez faire. Only at the end of the nineteenth century did two distinctively American economic figures emerge: Henry George and Thorstein Veblen.

Henry George (1839-1897)

In his time and into the 1920's Henry George was the most widely read of American economic writers. His major work, first published in 1879, was entitled "Progress and Poverty." Henry George's principle idea centered on the accidental and unjust enrichment that came from the ownership of land and the further meaning this had for the financing of the modern state. From his vantage point of San Francisco, Henry George saw the lush enrichment of landowners: as the frontier moved forward, the population increased, and economic development proceeded. David Ricardo had previously witnessed that the tendency of a growing society to enrich

Henry George

the holders of its land would have an adverse affect on the capitalist. However, to Henry George, the resulting contrast between wealth and misery was intolerable.

From this observation followed the remedy he prescribed; it was to tax away the unearned gain in land values that did not derive from the effort or intelligence of the owner but came in effortless fashion from the general advance of population and industry. The revenues that were collected, George believed, would more than cover the operating expenses of the State; all other taxes would be redundant. Thus, his great reform was given the name of, the "single tax."[6]

Needless to say, there were a very large number of wealthy landowners, who strongly motivated and politically powerful, were in opposition to the single tax idea. However, even today the beliefs of Henry George can be found in less formal conscious thought. The real estate developer or speculator encouraged by and encouraging an increase in land values is, quite possibly, the least praised of American entrepreneurs.

Thorstein Veblen (1857-1929)

Of the early twentieth century, economic writers, Thorstein Veblen is perhaps still the most notable. Just south of the small city of Northfield, Minnesota are 290 acres of land where Thorstein Veblen spent his childhood. From that background, Veblen went on to study at Johns Hopkins University and Yale, where among his principal mentors was William Graham Sumner.

Veblen established himself as a critic of the classical system, at first in a series of short papers published at the turn of the century. In these papers, Veblen argued that the central ideas of the classical system did not reflect a search for truth and realty; rather they were and are a celebration of approved belief. In Veblen's view, economic

Thorstein Veblen

institutions change; so does economic subject matter; there can be understanding only if one is in tune with change.[7]

A further Veblen contribution which was presented in "The Theory of Business Enterprise," published in 1904, identified a powerful conflict in the modern business organization between the engineers and scientists, who were professionals of great skill and productive potential, and the profit oriented businessmen. The businessmen, according to Veblen, keep the talents of the scientists and engineers under control and suppressed them as necessary in order to maintain prices and maximize profits. Today product managers and marketing people have continued this argument. Also, this argument can be extended to compare the propensity of many U.S. companies to manage in the short-term, i.e., from quarter to quarter, versus the Japanese propensity to manage for the long-term and to seek market share as their main goal.

From this view of the business firm Veblen developed his conclusion. If the business community could somehow release those who are technically and imaginatively proficient from the restraints imposed by the system, there would be unprecedented productivity and wealth in the economy.

Veblen's views on two other matters are also worthy of comment. First is his emphasis on the ordinary worker's concern for the quality of his performance, i.e., "I take pride in my work." This statement can be found in Veblen's "The Instinct of Workmanship," published in 1914. This attitude can be seen today in such things as:

- The Japanese team approach to management and process engineering.

- The new emphasis on service as a major part of a product.

Secondly, and in addition to his other contributions, Thorstein Veblen remains a resonant voice nearly a century after his most memorable book was published. This work was his superb examination of the manners and motives of the rich in "The Theory of the Leisure Class," published in 1899.

The two phrases that Veblen coined; "Conspicuous Leisure," and "Conspicuous Consumption," have permanently entered the American language and culture. They have affected the economic and social attitudes and behavior of countless thousands who have never heard of Veblen. As a consequence of Veblen's work, leisure for the affluent in the United States has come "to lack repute." No one is spared the question, "What do you do for a living?" Even more specifically, no forms of entertainment and no house, if sufficiently expensive or grand, are safe from the denigrating description "Conspicuous Consumption."[8]

Joseph A. Schumpeter (1883-1950)

Joseph Schumpeter

During the early decades of the twentieth century the classical tradition, was now above any challenge in England. Also, because of the influence of such disciples as Harvard's Frank W. Taussig (1859-1940), classical economics was fully accepted in the United States. Prices adjusted to marginal costs; costs, including that of labor, adjusted downward as necessary to ensure the employment of available plant, materials, and above all, workers. Say's Law, which states that supply creates its own demand, was widely accepted.

Although Alfred Marshall ruled in these early years, his system did receive some influential amendments. Joseph Schumpeter added a major dimension to the Marshallian equilibrium. This came from the central figure of Schumpeter's system, the

Basic Economics 91

entrepreneur, who aided by bank credit, challenges the established equilibrium with a new product, a new process or a new type of productive organization. The tendency then is to a new equilibrium; a new stability in what Schumpeter saw as a circular flow with production moving in one direction, and the money to fund the production in the other. This new equilibrium would inevitably be disturbed and broken by the next innovator. Therefore, economic life would continue and expand; for this is the nature of economic development.

Joseph Schumpeter was born in Austria in 1883. He studied law at the University of Vienna and attended lectures by the leading economist of the day. These economists included some of the founders of the Austrian school of economics. The Austrian school traces its origins to Karl Menger and Friedrich von Wieser who worked in Vienna in the latter part of the nineteenth century. In the twentieth century, the Austrian tradition was brought to the United States by Ludwig von Mises and Friedrich von Hayek among others. Today the Austrian school continues to have a strong following in the United States partly because of the theories of one of its close cousins, the Public Choice School of economics, which will be described in a later chapter.

In the view of the Austrian economists the spontaneous order of the marketplace is best viewed in terms of a market process that takes place continuously. The central player in the market process is the entrepreneur. It is the entrepreneur's efforts to move resources from less valued to more valued uses that is the source of profit for the capitalist.

In 1912 Schumpeter published his first book on economics entitled "The Theory of Economic Development." The book is about the way in which capitalism develops its propensity toward growth. The book starts with a description of a capitalist economy that lacks capital accumulation and growth is totally absent. Schumpeter's model pictures a society whose flow of production is perfectly static and absent of change, reproducing itself in a "circular flow" that never expands its ability to create wealth. Also, in the static flow of production, competition among the capitalists will remove all earnings that exceed their opportunity costs. In other words, economic profit would be zero with the economy in a static state. Workers would receive wages, landlords rent, and the capitalists would receive only their wages as managers.

Historically many economists had attempted to explain the source of profits in an economy. Schumpeter argued that profits did not arise from the exploitation of labor as Karl Marx had claimed, or from the "abstinence" of capitalists that was proposed by John Stuart Mill. Profits appeared in a static economy when the circular flow failed to follow its routine course. From the starting point of the circular flow some new force is required to break the inertia and this force is the introduction of technological or organizational innovations into the circular flow. As a result of these innovations, a flow of income arises that does not come from the contributions of the workers or the resources of the capitalist.[9]

A new product that obtains an initial monopoly position in the marketplace or a new manufacturing process that reduces unit costs can result in a profit for the capitalist that is substantially greater than their opportunity costs. In economic terms the capitalist receives an economic rent for his innovation. An innovation requires an innovator who is responsible for combining the factors of production in new ways. Schumpeter held that innovators do not necessarily come from any social class. He took an old word from the economic lexicon and used it to describe these revolutionists of production and product innovation. He called them entrepreneurs. Entrepreneurs, according to Schumpeter and their innovating activity were the source of profit and growth in the capitalist system.[10]

The Trend toward Oligopoly in Manufacturing

In 1933 two economists working separately developed the theory of oligopoly. They were Edward H. Chamberlin (1899-1967) of Harvard and Joan Robinson (1903-1983) of Cambridge. Chamberlin and Robinson both argued that between the general case of competition in the classical system and the exceptional case of monopoly, there was an array of intermediate possibilities. The most important case as an intermediate between pure competition and monopoly, was that of small numbers of participants in the same industry. This market structure they called oligopoly, which is a term that promptly entered the language of economics. The American automobile, petroleum, steel, chemical, rubber tire, machine tool and farm equipment industries, with a few giants in each industry, are cases in point.[11]

The intelligent oligopolist would, in setting his price, give thoughtful consideration to what would be most advantageous for all; so would the others in their industry. Therefore, the price and profit that would be arrived at by an oligopolist, would be somewhere between that of pure competition and monopoly.

The concept of oligopoly was considered a lesser threat to competition than that of the monopoly, and therefore, entered classical thought without any great difficulty. The large modern corporate sector of the economic system, where oligopoly ruled, was the dominant sector, and, monopoly or not, one could not declare it illegal. Also, while oligopoly was, in principle socially unjust, in actual performance, it aroused no great consumer resentment. While economists might argue that oligopoly was wrong in principle; in practice, it produced a whole spectrum of new and lower cost products. Therefore, economists came to view oligopoly with theoretical concern, but they dismissed the necessity for practical action in dealing with it. Although monopoly was still considered the one great flaw in the system oligopoly was accepted as a common business practice.

PRODUCTIVITY AND COMMUNISM

Just as the latter half of the nineteenth century saw the growth of formalized education for engineers, the twentieth century witnessed a great acceleration of formalized education for businessmen. Between 1900 and 1910 alone, 240 volumes of business management books were published, and in 1908, Harvard University founded its Graduate School of Business Administration.[12]

Therefore, what effectively ended the long run potential threat to Capitalism from Communism or more moderate forms of Socialism was the increase in the productivity of the workers. Increased output for man-hour meant increased profit for the owners of business. However, increased productivity through training created skilled knowledgeable workers who could command more wages. Also, labor unions began to gather some strength during the twentieth century which gave the workers the ability to control the supply of skilled labor. The result of these changes was an increase in the amount of the price received for a unit of production that went to the worker. In summary, there eventually was no need for a revolt because the skilled worker was becoming the Bourgeois, the middle class or in today's economy, the favorite target of the tax collector.

NOTES:

Chapter 7
Neoclassical Economics

1. Buchholz, Todd G., New Ideas from Dead Economists, New York, NY, The Penguin Group, 1987, p. 152.
2. Marshall, Alfred, Principles of Economics, 9th Edition, London, England, 1961, p. 316.
3. Buchholz, p. 160.
4. Marshall, p. 3.
5. Keynes, John Maynard, "Alfred Marshal," in Essays in Biography, London, England, Macmillan, 1972, p. 164.
6. Galbraith, John Kenneth, Economics in Perspective, Boston, MA, Houghton Mifflin Company, 1987, p. 167.
7. Galbraith, P. 171.
8. Galbraith, P. 176.
9. Heilbroner, Robert L. The Worldly Philosophers, New York, NY, Simon & Schuster, 1986, p. 295.
10. Heilbroner, P. 296.
11. Galbraith, P. 183.
12. Krooss, p. 362.

CHAPTER 8

FRANKLIN ROOSEVELT AND THE NEW DEAL

"The only thing we have to fear is fear itself." --Franklin Delano Roosevelt

CLASSICAL ECONOMICS AND DEPRESSION

A singular and significant feature of the classical system was the lack of a theory of depression. The equilibrium to which the economy adjusted itself was one of full employment. This was the result to which movements in wages and prices inevitably led.

From the classical theory, there could not be a remedy for a depression, if depression had been ruled out by the theory. Consequently, when the great depression struck after the stock market crash in October of 1929, economists stood aside. This was something to be waited out.

Through what remained the presidency of Herbert Hoover, until March of 1933, the economic policy of the United States followed the classical design. Recovery was expected and compulsively predicted. There was no need for action to advance the inevitable. Herbert Hoover was, in fact, in complete accord with the accepted economic ideas of his time.

However, in 1933, there was a full-fledged depression that had three undeniable features as follows:

- The first was the relentless deflation in prices, with its bankrupting effect on industry and agriculture. This was especially severe on any industry that had high fixed costs.

- The second feature was unemployment. By 1933 the unemployment rate was over one quarter of the working population.

- The third was the hardship depression brought for especially vulnerable groups of the old, the young, and those in poor health.

FRANKLIN D. ROOSEVELT

Franklin D. Roosevelt

When Franklin D. Roosevelt became president in March of 1933, the first broad line of his policy addressed the problem of prices; the second sought to aid the unemployed by providing them with jobs; and the third attempted to mitigate the hardships of the vulnerable. In this last line of policy was the idea of the Welfare State, which had come earlier to Europe and was by this time on its way to the United States. However, Roosevelt did not develop a new approach to stimulating a depressed economy in a vacuum. Roosevelt received assistance from a new breed of economic advisors who were not restrained by classical beliefs.

In Roosevelt's gubernatorial (New York) years, a small group of scholars rallied to support him. The economic advisors among these new scholars were from Columbia University and were part of a group of Roosevelt's advisors, who were often referred to as the "brain trust." Two members of the Roosevelt brain trust, Rex Tugwell and Adolph Berle, were figures of particular distinction. Rex Tugwell was a key participant in developing strategy for Roosevelt's presidential election and later served in the administration. With his academic credentials, Tugwell was in a good position to persuade Roosevelt that he could break with the classical tradition.

The second economic figure in the brain trust was Adolph Berle, who like Tugwell, was a professor at Columbia University. A lawyer, not an economist, by profession, Berle was the author, along with Gardner C. Means, a young economist at Columbia, of an attack on the classical system of economic analysis.

The Berle and Means publication was entitled "The Modern Corporation and Private Property." It was about the management and control of the large enterprise. Their book described the current concentration of business in America. According to Berle and Means, the professional managers were now extensively in control of the modern business enterprise and their objective was often self-enrichment. This is a subject that has been previously noted as one of the reasons why major industries in the 1920's produced more than could reasonably be sold.

In the imperfect or monopolistic competition of Joan Robinson and Edward Chamberlin, the capitalist or entrepreneur still ruled and profits were still maximized. The results were not socially optimal, but they could be adapted to classical thought. The views of Berle and Means could not.

Following Roosevelt's election to the presidency, Rex Tugwell and Gardner Means immediately took government posts. Berle joined the ranks a little later. By the time Roosevelt came to office, prices had been in a devastating three-year slump, and from across the country there were appeals for government action to reverse the trend. One of the first reactions by the Roosevelt administration was an attempt to stabilize the economy. These actions took the form of declaring a bank holiday in March of 1933, suspension of gold payments to increase exports, and policies developed to stabilize prices.

ACTIONS TO STABILIZE THE ECONOMY

Stabilizing the Banking Industry

By 1921, there were over 31,000 separate commercial banks in the United States. That number was reduced considerably because over 14,800 of these banks had failed by 1934. In 1932, there was a decline in the rate of bank failures from the previous year, but as 1933 began, pessimism started to set in and a new wave of bank failures threatened the collapse of the entire system. When the depression began, demand deposits held with commercial banks or savings and loan associations, were not insured by the federal government. Because they feared a loss of deposits if their bank failed, large numbers of people were going, into banks and demanding their deposits. In a fractional banking system, such as ours, deposits are put to work making loans. This results in a balance sheet where deposits are vastly in excess of actual currency. Banking is based on the theory that all depositors will not want to withdraw their funds at the same time. However, if a majority of a bank's depositors demanded an immediate withdrawal of funds, the bank would become insolvent and therefore, would be required to stop doing business.

By March 4, of 1933, a run on the nation's banks caused such a financial panic that most of the banks in all thirty-eight states were forced to close. On March 6, 1933, President Roosevelt declared a "Bank Holiday," which specifically forbid the nations' banks to make any payments in cash. The major purpose of closing the banks was to give them the opportunity to liquidate some of their assets, especially government securities. The Federal Reserve banks attempted to assist the commercial banks with their liquidity problems by issuing more Federal Reserve notes against the government bonds that were held by the banks. The banks were audited by government inspectors who were instructed to take an optimistic view of the current values of bank assets.

As banks were found to be in satisfactory condition, they were issued licenses by the treasury and then allowed to reopen. About 2,000 banks never reopened their doors after the holiday; however, public confidence in the banking industry was restored and the outflow of currency was halted. Cash started to flow into the banks, and the wave of bank failures was over. As the banks began to reopen, the government began to take steps to improve the quality of their assets. Large volumes of bank loan assets were sold to federal government agencies such as the Reconstruction Finance Corporation, the Home Owners' Loan Corporation, and the Federal Farm Mortgage Corporation. These agencies also made loans to commercial banks, and purchased some of their debt and equity issues.

While all of the changes to the banking industry outlined above were important, the most important and enduring improvement, was the creation of the Federal Deposit Insurance Corporation and the Federal Savings and Loan Insurance Corporation. These two federal agencies provided the commercial banks and savings and loan associations with federally backed insurance against individual bank deposits. All members of the Federal Reserve System were required to join the Federal Deposit Insurance Corporation, and nearly all of the state chartered banks became members on a voluntary basis. The result was a major improvement in the stability of the commercial banking system. Bank runs all but disappeared because depositors were assured of the safety of their deposits.[1]

The Suspension of Gold Payments

In the first days of the New Deal, Roosevelt ordered the suspension of gold payments by the banks and forbade the hoarding of gold. This action suspended the gold standard in the United States. Also, the order prohibited the holding of gold, in anticipation of its appreciation in dollars. Although commodity prices stirred upward briefly in the summer of 1933, there was nothing in the president's action that added to purchasing power and demand.

In the autumn of 1933 the administration began to offer progressively higher prices for newly mined gold, which was brought to the treasury to be traded into dollars. The dollar fell on the foreign markets as foreign currencies, which were still on the gold standard, could now be exchanged for more dollars. This resulted in a depreciation of the dollar. As a result of the cheaper American money there were some improvements in exports. However, the results of this action to stimulate export were minimal as the United States in the 1930's was basically a domestic economy.

ACTIONS TO RAISE PRICES

The first action to increase prices was a direct one that took place through the National Industrial Recovery Act. Under the provisions of this act, sellers were brought together to agree on minimum prices. They, in turn, were required to allow labor to bargain collectively and in good faith. Oligopoly, not competition, was now recognized as the industrial norm. Therefore, it was thought, that individual firms could strongly influence their own prices. The National Industrial Recovery Act provided the organizational framework of this program by instituting over 700 industrial codes that sought to stabilize production, employment, and prices. By agreement, the firms joining in an NRA code acted to arrest the downward spiral of prices. Market competition to reduce price was proclaimed by the NRA to be against the public interest, and monopoly; the conceded flaw in the classical system, was proclaimed acceptable. In fact, the NRA codes sought to create a monopoly pricing structure. At first, the ambitious effort at industrial coordination appeared to work; production, employment, and income grew during much of 1933. However, planning as a solution to the recovery problem never got a long-run test because the political difficulties of reconciling the conflicting interests of large manufacturers, small businessmen, and labor served seriously to reduce the effectiveness of the NRA. Then, on May 27, 1935, the Supreme Court invalidated the code making provisions of the National Recovery Act, thus bringing the experiment to an abrupt end.

The second major effort at price enhancement occurred in agriculture. Beginning in the last century, the United States government and the states, through land grant colleges and universities, had been supporting agricultural experiment and education. In the United States Department of Agriculture in Washington, there was a large and intellectually active center of research in the highly-regarded Bureau of Agricultural Economics.

The Bureau of Agricultural Economics, in its examination of farm prices, agricultural credit, farm markets and farm management, was highly pragmatic. This method of operation was, at the time, necessary to assure funding from Congress. Because of their practical orientation, these economists were not committed to the classical system. From the 1920's on, the principle concern of the Bureau was with economic problems, particularly the low prices paid to the farmers. Various scholars from Minnesota, Massachusetts, Montana, and California began an intense discussion of how to raise farm prices. Government, not just the marketplace, it was thought, should have a role in determining farm prices.

With the arrival of Roosevelt in 1933, the agricultural economists also came to Washington. Under their direction, the Agricultural Adjustment Administration (The Triple A) was born. One major provision of this act was a policy that sets minimum prices for most agricultural products, reduced farm production, and provided for the storage of any production that exceeded the established limit.

ACTIONS TO IMPROVE EMPLOYMENT

Most of Roosevelt's "New Deal" programs were aimed at treating the symptoms of the depression and not at finding a cure. While the cause of the depression was greatly reduced demand, for both industrial and consumer goods and services, the result was severe unemployment. The Roosevelt administration, unlike the Hoover administration, accepted responsibility for easing the plight of the unemployed. In May of 1933, the Federal Emergency Relief Administration, with Harry Hopkins as its director, officially came into existence. The purpose of the FERA was to assist the unemployed. The federal government decided that federal efforts to aid the unemployed would be concentrated on finding jobs. The Federal Emergency Relief Administration was empowered to make grants to the states to support their work relief efforts. Such FERA programs as the Civil Works Administration, the Works Progress Administration, and the Civilian Conservation Corps provided several million people with jobs each year.[2]

While some of these programs were said to be mere excuses to provide income to the unemployed, the basic concept was a response to the obvious hardships caused by the depression. The programs for the most part were designed to provide employment and income; however, many times the resulting products were not of a material consideration. The exception to this was the Public Works Administration. The responsibility of the PWA was not just to create jobs but to invest in public infrastructure, such as roads and dams. The primary emphasis of the PWA, under Secretary of the Interior Harold Ickes, was on the importance of the projects themselves. Every effort was made to complete these projects as efficiently as possible, regardless of the employment effects.

Although the PWA provided about seven hundred thousand jobs in 1936, this was far below the nearly five million employed under FERA programs at their maximum in 1934. However, many important and lasting improvements to our infrastructure such as the Hoover Dam on the Colorado River, was a direct result of the projects completed under the Federal Emergency Relief Administration. In total, during the depression years, federally funded employment programs, were directly responsible for creating more than eight million jobs. While FERA projects were not a cure for the headache of unemployment, for those employed by the program, it was certainly a great aspirin.

ACTIONS TO RELIEVE THE HARDSHIPS OF THE DEPRESSION

One of the most significant responses to the Great Depression in the United States was the creation of the welfare state. It would be the creation of the welfare state that would endure from the Roosevelt administration. However, the welfare state was not conceived in America. The welfare state was born in Germany of Count Otto von Bismarck (1815-1898). In the Prussian and German tradition, the state was competent, beneficent and highly prestigious. In 1884 and 1887, welfare legislation was passed in the Reichstag. The legislation provided for accident, sickness, old-age, and disability insurance.

A more comprehensive step in this process came in Britain twenty-five years after Bismarck's great initiative. Under the sponsorship of Lloyd George, the Chancellor of the Exchequer, legislation was passed in 1911 that provided for sickness and invalidism insurance and then unemployment insurance. A non-contributory system of old-age pensions had previously been written into law. In a very real sense, the success of Lloyd George in 1910 and 1911 paved the way for the American action a quarter of a century later. John R. Commons, of the University of Wisconsin, is the American companion to Bismarck and Lloyd George on the development of the welfare state.

John Commons' greatest achievement was in assembling and leading a group of colleagues who set out in a highly practical way to redress the evident social problems of the time. Their initiative began with the Wisconsin State Government in Madison. The Wisconsin Plan included a pioneer state civil service law, the effective regulation of public utility rates (a monopoly), a limit on usurious interest charges, support to the trade unions, and a state income tax. Also, an unemployment compensation system was developed in 1932. This had a penetrating effect on economic and political attitudes. This was the most important contribution to the federal legislation about welfare reforms that were enacted into law three years later.[3]

The Social Security Act

The Social Security Act of 1935 provided three types of relief from the hardship caused by the depression. First, there was direct aid to those unable to work: the old, handicapped, and dependent children. Secondly, it provided a system of accumulating income for retired workers; and finally, the act provided for unemployment insurance. The portion of the social security program that provided direct money payments to the needy was the forerunner of our current welfare system. The Social Security Act was the first explicit recognition in the United States that, in a market economy, there may be persons unable to provide for themselves.

The Social Security Act, which provided pensions for retired workers, was to be financed by taxes on both individual incomes and employers' payrolls. The contributions to fund worker pensions were to be shared equally between the employers and employees. However, since a payroll tax increases production costs, this expense would eventually be passed on to the consumer in higher prices. Social Security, however, did remove some of the hardships of old age. No longer was it necessary for people to work until they were almost dead. Prior to the Social Security Act the elderly who lacked adequate savings, often wiped out by the depression, faced a rather poor assortment of choices. They could depend on their children or turn to the public authorities for support. The Social Security Act provided a system of forced savings, with a federal government guarantee that the potential benefits could not be taken away by future depressions.

Another part of the Social Security Act was a system designed to provide income to the unemployed. A tax was levied on employers' payrolls and used to establish a fund from which payments could be made to those out of work. The length of time over which payments would be dispensed was limited for providing incentives for the unemployed to seek work. The plan was designed to encourage each state to set up its own program and to ensure conformity among the various state programs.

The principle that the Social Security (old-age pensions) accounts must be sustained by their own tax levies has remained nearly unchallenged ever since. The response from classical economists to the Social Security Act was relatively mild. Unemployment and economic disabilities of age did exist; perhaps these flaws should be remedied. The old-age pensions paid their own way; they were insurance, not a radical thing.

In total, the changes made by the Roosevelt administration during the depression years, in the basic workings of the American economy, were modest. The emphasis was largely on saving the market system, rather than replacing it with a socialist system. Although the changes were modest at first their effects remain well into the twenty-first century. Social welfare programs such as social security, unemployment insurance have been greatly expanded and have eased the burden of many of the people that receive the benefits of these programs. And these achievements were made against the advice of the leading economists of the time. Academics may argue who was the greatest president, but for those who elected him to four terms in office, Franklin D. Roosevelt was the greatest president of the twentieth century.

NOTES:

Chapter 8
Franklin Roosevelt and the New Deal (1929-1939)

1. Puth, Robert C., <u>American Economic History, Third Edition</u>, Fort Worth, TX, The Dryden Press, 1993, p. 569.
2. Chandler, L., <u>America's Greatest Depression, 1929-1941</u>, New York, N.Y., 1970, p. 196.
3. Galbraith, John Kenneth, <u>Economics in Perspective</u>, Boston, MA, Houghton Mifflin Company, 1987, p. 215.

CHAPTER 9

KEYNESIAN ECONOMICS

"In the long run we are all dead."—John Maynard Keynes

ECONOMICS IN ANTICIPATION OF KEYNES

In 1936, the fourth year of the Roosevelt administration's "New Deal," a very temporary recovery developed. However, 17 percent of the American labor force was still unemployed, and real gross national product was only 95 percent of the 1929 level. In 1937, there was another sharp slump. Since there was already a depression, a new name had to be found, and it was called a recession. Classical economic theory continued relentlessly to predict an eventual recovery from the depression. However, by this time a large portion of the population was beginning to wonder if the economy would ever return to normal. What was needed was a new theory to explain why the economy was not adjusting to lower wages and lower interest rates and therefore, returning to a level of full employment as the classical economists had promised. The public, in general, was just running out of patience. A new economic theory was required to explain the current circumstances. The new economic theory was developed by the distinguished British economist John Maynard Keynes in his 1936 publication, "The General Theory of Employment, Interest and Money." The essentials of Keynes' case were designed to release the fiscal policies of the British treasury and the Roosevelt administration from its classical economic constraints. The modern economy, Keynes held, does not necessarily find its equilibrium at full employment; it can find it with unemployment, i.e., the underemployment equilibrium.[1]

According to Keynes, it is not necessary to wait for the economy to adjust itself to a depression. The government can, and should, take steps to overcome a shortage of aggregate demand. In a depression, the desire of the federal government to balance their budget must give way to the need to stimulate aggregate demand. However, there were economists, who, by their actions, expressed the need for government intervention to stimulate demand well before Keynes. The most notable was the case of Sweden. Here for two generations, an alert group of economists took part in critical discussions of economic ideas as they were related to public affairs.

The independent minded Swedish scholars were men such as Gunnar Myrdal, Bertil Ohlin, Erik Lundberg, and Dag Hammarskjold. Dag Hammarskjold was later appointed to be the Secretary General of the United Nations. While these men all had full knowledge of the classical theory, they were more concerned with the practical problems of the Swedish economy. Instead on being constrained by a theory that just was not working, they advocated the deliberate use of the government budget to sustain demand and employment. The worldwide depression of the 1930's led the Stockholm economists to abandon hope that actions of the Central Bank to lower interest rates would materially expand investment expenditure and, therefore, aggregate demand. Instead, they held that in good times the public budget should be balanced, but in depression the budget should be unbalanced deliberately so that the excess of expenditure over income would sustain demand and employment. All of this was being done in Stockholm in the 1930's, well in advance of Keynes. By the middle of the decade, word of developments in Sweden was finding its way to Britain and to the United States. Sweden, with its now well developed social welfare system, was being pictured as the "Middle Way" between the classical economic system and Socialism and Communism.[2]

Finally, in anticipation of Keynes, there was a highly practical application of government deficit spending going on in the United States. Through most of the 1930's, the federal government ran a substantial deficit. Beginning in 1933, this was increased by expending for direct relief, public works, and other public forms of employment. This type of employment was managed through such agencies as the Federal Emergency Relief Administration, the Public Works Administration, and the Works Progress Administration. By 1936, the federal revenue receipts were only 59 percent of government expenditures. The deficit was four and two tenths of a percentage of the current gross national product. The hardships brought about by the depression had already made what Keynes was to urge necessary.

JOHN MAYNARD KEYNES: THE MAN BEHIND THE THEORY

Early advocacy of Keynesian policy included strong attempts at persuasion by Keynes. However, none of this earlier effort ranked in importance with the publication of "The General Theory," as his book began to be known, in 1936. It was, as Keynes had intended it to be, a lethal blow at the classical conclusions as to demand, production and employment and the resulting policy. Say's Law was dead, and a new theory developed by John Maynard Keynes had arrived to take its place.

The General Theory owed much of its acceptance to the Great Depression and to the failure of classical economics to contend with the problems brought about by that unsettling event. However, the acceptance that this book received owed much to Keynes' ability and reputation. No economist is ever more highly regarded than he regards himself or followed with more certainty than that which he himself manifests. The affect that The General Theory had in changing economic analysis owed much to the background, reputation and prestige of its author.

John Maynard Keynes (1883 - 1945)

John Maynard Keynes was born in 1883 into a Puritanical Victorian home. John Neville Keynes, his father, was a well-known economist at Cambridge University; but Keynes, unlike his parents, had little use for puritan values. Keynes attended King's College at Cambridge where he developed friendships and liaisons with other intellectuals and was invited to join the university's most select and secretive society, the Apostles. Later, Keynes and many of the other Apostles, formed the Bloomsbury Group, who's Anti-Victorian, and Bohemian attitudes powerfully affected the evolution of British culture.[3]

John M. Keynes

Keynes originally attended Cambridge to study mathematics. His introduction to economics was through Alfred Marshall's "The Principles of Economics." After a brief departure from Cambridge, Keynes returned to accept Marshall's offer as a lecturer in economics. In his early years at Cambridge, his economic beliefs did not extend far beyond those of Marshall and the classical tradition. During the 1920's, Keynes continued to teach, edit, write, and advise the British government. He corresponded with most of the prominent politicians, academicians, and artists of his time. A lot of skill and a little bit of luck assisted him as he accumulated a fortune trading in stocks and commodities. There is a question that is often asked of economists, which is; "If you know so much why aren't you rich?" Only David Ricardo would rank higher than Keynes in becoming rich and most other economists would flunk this test miserably.

Keynes on Savings and Investment

In economics, Keynes originally focused mostly on monetary policy, especially in his "Treatise on Money," published in 1930. The Treatise tied together much of Keynes' earlier work on investment, with some new discussion of the connection between savings and investment. The Treatise examined the question of what made the economy operate so unevenly. The question had received the attention of economists for decades. Malthus had considered that savings could somehow result in a general economic glut, but most other early nineteenth century economists rejected the idea. In the world of Ricardo and Mill, virtually the only people who could save were the wealthy and their savings were usually invested in their own businesses. Therefore, saving was properly called accumulation for it represented the amassing of a sum of money and the immediate use of those funds in purchasing new capital equipment.

After the American Civil War, the structure of the American and European economies changed. The distribution of wealth improved as those who had the technical skills required to operate the new factory machines could demand higher wages. At the same time, business organizations became larger and were increasingly searching beyond their owners for more investment capital. Commercial banks also entered the equation by performing the function of funneling consumer savings into business investment. Hence savings and investment became divorced from each other as they became separate operations carried out by different groups of people. However, this separation of savings and investing often led to economic problems because the funneling of savings into investment is not automatic. Business firms usually need savings to fund the expansion of their operations. This is because business cash flows are not sufficient to provide it with enough capital to build a new factory or to purchase an expensive piece of equipment. Consumer saving is not spending, because it reduces national income. If businesses invest the savings of consumers the economy usually grows; however, if these savings are not invested it could lead to depression. The Treatise was a masterful analysis of this seesaw of savings and investment and its potential effect on economic stability.

The Fall of Classical Economics

The early 1930's brought challenges to economics so perplexing that Keynes soon began to realize that he could not rest on his previous publications. From 1929 to 1933 in the United States, Adam Smith's invisible hand of the free market kicked prosperity in the backside. Unemployment went from 3 percent to 25 percent; national income was reduced by almost half and the economy came to a screeching halt. The popular song writer Yip Harburg echoed the frustration and disparity of the nation in his song "Brother, Can You Spare a Dime?"

The British treasury and the American government, especially under Hoover, prescribed patience and promised recovery in the long run. However, Keynes blasted the treasury view as he wrote in his "Tract on Monetary Reform." What is the point of having such a government? "In the long run, we are all dead." Keynes justified the advice he gave to politicians in his 1936 masterpiece. The General Theory smashed the classical theory of economics and presented a new framework for a new field of study to be called macroeconomics.[4]

THE ECONOMICS OF JOHN MAYNARD KEYNES

In the General Theory, Keynes denounces the classical model of a self adjusting economy. According to Keynes, the most nincompoopish belief was in Say's Law that, as previously discussed, states that the production of goods and services generates enough income to workers and suppliers for all the products to be purchased. However, if someone believes in Say's Law, according to Keynes, they cannot believe in long-term unemployment or depressions. The simultaneous occurrence of a self adjusting mechanism to prevent long-term unemployment, and the great depression of 1929 is, by definition, mutually exclusive. Only a schizophrenic could believe in both. Even Keynes would not accuse his colleagues of being schizophrenics. He gave them the benefit of the doubt and called them stupid.[5]

Keynes developed a two-pronged attack against the prime positions of the classical system. According to Keynes, the self adjusting system of classical economics did not work because there was no link between savings and investment and wages were not flexible. On the subject of savings and investment, Keynes held that consumers and businesses save and invest for entirely different reasons. Households save for many different reasons, but what determines how much they can save is their disposable income. Interest rates have very little to do with the amount that consumers save. Businesses may invest more if interest rates are low because some projects may become profitable with low interest rates. However, a business invests in fixed assets based on future expectations. If a business believes that there is no market for its products, they will not invest to increase production capacity. This business decision will be made without regard to the rate of interest.

If household savings exceed business investment, a decline in aggregate demand will result. Business inventories will increase and production will decrease as a result of reduced demand for the company's products. Companies will react to the reduced demand by reducing the size of their work force, leading to even less consumption. As income falls, consumers, especially those out of work, will start to liquidate their savings. Savings will eventually drop enough to equal investment, but not necessarily at full employment.

The central ideas of Keynes' theory are that the decisive problem of economics is how the levels of output and employment are determined. Keynes argued that there is a direct relationship between income and savings. As consumer disposable incomes increase, savings increase, and as incomes decrease, the portion of total income saved decreases. Keynes assumed that each time a consumer gets an additional dollar of income they have two choices; they can spend or save the income. Keynes calls the part spent the marginal propensity to consume, and the part saved the marginal propensity to save. When analyzing the U.S. gross domestic product, it becomes apparent that the largest portion of expenditure, i.e., 70.1 percent of total GDP in 2003, is personal consumption. Therefore, if incomes are reduced, as a result of a reduction in employment, consumption will also fall. In addition, since households make up the largest portion of total expenditures, a reduction of consumer expenditures will have the greatest effect on aggregate demand.

Businesses also buy goods and services. By investing in fixed assets and additions to inventory, businesses account for another substantial part of aggregate demand, i.e., 11.4 percent of GDP in 2009. However, the most important reason that businesses change their investment plans is their future profit expectations. Businessmen do not change their investment plans in response to short run changes in interest rates, and they especially do not increase their investment in production capacity when there is a reduced demand for their products.

Therefore, for an economy to operate to its potential production capacity with full employment, households must provide consumption and businesses must expand their investment in fixed assets and inventory. The expansion must be adequate for sales of goods to be brought into equilibrium with the number of items produced. Thus, if people were to spend all of their income, the marginal propensity to consume would be one. If all income is consumed, then the economy would function according to the classical economist self adjusting model. However, since people save some of their income, business investment must make up for the lack of personal consumption. If business investment does not equal savings, output will be greater than sales, inventories build, and employers will lay off workers. Therefore, per Keynes, depressions are caused by a drastic reduction in demand and one of the main culprits is savings.

In addition to his views of the relationship between savings and investment, Keynes did not agree with the classical theory on the flexibility of wages and prices. When unemployment occurred in the classical context, the accepted cause was wages that were too high or too rigid. With Keynes, this was no longer so; what was true for the individual employer was not true for all. If all employers were to lower wages in a time of unemployment, the flow of purchasing power, the aggregate of effective demand, would diminish. The result of this reduced purchasing power would be that consumers would not have enough income to buy the products produced. Therefore, unemployment could not be blamed on high wages or on the supply controlling effects of labor unions. Unemployment is a result of decreasing aggregate demand. Thus, per Keynes, the equilibrium situation in the economy is not necessarily at full employment; it can be at different and even severe levels of unemployment. This new theory by Keynes became known as the Underemployment Equilibrium.

The Keynesian Solution

In the past, critics of the capitalist system angrily pointed their finger at the robber barons. Keynes suggested that consumers who insist on increasing their savings, especially in times of recession, do more harm than the nefarious industrialist. In addition, this wicked deed of savings tends to compound itself through what Keynes called the "Multiplier." This theory states that an increase or decrease in spending has an affect on the economy that is greater than the original change in expenditures. This multiplier affect occurs because as money is spent on goods and services, those who receive the revenue now have additional income, part of which they spend.

Keynes provided a simple formula to calculate the multiplier with the key being the marginal propensity to consume:

Multiplier = 1/ [1-MPC] or 1/MPS

According to Keynes, the higher the degree of consumption, the higher the multiplier affect would be. On the basis of this formula, Keynes concluded that small reductions in investment may severely pressure the economy as a whole. Also, if deficient demand is the cause of a recession, the cure must be to stimulate more spending. However, if the MPC is known, spending can be injected into the economy, which will multiply throughout and end the recession by filling the original gap between output and consumption.[6]

Keynes estimated the United States multiplier to be about 2.5 times, and based on this estimate, he advocated massive federal spending programs. His recommendations were made in letters written directly to Roosevelt as well as publishing articles in magazines. According to Keynes, the United States could stimulate its economy directly through government spending projects. However, the amount of the injection could be less than the shortfall of consumer and business spending. For example, with a multiplier of 2.5, if the difference between the potential output and the actual output of an economy was $1 billion, the government would only have to inject $400 million in new expenditures to fill the output gap. Therefore, Keynes urged Roosevelt to raise the level of government spending. This meant that the federal government would have to run a deliberate deficit in order to pull the economy out of a depression. This alone would break the underemployment equilibrium, by increasing aggregate demand, through investing the savings of the private sector. It was a powerful affirmation of the wisdom of what was already being accomplished by the Roosevelt administration in order to relieve the hardships caused by the depression.

Keynes and Mars the God of War

For the Keynesian system World War II had major consequences. First, it brought a younger breed of economists into positions of power in Washington. Secondly, World War II demonstrated beyond comparison the power of Keynesian economics. In addition, these young Keynesian economists had the support of such established authority as Alvin Hansen, who came to the Federal Reserve Board, and John Maynard Keynes, who arrived from England to represent the British government.

The final contribution of World War II to the propagation of Keynes' beliefs was that it showed what his economics could accomplish through fiscal policy. Fiscal policy was defined as the actions of the federal government in changing expenditures and tax collections for the purpose of stimulating or slowing down an economy. From 1939 to 1944, the wartime peak, gross national product in constant dollars (1972 dollars adjusted for inflation), increased from $320 billion to $569 billion. Personal consumption expenditures increased from $220 to $255 billion. Unemployment was approximately 17.2 percent of the civilian labor force in 1939; in 1944 it was a nominal 1.2 percent. Overall, in the last full year of the war, Americans were living better than ever before. This was the result of the upward pressure of public demand on the economy. The federal government purchases of goods and services, in these years, increased from $22.8 billion in 1939 to $269.7 billion in 1944. No one could seriously doubt that Mars the God of War, had demonstrated how fiscal policy, could be used to stimulate an economy.

Also, World War II had a great and everlasting effect on the tax system of the United States. Taxes, by modern standards, had been insignificant before 1941. In 1939, federal revenues were just under $5 billion; by 1945, they were in excess of $44 billion. With the war, and in justification of these taxes, came the notion of an approach to the equity of sacrifice: the poor would pay with their military service or their toil; the affluent, especially the non-serving rich, would pay with their taxes. The principle of a strongly progressive tax, effectively income redistribution, is still a major topic of political debate in the 1990's.

As the World War II had affirmed Keynes, so it had dealt a heavy blow to classical laissez faire. In the economics profession, a new view of government and a new reliance on its intervention would be one of the major economic consequences of the war.[7]

KEYNES AFTER KEYNES

After the war the Keynesian economists retained their power in Washington and had found allies in the business world. Full employment would no longer be considered the autonomous consequence of the competitive economy. Keynes proved that the underemployment equilibrium was possible, and in the future, it would be the responsibility of the federal government to ensure full employment.

In January of 1945, with the end of the war in sight, four senators, Robert F. Wagner of New York, James E. Murray of Montana, Elbert Thomas of Utah and Joseph O'Mahoney of Wyoming, sponsored a bill that was designed to guarantee full employment. However, because of strong reaction by business interest, the bill as originally written could not be passed. Full employment was therefore reduced to a goal of high employment. The Employment Act was finally passed by congress and signed by President Truman in 1946. The bill stated that it now was the recognized responsibility of the federal government to provide an environment where those able, willing, and seeking to work, could find employment.

In addition, the Employment Act of 1946 created the Council of Economic Advisors to consult with the president on measures to enhance employment and economic policy. The passage of the employment Act of 1946, with its provision for a council of economic advisors, was very important to the history of economics. It established economics firmly in the center of modern American administration.[8]

The quarter century following the end of World War II, was very good in economic performance. In only three of these twenty-five years did the American gross domestic product fail to increase. Reinforcing domestic expenditures in the United States was an inflow of purchasing power from abroad as the country had a strongly favorable trade balance. After World War II, the United States was the only major industrial power that remained intact. This put America in a position of economic leadership that had no comparison in the twentieth century.

The World War II demands required a sizable advance in the growth of the economy and an enormous transfer of resources from peacetime to wartime needs. The average level of federal expenditure from 1942 through 1945 amounted to roughly one half of the net national product. The federal government, in contrast to its performance during World War I, made a determined effort to control inflation. Roosevelt initiated a program of price controls and rationing in January of 1942 and the Truman administration maintained it until June of 1946. The primary vehicle for implementing price control was the Office of Price Administration (OPA). As a result of the efforts of the OPA, price increases averaged only 6.4 percent, from 1939 to 1948. This was the result of an effective enforcement campaign, the popularity of the general war effort, and the unusual willingness with which Americans accepted price controls and rationing.

One of the curiosities of the postwar expansion was that it defied a restrictive government fiscal policy. The curtailment of government expenditures that began in 1946 continued throughout 1948, with expenditures declining to about one third of what they had been in 1945. However, government tax receipts decreased by less than 10 percent. This resulted in a government surplus of $8.4 billion by 1948.

After World War II, there was a great deal of concern in the United States that the nation would return to the depression of the 1930's. However, during the war two major things occurred to prevent a continued depression. First, there was the elimination of unemployment, and secondly, an expansion of the total number of persons employed. The war effort required a tremendous expansion of the production of military equipment. With the bulk of the young men recruited to fight the war, it was necessary to recruit millions of women to work in the factories that produced military equipment. In addition, government rationing programs restricted the supply of consumer goods that were available to purchase. This pattern of increased revenue and reduced products to purchase resulted in a large increase in savings. The end of World War II brought with it a release of pent-up consumer demand following the lifting of wartime restrictions, especially with regard to consumer durable goods and housing. The combination of pent-up consumer demand and the lifting of wartime restrictions resulted in a large increase in consumer demand that eliminated any possibility of a renewed depression. Because of the large accumulation of money and other highly liquid assets to support this demand, the public would have spent a great deal more on peacetime goods and services had the government not run a surplus.

Another expansive force was the increase in the stock of money, which grew at a rate of slightly more than 4 percent per year between January 1946 and August 1948. The weakness of policy during the late 1940's and the 1950's was more in the management of fiscal policy than in the use of monetary mechanisms. The Federal Reserve Board maintained a rather consistent posture throughout the period, in effect, working to keep the nation's money stock growing at a reasonable stable rate, one upon which other institutions and individuals could depend.

In 1964, there was a deliberate attempt to use Keynesian economics to prevent the economy from entering into a recession. It was the tax reduction of that year. This idea to stimulate demand was begun earlier by President Kennedy, and signed into law after Kennedy's death by President Lyndon Johnson. The highest rate on the personal income tax was reduced to 70 percent. Also, there was a reduction in other lower income brackets and the basic rate on the corporate income tax was reduced. This tax reduction was deliberately designed to expand consumer purchasing power which would stimulate aggregate demand and avoid a budget surplus at full employment. Also, the Federal Reserve accommodated fiscal policy by instituting a moderately simulative monetary policy. The results of the federal government's use of fiscal policy to stimulate the economy, was that the unemployment rate declined from 6.7 percent in 1961 to 3.8 percent in 1966. The first attempt by the federal government to use fiscal policy to increase aggregate demand and therefore, to reduce unemployment was a success and resulted in only a slight increase in the rate of inflation.

NOTES:

Chapter 9
Keynesian Economics

1. Galbraith, John, Kenneth, <u>Economics in Perspective</u>, Boston, MA, Houghton Mifflin Company, 1987, p. 222.
2. Galbraith, p. 225.
3. Buchholz, Todd, G., <u>New Ideas from Dead Economists</u>, New York, N.Y., Penguin Books, 1989, p. 205.
4. Buchholz, p. 206.
5. Buchholz, p. 207.
6. Buchholz, p. 212.
7. Galbraith, p. 249.
8. Galbraith, p. 255.

CHAPTER 10

NATIONAL INCOME ACCOUNTING AND FORECASTING

"Forecasting is very difficult, especially if it's about the future." --Edgar Fielder.

NATIONAL INCOME ACCOUNTING

Once the concept of macroeconomics was developed by John Maynard Keynes in the "General Theory," it became essential to create a terminology to describe its aggregate elements. During the 1940's, many of those who had been converted to Keynesian economics set out to develop a terminology and to measure the entire system of final output in the United States. Their work was the starting point for what today is called National Income Accounting. Simon Kuznets and Richard Stone received a Nobel Prize in Economics for their efforts to define a set of rules and definitions for measuring total economic activity.

National income accounting provides a way of measuring the total output of an economy over a designated period. The Department of Commerce, which gathers the necessary statistics, provides a measurement of economic activity each quarter called the Gross Domestic Product (GDP). GDP is widely reported in the media each quarter as an annualized figure. For example, if GDP grew by 1 percent in the first quarter of 2016, this would equate to a projected growth of 4 percent for the entire year. In national income accounting, aggregate economic production is broken down into two kinds of output, consumption and investment.

Consumption consists of goods and services bought by households for their personal use, such as new cars, and household goods and services. These various goods and services are often referred to as consumer goods. Investment goods are those purchased by business firms to start or to increase their production, by individuals to purchase new homes and by the government to build public infrastructures such as highways and bridges.

Accounting by definition is based on certain identities. For example, in a business, revenue must equal the total cost of producing plus a profit or in some cases a loss. All costs and revenue are kept track of through the use of double entry bookkeeping. In the national income accounts, whenever things are produced, income goes to the people who participated in the production of those goods and services. In other words, individual wealth is created by the production of goods and services. In financial accounting terms, for every use of funds in producing a product, there must be a source for those funds. In the national income accounts, we can define GDP as expenditures as a use of funds and GDP as income as a source of funds. GDP as expenditures, is divided into four main categories: Consumption expenditures, gross private investment, government purchases, and net exports

GDP as Expenditures

Consumption expenditures are the total of all goods and services that are purchased by households during the course of a single year. This category is further broken down into durable and non-durable goods. Durable goods are those products that last for periods greater than one year; for example, automobiles and household furniture. Non-durable goods are those that usually last for a period of less than one year. Consumption expenditures are by far the largest category of GDP.

Gross private investment expenditures are made by businesses and households for capital goods. When economists use the term investment, they refer to the nation's stock of capital assets. Financial assets such as corporate stocks and bonds are not considered capital assets. Gross private investment is broken down into two sub-categories called, fixed investment and changes in business inventory. Fixed investment is by far the largest portion of investment and includes investment in residential buildings, buildings used by business and government, and equipment such as machinery and computers. Inventory investment is the change in the aggregate value of the current stocks of finished goods that businesses have produced and have not yet sold.

Government purchases are divided into federal expenditures and state and local government purchases. Government purchases involve consumption and fixed investment as they can buy both bridges, highways, and pay their employees. The state and local government purchases combined are greater than the federal governments. However, the budget of the federal government is much larger than their total purchases. For example, for total year 2016, total federal expenditures were $3,688 billion and total purchases in the GDP accounts were $1,245 billion. The reason is that the largest part of the federal budget is mandated payments such as transfer payments or entitlements. For 2016 mandated payments totaled $2,301 billion. The remainder of the expenses for 2016 of $271 was for other federal expense and interest on the federal debt. Transfer payments take money from some Americans and transfer it to others, for example, from tax payers to Medicare recipients. However, the government does not spend the money on purchases and therefore transfer payments are not part of the GDP.[1]

Net exports are the final value of all goods and services that are sold to foreign individuals, businesses and governments less the amount of goods and services that are purchased from foreign sources. If we sell more goods and services abroad than we buy there is a positive balance of trade and as in recent years, if we buy more than we sell, a negative net export figure is entered into the GDP accounts.

GDP as Income

Domestic income is the total income earned by the residents and businesses in a country. However, the United States' federal government does not report domestic income in the GDP accounts. The government instead reports national income. National income is the total income earned by the citizens and businesses of a country. Since GDP is based on domestic income an adjustment to account for the foreign income that is paid and received must be made to reconcile the two methods of accounting. To move from domestic income to national income, you must add the difference between investments incomes received from abroad minus the income earned by foreigners. This adjustment to domestic income is called the net foreign factor and is necessary to convert gross domestic product to gross national product so that national income and expenditures can be compared.

National income consists of, compensation paid to employees, rents paid to individuals, interest payments paid by businesses to individuals, and business profits. Compensation paid to employees consists of wages and fringe benefits paid to individuals, adjusted for government income taxes, social security and unemployment insurance deductions. Compensation to employees makes up the largest category of GDP as income.

Rents are the income that is received by individuals for letting other people use their property. Rents received by business firms are not considered here because they are a part of the income and therefore the profit of businesses.

Interest payments are the income that businesses pay to households that have purchased financial assets from the firms. The largest providers of interest payments to households are the financial institutions that hold individual demand and time deposits.

Profits are the amounts left over after a business makes payments to the factors of production. Corporate profits are either paid out to shareholders in the form of dividends or held by the corporation as retained earnings. However, both dividends and retained earnings are owned by stockholders. Therefore, for national income accounting purposes, both are considered to be household income.[2]

To equate national income to gross national product, two additional adjustments must be made. GDP as income reflects net investment and GDP as expenditures show gross investment. To reconcile the two accounts, depreciation expenditures must be subtracted from gross investment. Also, GDP as expenditure contains indirect business taxes. Indirect business taxes include retail sales taxes, excise taxes, business property taxes, customs duties and license fees. These are all expenses of doing business, but they are not income flows to the factors of production and therefore, is not considered as part of the GDP as income accounts.

Basic Economics   123

Table 10-1

National Income Accounting Source and Use of Funds Statement Year 2016 (Dollars in Billions)

Source of Funds GDP as Income	$ Billions	Use of Funds GDP as Expense	$ Billions
Wage and Benefits	10,101	Durable Goods	1,403
Rental Income	705	Non-Durable	2,695
Interest Income	485	Services	8,660
Household Income	11,291	Consumer Exp.	12,758
		Residential Invest.	706
Corporate Profits	2,086	Business Invest.	2,309
Non-Corp. Profits	1,418	Inventory Changes	21
Business Income	3,504	Investment Expense	3,036
Business Taxes	1,335		
		Government Purchase	
National Income	16,130	Federal	1,245
		State & Local	2,031
Adjustments			
		Total Government	3,276
Depreciation Expense	2,910		
Net Foreign Factor	-207	Exports	2,232
Statistical Error	-264	Imports	2,734
Total Adjustments	2,439	Net Exports	-501
Total Sources	18,569	Total Uses	18,569

Source: Bureau of Economic Analysis Table 1.1.5, March 2017.

Table 10-1 is a source and use of funds statement for the year 2016. This statement shows in detail how the two accounts are reconciled. However, in calculating GDP using two different methods, there are bound to be some slight differences. These differences are reconciled by an account that is called statistical discrepancies. These discrepancies are caused by the different methods that the Department of Commerce uses to calculate GDP.

THE ROLE OF SAVINGS AND INVESTMENT

Growth is the norm in a capitalist economy. This is a function of the desire of businesses to expand by constantly seeking new markets, new products, and new ways to reduce the cost of production. As detailed in Table 10.1, gross domestic product as expenditures has four major economic sectors. The table below shows these sectors as a percent of total GDP for 2016 and 2015.

Description	% of	Total	GDP
	2015	2016	Change
Consumer Expenditures	68.3	68.7	.4
Investment Expenditures	16.8	16.3	-.5
Government Expenditures	17.7	17.7	.0
Net Exports	(2.8)	(2.7)	.1
Total GDP	100	100	0.0

Household expenditures on consumer goods are by far the largest section of GDP at 68.7 percent. The change from 2016 to 2015 shows a .5 percent decrease in investment expenditures. This was due to slow economic growth in 1016.

A key factor in an expanding economy is the ability of the private sector to invest in new structures, both residential and business, and new factory equipment. Business expansions are funded by both internally generated retained earnings and personal savings. Personal savings and undistributed corporate profits are reported in the National Income and Product Accounts. Table 10-2 details the relationship between National income, personal income and personal savings.

Table 10-2

National Income Accounts Personal Income and Savings

National Income Accounts	2015 ($ in billions)	2016 ($ in billions)
National Income	15,458	16,130
Less Corporate Profits	2,088	2,086
Business taxes	1,181	1,197
Other transfer payments	1,662	1,873
Plus		
Personal income receipts on assets	2,253	2,263
Personal current transfer receipts	2,679	2,775
Equals Personal Income	15,459	16,012
Less Personal current taxes	1,939	1,966
Equals Disposable personal income	13,520	14,046
Less: Personal outlays	12,736	13,227
Equals: Personal Savings	784	819
Personal savings as a percent of disposable income.	5.8	5.8

Source: Bureau of Economic Analysis – Table 2.1 Personal Income and its Distribution, March 2017.

For 2016 the personal savings rate averaged 5.8. Percent of disposable income compared to 5.8 percent for 2015. The size of consumer expenditures is predictable based on existing demand and future demand for household purchases. Therefore, the major question about GDP growth is what happens to the percent of consumer's disposable income that is saved.

Just as households buy their goods and services mainly out of earnings, the business sector funds its short-term operations from the cash it generates from sales. The major difference is that the business sector does not normally save a large portion of its cash receipts. Most companies that wish to expand their operations through capital investment expenditures must borrow at least a portion of the total cost of large expansion projects.

Household savings are borrowed by the business sector to finance the building of new capital goods and this becomes a primary means by which an economy increases its productivity. This leads to an explanation of how GDP grows and why it fluctuates as follows:

1. Gross domestic product grows because savings are converted into investment for capital equipment.
2. The savings that originate in the household sector are invested by the business sector.
3. GDP fluctuates because the process of transforming savings into investment is not always smooth or steady.[3]

THE GOVERNMENT SECTOR

Governments' in most industrialized countries share three economic goals: economic growth, full employment, and price stability. To achieve these goals, a government often redistributes income to social projects and to individuals. This government does through a system of taxing its citizens. The economic rational a government often uses for its redistribution of their citizen's income would fall into the categories of either positive or normative economics. Positive economics is based on the theory of economic efficiency or the distribution of the goods and services that an economy produces to its most productive resources. Normative economics is based on a question of fairness or who should receive the goods and services produced. Normative economic theory suggests that income should be redistributed from those who have more than they need to those that have less. The redistribution of income from those who are working to those who are not working in the form of Social Security, Medicare and Welfare are examples of normative economics. Therefore, a major role of government is to tax its citizens in order to fund this redistribution and to setup the mechanism, which will require administrative cost, to run the system.

An example of a government using positive economics is where, the market system does not allocate all resources in a way that the citizens of a country desire. A country requires a system of laws that direct its business activity. Without a dependable legal system, a market economy could not operate. Also, a market economy may not properly allocate resources to train and educate its people. Without an educated work force a county would not be able to compete with other industrialized economies. And finally, a modern economy needs to provide its citizens with protection from foreign invasion, criminal actions against its citizens and unsafe and the unfair practices of individual businesses. Therefore, the question is not; do we need government, but how much government and at what cost? An additional question is how can a government use both fiscal and monetary policy to help achieve its goals of full employment, price stability and economic growth? The government's use of fiscal policy was introduced in chapter 13 "Keynesian Economics." Monetary and fiscal policy will be covered in more detail in later chapters.

BUSINESS FLUCTUATIONS

In order to make the mass amounts of historical economic data useful it is helpful to categorize the various forms of fluctuations and to develop techniques of analyzing them. Economists usually classify business fluctuations by the trend, cycles, and seasonal variations. Each of these fluctuations is a result of a different class of factors, and discovering the nature of these causes is important to economic forecasting.

Seasonal variations occur because of changes in business conditions from one season of the year to the next. A seasonal variation exists when there is a regular pattern of variation in the series and this change occurs over a period of time that is usually one year. The trend is the persistent underlying movement that has taken place in a series of data over a period long enough to cover several business cycles. The long-term trend in real gross domestic product (GDP adjusted for inflation), has been gradually rising at a fairly constant rate. Economic growth is the result of increasing the quantity and/or the quality of a country's factors of production. For example, to increase the size of the labor force either the population must grow and/or the quality of the labor force must improve.

A business cycle is the movement of some aggregate measure of economic activity upward or downward over time. The length of time of the cyclical movements will vary, and the magnitude of the movement upward or downward will differ over time. A business cycle can be divided into four phases as the economy fluctuates around the long-term growth trend. The peak of the cycle is the point which real output reaches a maximum. The period during which real output falls is known as the contraction phase. At the end of the contraction, real output reaches a minimum known as the trough of the cycle. After the trough, real output begins to grow again and the economy enters an expansion that lasts until a new peak is reached.

Joseph Schumpeter drew on the work of other economists and concluded that there were three distinct cycle lengths. He named the cycles after the economist that was most associated with these cycles. The Kondratieff cycles consisted of long waves averaging fifty-four years and oscillated around the economic trend. The second of these cycles, Schumpeter called Juglar cycles. These cycles oscillate around the Kondratieff waves and are nine to ten years in duration. Schumpeter named the third cycle, Kitchin cycles which lasted about forty months. The forty-month cycle approximates the average length of most post World War II short term business cycles. The principle reason for the Kitchin cycles is the accumulation and eventual reduction of business inventories as aggregate demand changes. However, longer cycles are affected more by the level of investment in long-term fixed capital and business innovations.

Innovations, according to Schumpeter, can be put into five classes, which require the introduction into the economic system of one or more of the following:

- New products, capital goods or consumer goods.

- New methods of producing goods or services.

- New markets for commodities.

Basic Economics   129

- The exploration of newly discovered sources of raw materials.

- New means of organizing business activity.

According to Schumpeter, the first Kondratieff wave started in the late 1780's and was associated with the industrial revolution and the development of steam power, iron and cotton textile mills. The second wave started in the late 1840's as a result of the expansion of the railroads. This expansion of railroad transportation created opportunities for mass marketing. The third Kondratieff cycle, started around the turn of the twentieth century. This cycle marked the introduction of electricity into the homes and factories and with the mass assembly of automobiles.[4]

In modern times, we can make a good case for the fourth Kondratieff wave in the invention of the jet airplane and the microcomputer. The invention of the microprocessor in 1971 by Intel has changed the organization of every business from the small establishment to the giant multinational corporation. The jet airplane brought with it tourism, which by the 1960's was the largest single industry in the world and made multinational giants out of several American corporations.

An examination of economic history reveals periods of great prosperity, often lasting a decade or more, followed by equally long periods of very slow, zero or even negative growth. The most accepted explanation of this phenomenon is that technology and innovation opens a whole level of opportunities for economic growth. Therefore, improving technology as a result of capital investment and innovation must be considered when developing an economic or business forecast.

ECONOMICS AND BUSINESS FORECASTING

Prior to 1970, economics was basically used to explain current events. There was, for all practical purposes, no attempt to forecast economic events into the future. However, there were two developments in this period that changed the future value and use of economic data. The first was the Input/output analysis of Wassily W. Leontief. The Leontief tables showed the value of what each industry and subsections of each industry sold to each other and received from each other. The resulting great complex, showed how any given change is distributed through the economic system. For example, what an increase in automobile production would mean in extra sales to the steel industry.

The second development was a product of the great engineering advances in data storage. This was the development of the econometric or computer models of the economy. Going beyond Keynes, and Leontief, these economic models seek to emulate the effects of all major changes in the economic system. Changes in public expenditures, taxes, interest rates, wages, profits, industrial production by individual industries, and housing construction were captured. With this data, the changes that were measured were associated with other changes that were occurring throughout the economy.

From the models came forecasts and more specific information relevant to corporate decisions. Each day, business executives and government officials, make decisions that require assumptions about the future. The modern large business enterprise must plan. Planning always involves the future. The forecasts help establish probable magnitudes of demand for a firm's products and keep decisions within the range of plausibility.

However, when preparing a forecast, the business or government planner would be wise to use the rules of forecasting that were first developed by Edgar Fiedler.[5]

- Forecasting is very difficult, especially if it's about the future.

- The moment you forecast you know that you are going to be wrong: you don't know when and in which direction.

- The forecasters best defense is a good offense, so; if you have to forecast, forecast often.

- But if you're ever right, never let 'em forget it!

Basic ECONOMICS

NOTES:

Chapter 10
National Income Accounting and Forecasting

1. Colander, David, C., <u>Economics</u>, Burr Ridge, IL, Richard D. Irwin, Inc., 1994, p. 166.
2. Colander, p. 171.
3. Valentine, Lloyd M., <u>Business Cycles and Forecasting</u>, Cincinnati, OH, South-Western Publishing Co., 1991, p. 126.
4. Heilbroner, Robert, Thurow, Lester, Economics explained, NYC, NY, Simon & Schuster, 1994, p. 89.
5. Fiedler, Edgar, <u>Across The Board</u>, New York, N.Y., The Conference Board, 1977.

CHAPTER 11

INFLATION AND MONETARISM

"His [Keynes] disciples, as disciples will, went much farther than the master. The view became widespread that money does not matter." -- Milton Friedman

THE ECONOMICS OF INFLATION

Gross Domestic Product can be defined as the aggregates of all revenue that is received for the sale of goods and services that are produced in an economy in one year. In addition, GDP can be represented using the simple equation of: "R = P x Q," where:

R = Total Revenue = GDP,
P = Aggregate prices of all goods and services,
Q = Aggregate quantity of all goods and services produced.

Nominal GDP is the total value of goods and services reported at current prices. Real GDP is the term that economists use to describe the total amount of goods and services produced, adjusted for price level changes, i.e., nominal GDP = P x Q, and real GDP = Q.

For example, between 2009, the year currently used by the Department of Commerce as the base year, and 2016 the U.S. gross domestic product, measured in nominal terms, increased from $14,418 to $18,569 billion, an increase of 4,151 billion or 28.7 percent. However, a major portion of the dollar value of GDP reflected an increase in the prices at which goods and services were actually sold. For comparison, the Department of Commerce sets the base year, in this case 2009, at 100. The GDP deflator is then used to adjust nominal GDP to real GDP. The GDP deflator is used to adjust gross domestic

Basic Economics

product to account for the effects of inflation because it is the most broadly based measure of price changes in the U.S. economy. For 2016, the GDP deflator was 114.4 or 11.4 percent higher than it was in 2009. To adjust nominal GDP to real GDP, nominal GDP is divided by the GDP price deflator as follows:

Table 11-1 Nominal and Real GDP

Description		($ in Billions)	($ in Billions)	($ in Billions)
Nominal GDP			$18,569	
----------------- =	Real GDP		----------	$16,662
GDP Deflator			1.144	
Description		2009	2016	Change
Nominal GDP		$14,418	$18,569	$4,151
Real GDP		$14,418	$16,662	$2,244

Therefore, the increase in GDP from 2009 through 2016 can be broken down into its two fundamental elements as follows:

Increase due to	$ (Billions)	% Increase
Price (P)	$2,897	20.1
Quantity (Q)	$2,244	15.6
Total Increase		35.7

During this six-year period, GDP increased by an average of 4.1 percent. The average increase due to price changes was 2.3 percent and the increase in real output averaged only 1.8 percent. This is an indication of a period of slow growth in output and a moderate rate of inflation.

Inflation is defined by economists as a long-term sustained increase in the general level of prices. The most often used measures of changes in the price level are the GDP deflator, the producer price index and the consumer price index. The GDP deflator, used in the above example, is a weighted average of the prices of all final goods and services produced in the economy in one year. The producer price index is a ratio of a composite of prices based on a sample of goods and services bought by business firms. Economists use the PPI as an early indication of the future direction of inflation. This is because many of the producer prices are those of the raw materials used as inputs in the production of consumer goods.

The most widely reported measure of inflation is the consumer price index. The CPI is often used to index wages in labor contracts and is also used by the federal government to decide the yearly increase in social security payments and the salaries paid to many government workers. To determine the CPI, the government records the prices of approximately 90,000 different consumer purchases in seven different groups each month. The major groups of consumer purchases are entertainment, medical care, housing, food and beverage, transportation, apparel, and other goods and services. The data is collected and compiled by the U.S. Department of Labor Statistics that has about 680 workers and 360 part-time collectors who survey prices in eighty-five cities. The annual budget for developing the CPI monthly is about $35 million.

THE ROOTS OF INFLATION IN AMERICA

The result of the simultaneous use of expansive fiscal and monetary policies that was started in 1964, was the achievement of an exceptionally low rate of unemployment. However, the low unemployment rate came at the expense of future price increases. At the beginning of 1966, unemployment moved below 4 percent for the first time since 1957 and remained below that level until the first quarter of 1970. However, the increasing aggregate demand that reduced unemployment, also placed pressure on the economy's production capability. The combination of increased consumer disposable income and the expansion of the money supply created a situation where there was more marginal money available to spend than products available for purchase. This occurrence of "too much money chasing too few goods," as economists called it, accelerated the rate of price increases and created a widespread anticipation of further price increases. This created a psychology of inflation among American businesses who became more concerned with increases in revenue than with controlling operating expenses. The attitude of many producers and even commercial banks was that, if they could pass along price increases to consumers, why should they worry about controlling costs.

In the Keynes system deflation and unemployment called for higher public expenditure and lower taxes, which were politically acceptable actions. Price inflation, on the other hand, called for lower government expenditure and higher taxes, which were far from politically agreeable. Therefore, the economics of John Maynard Keynes, while acceptable in theory, was not effective in controlling inflation. Keynesian policy was a one-way street, an avenue that presented a politically pleasant remedy for curing a recession, but a politically unpalatable solution to the problem of inflation. After 1966 the rate of inflation began to accelerate; it went up more than 6 percentage points between 1969 and 1970, nearly 8 percent between 1972 and 1973 and nearly 14 percent from 1974 to 1975. In 1975 the phrase "double digit inflation," was introduced to American economic terminology.

A further and yet more serious problem in all the industrial countries was the new form of inflation. This was price and wage increases coming from the interaction in the modern economy and its large corporate organizations. With industrial concentration, corporations had achieved a very substantial measure of control over their prices. Also, trade unions, by controlling the supply of labor to large manufacturing corporations, had achieved substantial authority over the wages and associated benefits paid to their members. From the interaction of these entities came a new and powerful inflationary force. This was the upward pressure of wage settlements on prices, and the upward pull of living costs on wages. This was the interacting dynamic that came to be called the "wage-price spiral."[1]

In 1965, with the economy running at nearly full capacity, President Lyndon Johnson instituted his "Great Society" social welfare program. At the same time, America, had begun a military involvement in the civil war between North and South Vietnam. However, based on excessively optimistic forecasts of military and domestic expenses, the total cost of this joint program was badly underestimated. The Johnson administration began to realize that taxes would have to be raised to prevent further inflation. However, no tax increase was enacted until 1968, when inflation was already well established. The new taxes were introduced as a surcharge rather then a part of the permanent tax tables. The reaction of consumers to a temporary increase in tax rates was a decrease in savings. The decrease in savings increased the marginal propensity to consume which offset the effects of the tax increase. This change in consumer spending habits made the tax increase totally ineffective.

Policies of the Nixon and Ford Administrations

In 1969, Richard Nixon became the thirty-seventh president of the United States. The Nixon administration found it necessary to maintain the tax surcharge throughout 1969, and then the surcharge was removed in stages. After all, politicians do not like to give up increased taxes. Meanwhile, the Federal Reserve began to implement policy designed to tighten the money supply. The result of the Feds policy was a sharp reduction in the growth of the nation's money supply and an end to the economic expansion that had begun in 1962. By 1970, a recession had replaced the long economic expansion in the United States and recessions bring about an event that often puts fear in the heart of politicians, i.e., unemployment.

A combination of 6 percent unemployment and 5 percent inflation created a real problem for politicians about to launch a reelection campaign. The problem for the administration was how to reduce unemployment and inflation at the same time. Remember, both monetary and fiscal policies, which are designed to effect recession or inflation, work on one side of the problem at a time. President Nixon's answer to this dual problem was the announcement of a "New Economic Policy." The most important part of the new economic policy was an immediate freeze on all wages and prices. Although the price controls received widespread political support when they were announced, they proved mostly ineffective. Employers and workers quickly found ways to limit the effect of these controls. Many goods that were normally sold domestically were exported to avoid the price controls. Companies found ways to avoid the wage controls by promoting key employees or by changing job titles.

The result of the first peacetime attempt to establish wage and price controls was, for the most part, a failure. The controls were designed to cure inflation by treating its symptoms, while at the same time other government policies exacerbated the causes of the inflation. Most wage and price controls were dropped in mid-1973. However, since the factors that cause inflation had not been addressed, the result was an increase in inflation after the controls were lifted. Finally, beginning at the end of 1973, there came the large increase in oil prices, the results of the cartel action of the Oil Producing States (OPEC). Between 1972 and 1981, the index of prices of household fuels in the United States climbed from 118.5 (1967=100) to 675.9, an increase of almost 600 percent.

In 1975, President Gerald Ford called into conference some of the country's better known economists to prescribe for inflation (There was a 13.5 percent increase in the consumer price index in that year). The full group agreed on only one remedy: government should remove any impediments to market competition. For practical effect, this was no better than the president's own prescription, which was the wearing of buttons inscribed with the insignia (WIN - Whip Inflation Now). The Keynes system of using fiscal policy while theoretically logical, was in practice of limited value. Congress was not going to vote to increase taxes or to reduce expenditures to decrease inflation. This is because most congressmen run for office on a platform emphasizing the amount of increased government programs that they can obtain for their district. The way that politicians get elected to office in the United States, was found to be mutually exclusive with the requirements of Keynes economics, during periods of inflation. Consequently, there remained only one viable course of action: to use monetary policy to control inflation.[2]

MONETARY POLICY

In 1979, President Jimmy Carter appointed Paul Volcker as the Chairman of the Federal Reserve System. Under Volcker, the Federal Reserve began a policy that was determined to control inflation.

However, before we examine the effects of this new policy, it would be beneficial to explain just how monetary policy works and to illustrate how the Fed uses its monetary tools to implement the policy.

Monetary policy operates against inflation by raising interest rates. As interest rates increase, consumer durable goods such as new homes and automobiles become too expensive to purchase and business organizations reduce investment spending as the expected return on investment for new projects does not meet the companies' minimum return on investment requirements. This, in turn, reduces bank lending, the resulting deposit of funds and the creation of money.

Monetary Policy and the Federal Reserve System

Monetary policy is executed by the Federal Reserve System in the United States. The Federal Reserve System is divided into twelve district banks that are directed by a nine-person board of directors with three coming from commercial banks, three from non-banking business interest and three appointed by the Federal Reserve Board. The Federal Open Market Committee is the official policy making body of the Federal Reserve System. The committee is made up of the seven members of the Board plus five of the twelve district bank presidents. Since the New York Federal Reserve Bank actually carries out monetary policy, the president of the Federal Reserve Bank of New York, is a permanent member of the committee.

The major responsibility of the Federal Open Market Committee is to set monetary policy goals that, in theory, would lead to long-term economic growth and stable prices. The Fed controls the money supply, which in turn, affects the nation's gross domestic product and the level of prices. The Federal Open Market Committee sets monetary targets and then implements them through the Federal Reserve Bank of New York. Each FOMC directive outlines the conduct of monetary policy over a six to eight weeks' period.

The Federal Reserve controls the money supply by changing the reserves of its member banks. There are three ways that Federal Reserve action can affect the money supply. These tools are an adjustment to banks reserve requirements, changes in the Federal

Reserve Discount Rate and Open Market Operations. These tools work as follows:

Reserve Requirement

The Fed requires banks to hold a fraction of their deposits on reserve. This fraction is the required reserve and was last changed in 1992 to 10 percent of demand deposits. Legal reserves are the sum of a bank's vault cash and deposits in the Federal Reserve Bank. When legal reserves equal required reserves, the bank has no excess reserves and can make no new loans. If the Fed lowers the reserve requirement, as it did in 1992 from 12 to 10 percent on transaction accounts, a portion of what was previously required reserves becomes excess reserves. Excess reserves can be used by commercial banks to make loans and in turn, to expand the money supply. Also, if the Fed wants to fight inflation, it can increase reserve requirements which will reduce excess reserves and reduce the money supply.

Discount Rate

The Discount rate is the interest the Fed charges its member banks who borrow directly from the Federal Reserve. When the Fed raises the discount rate, it raises the cost of borrowing. This action reduces the amount of reserves borrowed by member banks. If the Fed reduces the discount rate the excess reserves at commercial banks will tend to increase. This, however, is not a very effective tool for controlling the money supply, for banks usually borrow from the Fed only to satisfy seasonal needs and as a last resort.

Open Market Operations

This is the major tool of monetary policy. If the Fed wants to Increase bank reserves, the Federal Open Market Committee issues a directive to the bond trading desk at the New York Fed, to buy bonds. The bonds are purchased from private bond dealers. The dealers are paid with checks drawn on the Federal Reserve, which then are deposited in the dealers' accounts at commercial banks. As bank deposits and reserves increase, banks are able to make new loans. To the extent that the banks use these new reserves to make loans, the money supply expands. If the Fed wants to decrease the money supply, it sells bonds.

The expansion of the money supply depends on the amount of new purchases of securities by the Fed and the banking system's willingness to make new loans. If the banks choose to use excess reserves to buy securities for their own portfolio, then the money supply is not increased.

Also, when the Fed talks of controlling the money supply, they are not just referring to cash in consumers' pockets. The Fed defines money in terms of M1 and M2. M1 is called the money stock and is defined as Federal Reserve notes in circulation plus transaction deposits. Transaction deposits are made up mostly of demand deposits kept with commercial banks. M2 is defined as M1 plus short term liquid assets that cannot be used directly as a medium of exchange but can be easily converted into cash or checkable deposits. The money supply, referred to as M2, includes M1 plus money market demand deposits at banks, money market mutual fund accounts, savings accounts and certificates of deposit that are under one hundred thousand dollars. When the Federal Reserve announces that they are targeting the money supply they are referring to the monetary items in M2. What the Fed normally targets are a range of yearly growth of the money supply, for example, between 4 and 8 percent per year.

Monetary Policy and Inflation

As the 1970's passed, inflation persisted. The administration of President Jimmy Carter initiated a strong monetarist action. During the early 1980's another word was added to the economist's vocabulary, "Stagflation," that describes a stagnant economy in association with continuing inflation. In the early 1980's, interest rates were brought to unprecedented levels, in the United States. This resulted in the unwanted combination of double-digit inflation and double digit interest rates. Double digit interest rates curtailed demand for new housing construction and for automobiles and other credit supported purchases. In 1982 and 1983, they brought a sharp restriction in business investment expenditure. The sharp reduction in business investment resulted in a large increase in unemployment, i.e., 10.7 percent in late 1982. Further, the high interest rates brought in a strong flow of foreign funds, which bid up the value of the dollar, curtailed American exports, and strongly encouraged imports, especially from Japan. The overall result of the use of monetary policy to curtail inflation was the deepest economic recession since the Great Depression of the 1930's. [3]

However, by the end of 1984, the consumer price index was nearly stable. Inflation had been substantially reduced. Monetary policy had worked to control inflation, by producing a severe economic slump. There remained a question as to rather the cure was worst than the disease. One way to answer this question is to analyze the results of the 1980 in the form of GDP growth. Gross domestic product increase from $ 3,131 billion in 1981 to $5,489 in 1989 an increase of over 75 percent an average increase of over 9 percent. In comparison, by 1988 the CPI index had fallen to 4.1 percent.

MILTON FRIEDMAN AND MONETARISM

Many economists believe that the equation of exchange provides important insights into the way the economy functions and the way monetary policy can affect price levels in the long run. Monetarism is a theory of long-term macroeconomic equilibrium based on the equation of exchange. According to the equation of exchange, shifts in the velocity of money are reasonably predictable. The equation of exchange was first introduced into economics in 1911, by Irving Fisher of Yale University. The most popular version of the equation of exchange is the "Quantity Theory of Money" with its simple equation of $MV=PQ$. The M in this equation represents the money stock and the V is the velocity of money. The velocity of money is defined as the amount of times money is spent during the course of one year. The P in the equation represents the general price level and the Q is the amount of goods and services actually produced by an economy in one year. Therefore, according to the equation, the stock of money multiplied by the number of times money turns over equals the dollar value of all goods and services produced in that year.

Monetary Economics

The basis for the monetarist theory is as follows:

- Velocity of money is constant or at least predictable.

- The amount of goods and services that can be produced in the short run is fixed because organizations require time to increase their production capability.

- Increases in the supply of money, in the long-run, will only result in an offsetting increase in price levels. The quantity theory essentially eliminates velocity and quantity from the equation, and concludes that any change in the money stock will be felt only in the price level.

Monetarists usually agree that short term changes in the supply of money can affect economic activity. For example, the Federal Reserve can increase the money supply that will lower interest rates. In times of recession, the lower interest rates will stimulate additional consumer purchases of durable goods and increases in business spending. The reason for the increased spending is because many consumer items that are purchased on credit become more affordable with lower interest rates. Also, business projects that did not provide an acceptable rate of return under assumptions of high interest rates, may be approved when the cost of funding the proposed projects is reduced. There is one other key ingredient that determines whether monetary policy will be effective. Monetary economics works through the extension of bank credit. Therefore, the commercial banking systems must be willing to make loans if monetary policy is to have any influence on economic growth.

While monetarists concede that the Federal Reserve System can affect economic growth, they argue that these benefits are only short-term. In the long-term, they hold, changes in the money supply can only change price levels. Assuming the velocity of money is constant, the classical quantity theory of money implies that, over the long-run, rapid inflation can be caused by growth of the money stock, if that growth is in excess of the long-term growth rate of the gross domestic product. This implies that monetary policy can keep inflation under control over the long-run by making sure the growth rate of the money stock does not exceed the growth rate of an economy's ability to produce.

Milton Friedman (1912-2006)

Milton Friedman

Milton Friedman was a diligent advocate of the policy that was to fill the post-Keynesian void. Friedman was the leading American exponent of the classical competitive market, which he claimed still exists, except as it suffered from ill-advised government intrusion. He was a powerful opponent of government regulation and government in general. According to Friedman, the key to a healthy, stable economy is for the money supply to expand, at a constant rate, in accordance with the growth of an economy's production capability. He is a believer in laissez faire capitalism and a fan of Adam Smith. For his work, he received the Nobel Prize in Economics in 1976. Friedman's books include "A Monetary History of the United States, Capitalism and Freedom, and Free to Choose." Friedman taught at the University of Chicago for 30 years. He retired in 1977 and currently works out of the Hoover Institute at Stanford University.

In a series of studies Friedman rescued the quantity theory of money from the attacks of Keynesian economists. In 1956, Friedman published a set of essays that were designed to test the quantity theory. Per Friedman, demand for money and in turn the velocity of money is stable. The demand for money depends on long-term factors such as health, education, and individual income expectations. Since consumers do not vary their long run expectations very often, the amount of times each year that they spend their money does not vary widely. In other words, velocity remains constant in the long-run.

Consumers will not let a bad week or month or even a year alter their spending patterns. They will simply use up some of their savings.[4]

To test his theory of long-run stable velocity of money, Friedman, with Anna J. Schwartz, published "A Monetary History of the United States, 1867-1960." This publication pointed out that between the years 1929 and 1933, the quantity of money available in the United States, had plunged by one-third. Per Friedman and Schwartz, one of the major causes of the Great Depression was the refusal of the Federal Reserve to provide liquidity to the nation's banks when panic stricken depositors demanded redemption of their deposits. In summary, Friedman claimed that poor policy execution by the Federal Reserve has accompanied every severe recession and every significant inflationary occurrence in the twentieth century. Milton Friedman, passed away On November 12th 2006 at the age of 94. Friedman will be remembered as the leader of the Chicago School of monetary economics, which stresses the importance of the quantity of money as an instrument of government policy and as a determinant of business cycles and inflation

In addition to explaining the power of money and breathing new life into the quantity theory, Friedman attempted to challenge Keynes' claim that government spending could spur the economy. However, to prove this point, monetarist had to show that the Keynesian expenditure multiplier did not exist. Monetarist, when analyzing the Keynesian prescription for stimulating an economy, ask one simple question: Where does the money come from? If the money supply remains constant and the government increases its expenditures, then either consumers or businesses must spend less. Therefore, increased government spending must take the place of business or consumer spending. Economists refer to the replacement of consumer and business expenditures with government spending as the "Crowding Out" effect.

Keynesians do not deny that crowding out takes place. However, they propose that crowding out does not completely offset government spending, especially during a recession. Therefore, the debate between the monetarist and Keynesians revolves around the question of the size of the multiplier and whether it is consistent during different levels of economic growth and recession. Data Resources Corporation

Basic Economics 145

has developed a large computer model of gross domestic product and its many components. According to the DRI model, the multiplier is estimated to be about 1.6 the first year of the increased government expenditures and steadily dropping after that.[5]

By the late 1970's, the monetarists were no longer receiving the butt of jokes from the economics' profession. Many of the views of Milton Friedman and the monetarist were being recognized. Central Banks throughout the world began to closely monitor their country's money supply. Main-stream economists absorbed many of the monetarists' views and began to shed their insistence on the use of fiscal policy alone. An even congress was rescued, as the Federal Reserve provided them with a set of tools for fighting inflation without the difficult task of having to reduce their spending habits.

NOTES:

Chapter 11
Inflation and Monetarism

1. Galbraith, John Kenneth, <u>Economics in Perspective</u>, Boston, MA, Houghton Mifflin Company, 1987. p. 267.
2. Galbraith, p. 270.
3. Galbraith, p. 275.
4. Buchholz, Tod, G. <u>New Ideas from Dead Economists</u>, New York, N.Y., Penguin Books, 1989, p. 231.
5. Buchholz, p. 234.
6. Niskanen, William A. & Moore, Stephen, <u>Supply-Side Tax Cuts and the Truth About the Reagan Economic Record</u>, Washington, DC, The Cato Institute, 1996, p. 3-5.

CHAPTER 12

RONALD REAGAN AND THE 1980's

General Secretary Gorbachev, if you seek peace, if you seek prosperity for the Soviet Union and Eastern Europe, if you seek liberalization: Come here to this gate! Mr. Gorbachev, open this gate! Mr. Gorbachev, tear down this wall—Ronald Reagan

RONALD REAGAN (1911-2004)

Ronald Reagan

The 1980s will be remembered in America as the era of conservative politics with Ronald Reagan as its chief advocate. Ronald Reagan was not merely a successful president, he was a great president. Not all intellectuals agree with this statement, however, the majority of American voters who overwhelming elected him to two terms in office would agree. Reagan dominated American politics in the second half of the twentieth century in much the way Franklin D. Roosevelt dominated the first. Clare Booth Luce once said that history will remember each president by a single line: "Lincoln freed the slaves," or "FDR brought the country out of depression" for example. Margaret Thatcher, the British Prime Minister during the 1980s, came close to composing Reagan's legacy when she said, "Ronald Reagan won the cold war without firing a shot."

When Reagan came to office in 1981, America was on a downward spiral in economic well-being and global influence. He faced

Basic Economics 147

several problems including rapid inflation, the energy crisis, unemployment, and government over-regulation.

Inflation had been accelerating since the 1960s and reached double digits in the 70s. At a rate of 12 percent in 1979-1980, inflation would double the prices of basic goods and cut in half the value of savings and pension plans in just a few years. The energy problem, with rising gasoline prices and fuel shortages, also contributed to higher prices. Gasoline prices had soared from about 35 cents a gallon in 1970 to more that $1.50 in 1980.

Interest rates had peaked at 21 percent in 1980, making it difficult for most families to buy homes and for companies to fund the purchase of long-term assets such as new factories and equipment. Unemployment and poverty rates were high, and industrial productivity was down to about 1.5 percent per year. Consumer confidence was low and economic growth had ground to a halt resulting in the worst economy since the great depression.

A policy analysis study by the Cato Institute highlighted some of Reagan's economic achievements during the years 1981 through 1989. The average annual growth rate of real gross domestic product (in 1987 dollars) from 1981 to 1989 was 3.2 percent per year, compared to 2.8 percent from 1974 to 1981. Real median household income rose by $4,000 in the period, from $37,868 in 1981 to $42,049 in 1989. From 1981 through 1989 the U.S. economy produced 17 million new jobs, or roughly 2 million jobs per year. When Reagan took office, the unemployment rate was 7.6 percent. In the recession of 1981-82, that rate peaked at 9.7 percent. When Reagan left office, the unemployment rate was 5.5 percent. In 1980 the consumer price index (CPI) rose to 13.5 percent. By Reagan's second year in office, the inflation rate fell by more than half to 6.2 percent. In 1988, the CPI had fallen to 4.1 percent. In 1981 the prime rate (lending rate to high credit quality businesses) was over 18 percent. By 1987 the prime rate had fallen to 8.2 percent. The stock market as reflected in the Dow Jones Industrial Index, doubled in value and the United States reaffirmed its position as the world's preeminent economy.[1]

Reagan's achievements on stopping the advance of communism were even more amazing. When Reagan was elected president, democracy was on the retreat in much of the world. Soviet Premier

Khrushchev's boast that the Soviets would "bury the West" seemed a real possibility. In South and Central America, guerrilla revolutions, fueled by popular discontent against the old dictatorships led to a socialist rebellion in many parts of the region. For the first time, the Soviet nuclear arsenal surpassed that of the United States.

During the Reagan administration, the communist influence in the region began to decline as dictatorships collapsed in Chile, Haiti, and Panama. In addition, eight more Latin America countries, Bolivia, Honduras, Argentina, Grenada, El Salvador, Uruguay, Brazil and Guatemala, elected democratic leaders. Fewer than one-third of the countries in Latin America were democratic in 1981: more than 90 percent of the region developed democratic governments by 1989.[2]

The freedom revolution soon penetrated the Soviet countries. Poland held free elections, and Lech Walsea, the president of the country's largest labor union, was elected president. The march toward democracy continued until the majority of the countries in the Soviet bloc declared their freedom, and in 1989, the Berlin Wall, long the symbol of communist domination, came down.

In 1991, the Soviet Union abolished itself, and Boris Yeltsin became the first freely elected president of Russia. An era of friendship between the United States and Russia was made possible by the diminished nuclear rivalry between the two nations as Russia strives towards democracy and the century old debate between Capitalism and Communism was resolved.

Reagan did not achieve this success alone, others such as Margaret Thatcher, Pope John Paul II, Vaclav Havel, Lech Walesa, and especially Soviet General Secretary Mikhail Gorbachev, played a key role. However, Reagan was the catalyst; he was the chief architect of this change.

Dinesh D'Souza, a domestic policy analyst in the Reagan administration, in his book "Ronald Reagan: How an Ordinary Man Became an Extraordinary Leader" summarized his and many others' opinions as to Reagan's achievements by writing "Reagan's greatness derives in large part from the fact that he was a visionary, a conceptualizer who was able to see the world differently from the way it was. Reagan understood Soviet Communism with the same moral clarity that Lincoln had in understanding slavery. Both men were fundamentally motivated not by political calculation but by a basic sense of right and wrong."[3]

SUPPLY SIDE ECONOMICS

In the 1970s and early 1980s, two economists revised the classical economic system and refurbished it to fit the modern would. The two men were Robert Mundell and Arthur Laffer. The economic system was named supply side economics. Robert Mundell was the first economist to predict the rise in inflation that occurred in America and the rest of the world during the 1970s. Keynesian economic theorists during the 1970s were baffled by the recurring combination of high inflation and high unemployment. They couldn't solve the problem of stagflation. Mundell turned the Keynesian demand model upside down. Instead of the philosophy that taxes should be raised to curb excess demand, Mundell argued that inflation is a monetary problem that can only be cured by an increase in dollar purchasing power value. Mundell wrote that only tax-rate reduction would restore the necessary worker rewards and investment incentives to increase the supply of new jobs, production capital formation and growth. Robert Mundell, currently a professor at Columbia University, received the Nobel Prize in Economics in 1999.

Arthur Laffer, a protégé of Mundell's, extended the theory by developing what became known as the Laffer curve. The Laffer curve suggests that there is an optimal tax rate that maximizes government revenue from taxation. Laffer argued that as taxes increased from fairly low levels, tax revenues received by the government would also increase. However, he stated that as tax rates rose, there would come a point (on the curve he designed) where people would regard it as not worth working so hard. Essentially, the marginal returns to working harder would become lower because tax rates are higher at higher incomes. Therefore, Laffer suggested that, if high tax rates were decreased, this would provide increased incentives for people to work harder and, thereby, increase total tax revenues for the government.

The basic premise of supply-side economics is that it places supply over demand in the hierarchy of economics and, therefore, deals with enhancing economic production, efficiency, and growth within the context of the marketplace. Supply-side economics focuses largely on relative prices, such as incentives for working, saving, investing, and risk-taking. Supply-side economics falls under the broader category of free-market economics. Therefore, supply-siders hold the same skepticism of government, as do their free-market cousins, such as public choice, monetarists, and Austrian economists. They argue that production for the sake of production is fruitless. Production must meet current demands or create new ones. Value must be created. Supply-side economists recognize that government lacks the requisite experience, knowledge, and incentive to make resources allocations that create value.

REAGANOMICS

In 1981 Reagan advisors, such as Arthur Laffer, Norman Ture, Martin Anderson and Jack Kemp, urged him to implement supply-side tax cuts. This change in economic policy became known as Reaganomics and consisted of four key elements designed to reverse the high-inflation, slow growth economic record of the 1970s. The key elements were as follows: (1) A restrictive monetary policy engineered through Federal Reserve Chairman Paul Volker; (2) The Economic Recovery Tax Act of 1981 including a 25 percent across-the-board tax cut designed to spur savings, investment, work, and economic efficiency; (3) A promise to balance the budget through domestic spending restraint; (4) An agenda to roll back government regulation.

Fiscal Policy Achievements

The economic achievements of the Reagan years as previously outlined were impressive. The fiscal record of the 1980s was not as impressive. The national public debt in real dollars (adjusted for inflation in 1987 dollars) doubled from $1,004 billion in 1981 to $2,028 billion in 1989. The rise in the national debt imposed significant repayment costs to future generations. Nominal federal revenues doubled in the 1980s from $518 billion to $1,031 billion. As a share of GDP, however, federal tax revenues fell by 1 percent during the period. The federal budget was not cut under Reagan. In fact, it was 69 percent larger when Reagan left office than when he entered it. As a share of GDP, federal outlays declined by less than 1 percent. Overall domestic spending growth was relatively constrained during the Reagan presidency. Domestic outlays as a share of GDP fell from 15.3 percent to 12.9 percent from 1981 to 1989. However, the reductions in domestic spending as a percent of GDP were much smaller than the amounts needed to balance the federal budget, cut taxes and finance a military build-up.

Analysis of the data from 1981 points a finger directly at the defense build-up as the main reason for the deficits of the Reagan era. The cumulative increase in defense spending from 1981 to 1989 was $809 billion. The commutative buildup in the deficit for the same period was $779 billion. If the defense spending had been held to an inflation rate of 3 percent during the period of 1981 to 1989, the total real deficit would have fallen rather than risen.[4]

In conclusion, when the facts are analyzed a case can be firmly stated that the Reagan tax cuts were not a primary cause of the expansion of the deficit in the 1980s. The two main causes were an unexpectedly sharp reduction in inflation in the early 1980s that led to large real increases in federal spending, and a nearly $1 trillion military build-up during the last phase of the cold war. If the entire accumulation of debt in the 1980s went to finance the Reagan defense build-up, the key policy question would shift to whether it was appropriate to borrow for those large military expenditures. Was the Reagan administration justified in paying for the one-time increase in "public investment" spending through debt rather than taxes? Or, put another way; was it appropriate to have asked our children and grandchildren to help defray the cost of defeating the Soviet Empire? The answer to that question rests to some extent on the issue of whether the defense build-up materially contributed to the collapse of the Soviet Union. If the Reagan defense buildup contributed to the fall of the Soviet Union, and many Soviet leaders, including General Secretary Mikhail Gorbachev, have indicated that it was a major factor, then the value to our children of establishing an economic partnership with the new Russia and presidents Boris Yeltzin and currently Vladimir Putin should far out way any cost.

Deregulation

Reagan reappointed Paul Volker chairman of the Federal Reserve Board and later appointed Alan Greenspan who remains the current chairman. He gave them both the authority to do what it took and encouraged them to deregulate the economy. Reagan also turned around the labor situation in the Federal government by standing up to the air traffic controllers union (PATCO) and settled their dispute firmly as he refused to allow a materialistic union to strike against the American public. Reagan's first official act as president was, by executive order, to immediately terminate oil price controls, a policy that instantly reenergized America's domestic exploration and production of oil. Virtually every energy policy in the 1970s exacerbated the energy crisis, from the windfall profits tax to energy price controls. Reagan hastened the end of the energy crisis by repealing virtually all of these policies. Reagan was instrumental in deregulating the transportation industry and the banking and financial services industry. He was instrumental in setting lose the forces that led to the deregulation of telecommunications, and more recently, utilities. It was Reagan who engineered a free trade agreement with Canada, which was later, under President Clinton, expanded to include Mexico to form the NAFTA agreement. Reagan also floated the notion of hemispheric free trade where, at some point in the future, Canada, the United States, Mexico, and all of Latin America would be linked into a free trading zone. Creating a free America trade zone is still a topic for discussion among the many countries of the Americas.5

THE FALL OF COMMUNISM

At the end of World War II, there were two military superpowers, the United States and the Soviet Union. However, there was only one economic superpower, the United States. In any economy, certain items can be produced at the expense of other products. When the Reagan administration increased its defense spending in the middle 1980's, the Soviet Union had to increase their spending on defense in order to maintain military equity. Since the Soviet Union was not an economic superpower, their increased defense expenditures had to be funded through a decreased investment in civilian consumption. However, the reason for the fall of communism in the Soviet Union was even more fundamental than the trade-off between civilian and defense spending. The reason that Communism failed is due to the faults of the system itself.

The Soviet system, unlike capitalism, did not evolve gradually over time. The system came into being after the revolution of 1917. A semi-feudal society was taken over by a group of revolutionaries who were driven by the philosophy of Karl Marx. Per Marx, after the revolution, a temporary regime known as the "dictatorship of the proletariat," would take over the transition from capitalism to socialism. Once government was organized, a planned socialist economy would emerge that would set up the organization that was necessary for the production and distribution of goods and services. However, the revolution presented, Lenin, Trotsky and the other leaders of the new Soviet Union with problems far more complex than Marx's utopian design. One of the major problems of the new government was how to distribute food from the farms to the factory workers.

In 1927, Joseph Stalin became the new leader of the Soviet Union. Stalin decided to solve the food distribution problem by taking over the farms. While the process of collectivizing both agriculture and industry solved the distribution problem, there was a tremendous social and economic cost. Many peasants slaughtered their livestock rather then hand them over to the new collective farms and others just refused to cooperate with the new system. In reprisal, Stalin acted with brutal force. Farmers that would not cooperate were executed or put in labor camps. In the cities, factory workers were given tasks by the central authorities. The right to strike was forbidden and trade unions were eliminated. Under Stalin, the Soviet Union was transferred from a utopian form of socialism, as advocated by Karl Marx, to a dictatorship.

Economists often define socialism as a system where the productive resources are owned by government. In a capitalist system, the market through the price system is used to produce and distribute goods and services. In the absence of a market, direct orders from a central planning agency must be used to distribute society's products. In a socialist economy, planners not consumers determine the demand for products. In a totally planned economy, every item that goes into the final plan must be in great detail. Schedules of production are needed down to the smallest items. Supplies of labor must also be planned. Thus, the master plan must be accompanied by a whole hierarchy of smaller plans in order to achieve the smallest of objectives. Even one little planning error can have disastrous affects, if it is part of the strategic link in the chain of production and distribution. In short, to effectively run a socialist system, the leaders of the system would have to know all the possible available alternatives. The probability of success of such a system approximates the possibility that one group of people knows all the answers to all of the problems inherent in an economy. While it is possible to develop strategy for even a large economy, it is the execution of the plan that requires an ability greater than that, which could be possessed by a small group of people.

With all its improbabilities, central planning worked in the years following World War II. However, after the war, the inherent problems of a socialist system began to appear. The problem of developing and implementing the basic framework of a modern industrial state became increasingly difficult. Under Stalin's successors Nikita Khrushchev and Leonid Brezhnev, the Soviet system began to show signs of failure. The system was becoming bogged down with a large bureaucracy. Consumer goods were produced in sufficient quantity, but they were of such poor quality that warehouses bulged with unusable shoes and shoddy clothes. Although the Soviet Union produced almost twice as much steel per capita as the United States, there was a chronic steel shortage because the material was used so wastefully. In summary, by the time that Mikhail Gorbachev began to speak of "Glasnost" (openness) and "Perestroika" (the fundamental restructuring of the economic system) in 1985, the Russian system was apparently becoming an economic failure.

According to Margate Thatcher, the meeting between Soviet General Secretary Mikhail Gorbachev and President Reagan at Reykjavik in October of 1986 was the turning point in the cold war. Finally, Gorbachev realized that he had a choice: continue a no-win arms race, which would utterly cripple the Soviet economy, or give up the struggle for global domination and establish peaceful relations with the West. In December 1987, Gorbachev visited Washington, DC to sign the INF treaty in which the superpowers agreed to reduce their intermediate-range nuclear missiles to zero. For the first time in history, the United States and the Soviet Union had agreed to eliminate an entire class of nuclear weapons.

On June 12, 1987, Reagan made a trip to the Brandenburg Gate in Berlin, Germany. The purpose of the trip was to encourage Gorbachev's reform efforts. Reagan used this speech to drive Gorbachev into an awkward political position, to compel him to prove his sincerity before the world. The most memorable part of the speech was when Reagan said: "General Secretary Gorbachev, if you seek peace, if you seek prosperity for the Soviet Union and Eastern Europe, if you seek liberalization: Come here to this gate! Mr. Gorbachev, open this gate! Mr. Gorbachev, tear down this wall."

The collapse of the Soviet empire in Eastern Europe occurred shortly after Reagan left office. The revolt began in Poland, where the Communists were routed in a public election and Lech Walesa became president of Poland. Next, Hungary claimed itself to be a free republic. On November 9, 1989, shortly after Reagan left office, demonstrators in East Germany removed the communist dictator Eric Honecker and the Berlin Wall were torn down.

In November of 1994, Reagan revealed to the world that he was suffering from the memory destroying neurological illness known as Alzheimer's disease. There is a bitter irony in the fact that Reagan, once a brilliant storyteller who was so delighted in entertaining friends and aides with stories of his past, had been robbed of the ability to access those tales. The man, who left the White House with the highest approval rating of any modern president, reportedly had little memory of having lived there. In a touching epistle to the citizens who twice elected him their leader, Reagan wrote, "I now begin the journey that will lead me into the sunset of my life. "

Ronald Reagan Died at his home in Bel Air, California on June 5, 2004 of pneumonia as a complication of Alzheimer' s. Reagan's body would lie in repose on Monday and Tuesday at the Reagan library. His casket would lie in state in the U.S. Capitol in Washington and he was buried at the Reagan presidential library in Simi Valley, California on Friday June 11th. All week long the world sent praise for America's 40 president. Below is just a sample:

- **Former Soviet Mikhail Gorbachev**: "I deem Ronald Reagan a great president, with whom the Soviet leadership was able to launch a very difficult but important dialogue."
- **Former Prime Minister Margaret Thatcher**: "He will be missed not only by those who knew him and not only by the nation that he served so proudly and loved so deeply, but also by millions of men and women who live in freedom today because of the policies he pursued."
- **Senate Majority Leader Bill Frist**: "President Reagan's bold leadership in difficult times provided Americans with tremendous strength and inspiration."
- **Senate Minority Leader Tom Dashle**: "America has lost an icon. Ronald Reagan's leadership will inspire Americans for generations to come. His patriotism and devotion to our country will never be forgotten."
- **Lt. Col. Oliver North**: "Ronald Reagan was easily the greatest president of my lifetime—and he will be regarded as one of the greatest leaders this country has ever had."
- **Former President George H.W. Bush**: "We had been political opponents and became close friends. Reagan could take a stand and do it without creating bitterness or creating enmity on the part of other people.
- **Former President Bill Clinton**: "It is fitting that a piece of the Berlin Wall adorns the Ronald Reagan Building in Washington."
- **President George W. Bush**: "Ronald Reagan won America's respect with his greatness, and won its love with his goodness. He had the confidence that comes with conviction, the strength that comes with character, the grace that comes with humility, and the humor that comes with wisdom."
- **Nancy Reagan:** "I think they broke the mold when they made Ronnie. He had absolutely no ego, and he was very
- Comfortable in his own shin; therefore, he didn't feel he ever had to prove anything to anyone."

NOTES:

Chapter 12
Ronald Reagan and the 1980s

1. Niskanen, William A. & Moore, Stephen, <u>Supply-Side Tax Cuts and the Truth About the Reagan Economic Record</u>, Washington, DC, The Cato Institute, 1996, p. 3-5.
2. D'Souza, Dinesh, <u>Ronald Reagan: How an Ordinary Man Became an Extraordinary Leader,</u> New York, NY, Touchtone, 1999, p. 26.
3. D'Souza, P. 28
4. Niskanen & Moore, P. 9.

CHAPTER 13

NATIONAL DEBT AND INTERNATIONAL TRADE DEFICITS

"I saw a startling sight today, a politician with his hands in his own pockets." — Mark Twain

THE TWIN DEFICITS

During the severe recession of the early 1980's in the United States the production of goods and services declined over a broad range. With the exception of adequate housing, no one was thought to suffer because of what was not produced. All suffering was identified with the interruption in the flow of income, i.e., with the loss of employment. That, not prices or the unequal distribution of income, is demonstrably the prime social anxiety of our time. In the modern industrial economy production is of first importance not for the goods it produces but for the employment and income it produces. Economics in the 1980's concerns itself with the elements of national income (wages, rents, interest and profits), more than national product. Say's Law has, for all practical purposes, been reversed. That is demand creates its own supply.

  Unemployment, in the past, has been seen as a macroeconomic problem. Unemployment was something caused or remedied by the overall design and management of fiscal and monetary policy. This also will cease to be so; increasingly it will be seen that unemployment arises from the non-optimal performance and the changing competitive position of individual industries. In the United States, coal mining, steel making, automobile, and textile and apparel manufacturing are examples of industries that are losing market share to foreign competitors. While macroeconomic policies can increase or decrease general unemployment, they cannot remedy it, given the specifics of these industries.

Money spent abroad for goods and services and travel by American residents in excess of what foreigners were spending in the United States had an economic effect precisely opposite from the expansive public deficit of the Reagan administration. The Keynesian effect of economic stimulation through increased government spending was thus to a large extent offset in the 1980's by the negative effect of the large trade deficit.

The Trade Deficit

The world may change, but the need for economics to explain the change remains. The world of the 1990's and beyond will be almost as different from the world of the 1950's as the industrial revolution was from merchant capitalism. The United States has gone from a point where they were the world's largest creditor after World War II to the world's largest debtor in the 1990's. From 2011 through 2016 the United States has run a huge current account deficit with the four Asian countries shown in Table 13-1.

Table 13-1
U. S. Asian Trade ($ in billions)

Trade Deficit	2011	2012	2013	2014	2015	2016
China	318	333	296	315	338	334
Japan	81	94	58	53	57	78
South Korea	5	8	11	14	17	18
Taiwan	13	15	15	17	21	20
	-------	-------	-------	-------	-------	-------
Total	417	450	380	399	433	450

As a comparison, the current account balance in goods and services, for the United States in the year 2016, was a negative $481 billion. Of this total, $450 billion or 94 percent of the trade deficit was with four Asian Countries. Another way to examine the trade deficit is by region. For 2016 the current account balance of payments trade deficit by geographical region was as follows:

Geographic Region	2016 Current Account Balance ($ billions)
Asian Countries	-450
European Union	-5
NAFTA (Canada & Mexico)	-68
OPEC Countries	9
Remainder of the World	33
Total Current Account	-481

Source: Bureau of Economic Analysis Tables: April 2017

Four geographic regions account for $514 billion of the total current account deficit of $481 billion or over 100 percent. The OPEC countries had current account surplus $9 million as the U.S. has become less dependent on OPEC oil. In addition, OPEC countries are large purchasers of goods and services from the U.S. NAFTA had a deficit current account balance of $68 million as Mexico showed a positive trade balance (a negative balance for the U.S.) of $79 billion.

The International Balance of Payments Accounts

One way to help understand the international balance of payments accounts is to start with an analysis of the basic components of GDP as expenditures. The last component in the GDP as expenditures account is net exports.

The net export's component of GDP is derived from a country's balance of payments account. The balance of payments is a record of a country's trade in goods, services, and financial assets with the rest of the world. There are two basic categories in the balance of payments account; the current account and the capital account.

GDP As Expense By Component	Dollar Amount	($ in billions)
	2015	**2016**
Personal Consumption Expenditures	12,284	12,758
Gross Private Domestic Investment	3,057	3,036
Government Purchases	3,218	3,276
Net Exports	(522)	(501)
Total GDP	18,037	18,569

The current account is the sum of the balances in the merchandise, services, net investment and net transfer receipts accounts. The merchandise account records all transactions involving goods. U.S. exports of goods are merchandise credits; U.S. imports of foreign goods are merchandise debits. The services account includes travel and tourism, royalties, transportation costs, and insurance premiums. The sum of the total merchandise and services accounts is equal to the GDP net exports. One of the largest components of the current account is the return on investments. The income earned from investments in foreign countries is a source of funds and the income paid on foreign-owned investments in the United States is a use of funds. The final component of the current account is net transfer receipts, which include foreign aid, gifts, and other payments to individuals that are not exchanged for goods or services.

The capital account is where trade involving financial assets is recorded. The capital, in this account, refers to financial flows such as bank deposits, purchases and sales of stocks and bonds, and loans. A source of funds is the sale of an asset to a foreign resident or a loan from a foreign organization such as a commercial bank. A use of funds is a purchase of assets that are owned by a foreign citizen or a loan to someone in that country. The total of source and use of funds must agree in order to balance the books between countries. A simple example, of an international source and uses of funds statement, is shown below in Table 13-3.

Sources of Funds	Uses of Funds
Sale of an asset	Purchase of an asset
Borrowing from a country	Lending to a country
Total Sources	**Total Uses of Funds**

When countries import more than they export, the difference must be made up in the capital account. To finance net imports, a nation has only two basic choices; that is to either sell some of its assets or to borrow from a country that has a positive position in net exports. Because of its propensity to consume more foreign goods than it sells, the United States has been forced to accumulate large amounts of foreign debt or to sell large amounts of its assets to foreigners. From 1990 through 2016, the United States has imported more than it exported every year. The resulting negative net export data from the Commerce Department is detailed in Table 13-2. In addition, Table 13-3 provides an example of an international sources and uses of funds statement. The difference between the net exports on a GDP basis and the current account balance is that the current account adds financial transfers to the Net Exports shown in the GDP accounts. For example, for 2016 (Net Investment Income minus Unilateral Transfers totaling = $20 + Net Exports of $-501) = Current Account Balance of $-481.

From 1990 through 2016 the United States accumulated $9,888.8 billion dollars in negative net exports on a current account basis. This is dollars that was owed and paid from American businesses to the rest of the world.

Table 13-2

GDP Net Exports from 1990 through 2016 ($ in Billions)

Year	Exports	Imports	Net Exports
1990	$557.1	$628.5	$ -71.4
1991	$601.5	$621.1	$-19.6
1992	$640.5	$671.5	$-31.0
1993	$660.1	$725.8	$-65.7
1994	$722.0	$818.4	$-96.4
1995	$818.6	$902.8	$-84.2
1996	$875.2	$963.1	$-87.9
1997	$966.4	$1,055.8	$-89.4
1998	$964.9	$1,116.7	$-151.7
1999	$989.8	$1,240.7	$-250.9
2000	$1,069.0	$1,438.0	$-369.0
2001	$1,050.3	$1,380.1	$-329.8
2002	$1,014.9	$1,438.5	$-423.6
2003	$1,049.0	$1,543.9	$-494.9
2004	$1,147.0	$1,764.0	$-617.0
2005	$1,740.9	$2,545.8	$-804.9
2006	$2,096.2	$2,907.7	$-811.5
2007	$2,410.6	$3,149.2	$-738.6
2008	$2,591.3	$3,264.6	$-673.3
2009	$2,115.9	$2,535.8	$-419.9
2010	$2,496.6	$2,966.8	$-470.2
2011	$2,843.8	$3,317.2	$-473.4
2012	$2,936.5	$3,411.5	$-475.0
2013	$2,927.3	$3,306.6	$-379.3
2014	$2,341.9	$2,871.9	$-530.0
2015	$2,253.4	$2,782.3	$-528.9
2016	$2,232.4	$2,733.7	$-501.3
Total 22 Years	Accumulated	Trade Deficit	**$-9,888.8**

Source Bureau of Economic Analysis Tables March, 2017

Table 13-3
U.S. Balance of Payments for 2016 ($ in Billions)

Balance of Payments	Sources	Uses	Balance
Current Account			
Merchandise Balance			
Exports	$1,460		
Imports		$2,210	
Balance of Trade			$-750
Service Balances	752	503	249
GDP Net Exports	2,212	2,713	-501
Investment Income	802	621	181
Unilateral Transfers	128	289	-161
Total Current Account	$3,142	$3,623	$-481
Capital Account			
Capital Inflows	$759		
Capital Outflows		$331	
Capital Account Transactions		22	
Statistical Error	75		
Total Capital Account	$834	$353	$481
Total Sources and Uses			$0
			====

Source: Bureau of Economic Analysis – U.S. International Transactions Table 1, March 2017.

Gross Federal Debt Outstanding

Basic Economics   165

Federal debt managed by the Bureau of the Public Debt (BPD) comprises debt held by the public and debt held by certain federal government account, the latter of which is referred to as intragovernmental debt holdings. As of September 30, 2016, and 2015, outstanding gross federal debt managed by BPD totaled $19,560 and $18,138 billion, respectively. The increase in gross federal debt of $1,422 billion during fiscal year 2016 was due to an increase in gross intragovernmental debt holdings of $373 billion and an increase in gross debt held by the public of $1,049 billion. As table 13-4 illustrates, both intragovernmental debt holdings and debt held by the public have increased since fiscal year 2008. The primary reason for the increases in intragovernmental debt holdings is the excess annual receipts (including interest earnings) over disbursements in the Federal Old-Age and Survivors Insurance Trust Fund, Civil Service Retirement and Disability Fund, Military Retirement Fund, and DOD Medicare-Eligible Retiree Health Care Fund. The increases in debt held by the public are due primarily to total federal government spending exceeding total federal revenues. As of September 30, 2016, gross debt held by the public totaled $14,173 billion and gross intragovernmental debt holdings totaled $5,387 billion.

Changes to the Statutory Debt Ceiling

As of September 30, 2013, the statutory debt limitations were $16,699. A delay in raising the statutory debt limit existed at the end of fiscal year 2013 and lasted until October 17, 2013 when the Continuing Appropriations Act of 2014 was enacted. This act established a process that resulted in an increase of the statutory debt limit on February 8, 2014 to $17,212 billion. On February 15, 2014, the Temporary Debt Limit Extension Act suspended the statutory debt limit through March 15, 2015. The Budget Act of November 2, 2015 suspended the debt limit from that date through March, 15, 2017.

Table 13-4-A
Total Federal Debt Fiscal Years Ending Sept. 30, 2006 – 2016

Year	Deb Held by Public	Intragovernmental Debt Holdings	Total Federal Debt Outstanding
2008	5,809	4,202	10,011
2009	7,552	4,346	11,898
2010	9,023	4,528	13,551
2011	10,127	4,654	14,781
2012	11,270	4,789	16,059
2013	11,976	4,756	16,732
2014	12,785	5,025	17,810
2015	13,124	5,014	18,138
2016	14,173	5,387	19,560

Interest Expense

The primary components of interest expense are interest paid on the debt held by the public and interest credited to federal government trust funds and other federal government accounts that hold Treasury securities. The interest paid on the debt held by the public affects the current spending of the federal government and represents the burden of servicing its debt (i.e., payments to outside creditors). Interest credited to federal government trust funds and other federal government accounts, on the other hand, does not result in an immediate outlay of the Federal Government because one part of the government pays the interest and another part receives it. However, this interest represents a claim on future budgetary resources and hence an obligation on future taxpayers. This interest, when reinvested by the trust funds and other federal government accounts, is included in the programs' excess funds not currently needed in operations, which are invested in federal securities. For fiscal year 2016, interest expense incurred totaled $430 billion, interest expense on debt held by the public was $273 billion, and $157 billion was interest incurred for intragovernmental debt holdings. Interest expense for fiscal years 2004 through 2016 are listed in table 13-4 B below.

Table 13-4-B
Interest on Federal Debt Fiscal Years Ending September 30, 2004 – 2016

Year	Debt Held by Public	Intra-Govt. Debt	Gross Federal Debt
2004	$158	$164	$322
2005	$181	$174	$355
2006	$221	$183	$404
2007	$239	$194	$433
2008	$242	$212	$454
2009	$189	$192	$381
2010	$215	$198	$413
2011	$251	203	$454
2012	$245	$187	$432
2013	$247	$178	$425
2014	$260	$173	$433
2015	$251	$156	$407
2016	$273	$157	$430

Holders of the Federal Debt

Federal Debt Held by the Public includes federal debt held by U.S. citizens, corporations and government agencies and federal debt held outside of the U. S. government by individuals, corporations, Federal Reserve Banks, state and local governments, and foreign governments and central banks. A continuing trend is the increase in reported foreign ownership of Treasury securities.

Treasury reporting shows that foreign ownership of Treasury securities represents a significant portion of debt held by the public. As of June 30, 2016, the reported amount of Treasury securities held by foreign and international investors represented an estimated 45 percent of debt held by the public. This percentage is slightly lower than the 47 percent as of June 30, 2015, but remains considerably higher than the estimated 30 percent of debt held by the public as of June 30, 2001. Treasury estimates that the amount of Treasury securities held by foreign and international investors has increased from $983 billion as of June 30, 2001, to $ 6,281 billion as of June 30, 2016, an increase of $5,298 billion. Estimates of foreign ownership of Treasury securities are derived from information reported under the Treasury International Capital reporting system.

Debt Held by the Public

Debt held by the public primarily represents the amount the Federal Government has borrowed to finance cumulative cash deficits. During fiscal year 2016, Treasury primarily used the existing suite of securities to meet the borrowing needs of the Federal Government while its offerings of long term securities extended the average length of maturity. As a result, Treasury notes increased by $258 billion, bonds by $134 billion and TIPS (treasury inflation protection securities) by $74 billion. Also, Treasury bills increased by $290 billion to take advantage of lower short term rates. As of September 30, 2016, gross debt held by the public totaled $14,173 billion an increase of $1,049 billion over 2015. This increase was primarily the result of borrowings needed to finance the government's fiscal year 2016 deficit.

The Federal Reserve Banks (FRBs) act as fiscal agents for Treasury, as permitted by the Federal Reserve Act. As fiscal agents for Treasury, the FRBs play a significant role in the processing of marketable book-entry securities and paper U.S. savings bonds. For marketable book-entry securities, selected FRBs receive bids; issue book-entry securities to awarded bidders and collect payments on behalf of Treasury; and make interest and redemption payments from Treasury's account to the accounts of security holders. For paper U.S. savings bonds, selected FRBs sell, print, and deliver savings bonds; redeem savings bonds; and handle the related transfers of cash.

Intragovernmental Debt Holdings

Intragovernmental debt holdings represent balances of Treasury securities held by over 239 individual federal government accounts with either the authority or the requirement to invest excess receipts in special U.S. Treasury securities that are guaranteed for principal and interest by the full faith and credit of the U.S. Government. Intragovernmental debt holdings primarily consist of balances in the Social Security, Medicare, Military Retirement and Health Care, and Civil Service Retirement and Disability trust funds. As of September 30, 2016, such funds accounted for $4,777 billion, or 89 percent, of the $5,387 billion intragovernmental debt holdings balances.

As of September 30, 2016, and 2015, gross intragovernmental debt holdings totaled $5,387 billion and $5,014 billion, respectively an increase of $373 billion. The majority of intragovernmental debt holdings are Government Account Series (GAS) securities. GAS securities consist of par value securities and market-based securities, with terms ranging from on demand out to 30 years.

The Social Security trust funds consist of the Federal Old-Age and Survivors Insurance Trust Fund and the Federal Disability Insurance Trust Fund. The Medicare trust funds are made up of the Federal Hospital Insurance Trust Fund and the Federal Supplementary Medical Insurance Trust Fund. The Military Retirement and Health Care Funds consist of the Military Retirement Fund and the DOD Medicare-Eligible Retiree Health

Historical Perspective

Federal debt outstanding is one of the largest legally binding obligations of the Federal Government. Nearly all the federal debt has been issued by the Treasury with a small portion being issued by other federal government agencies. Treasury issues debt securities for two principal reasons, (1) to borrow needed funds to finance the current operations of the Federal Government and (2) to provide an investment and accounting mechanism for certain federal government accounts' (primarily federal trust funds) excess receipts. Total gross federal debt outstanding has dramatically increased over the past 25 years from $2,125 billion as of September 30, 1986, to $19,560 billion as of September 30, 2016, Large budget deficits emerged during the 1980's due to tax policy decisions and increased outlays for defense and domestic programs.

Through fiscal year 1997, annual federal deficits continued to be large and debt continued to grow at a rapid pace. As a result, total federal debt more than doubled between 1986 and 1997. By fiscal year 1998, federal debt held by the public was beginning to decline. In fiscal years 1998 through 2001, the amount of debt held by the public fell by $476 billion, from $3,815 billion to $3,339 billion. However, federal debt held by the public began to increase in fiscal year 2002, primarily as a result of higher federal outlays. From fiscal year 2008 through fiscal year 2016, federal debt held by the public increased by $8,364 billion. For the same period, intra-government holdings increased by $1,185 billion. This resulted in an increase in total federal government debt outstanding of $9,549 trillion.

Figure 13-1 Gross Federal Debt Outstanding

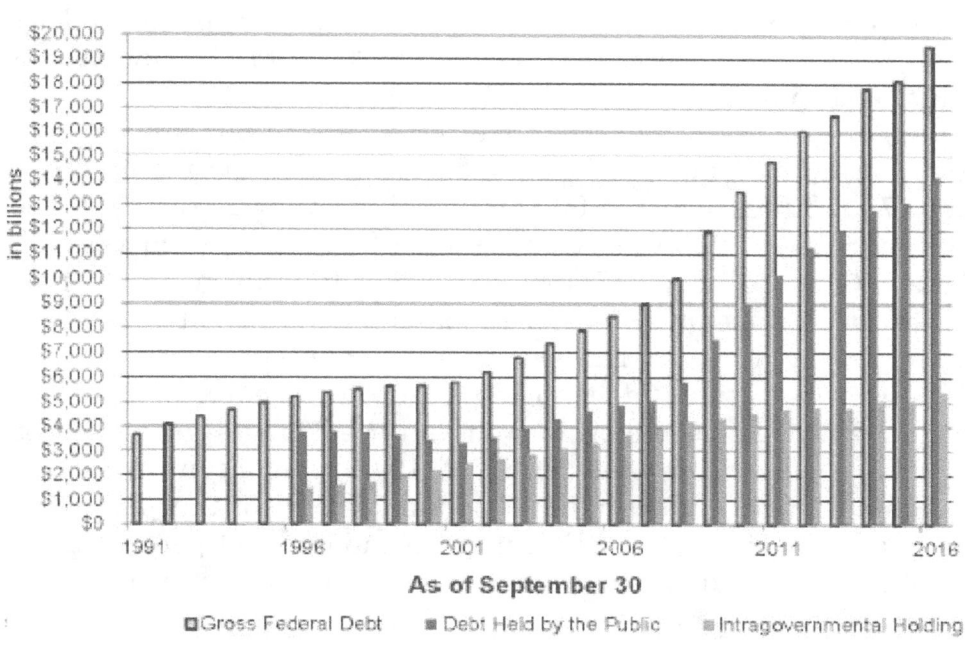

Source: GAO United States Government Accountability Office Report to the Secretary of the Treasury, Nov. 2016

The Size of the Federal Debt

Basic Economics   171

Many economists and politicians have pondered the question about the size of the gross federal debt in the United States. One of the major questions that are asked about the gross national debt is its size. One way to answer this question is to compare the debt with something. The best vehicle available for comparing a nation's gross accumulated debt is that country's ability to produce goods and services, i.e., their gross domestic product. Table 13-5 shows the gross federal debt compared to the gross domestic product from 1990 through 2016. The gross domestic product data for 2016 is an advanced forecast for the third quarter of 1016 and is subject to future government revisions. The gross federal debt increased as a percentage of gross domestic product from 1991 through 1996 as the federal government produced deficits in each of these years. The gross domestic product continued to increase after 1996, however, the federal debt was reduced as a percent of GDP in 1996 and the deficit was turned into a surplus in 1998.

In 2008 the American economy descended into a recession. This reversed the recent trend of reduced deficit spending and resulted in a deficit of $760 billion. From 2009 through fiscal year 2016 the deficit increased by $7,662 billion an average of $1,095 billion each year. To determine rather the United States has begun to manage its debt we can look to the European Union for guidance. Under the terms of the Maastricht Treaty, by 1999 European Union countries would have to reduce their gross national debt to GDP ratio to 60 percent to qualify for the new European common currency. Based on its gross federal debt to gross domestic product ratio of 104.9 percent in 2016, the United States might not qualify for admission to the European common currency. However, this European guide of 60 percent gross federal debt and gross domestic product will probably increase as most of the European economies were still recovering from recession in 2016.

The major portion of the net public debt is the internal debt. The internal debt is the portion of the debt owed to the citizens of the United States. The remainder is the nation's external debt, that portion of the debt that is owed to citizens of other nations.

Table 13-5

Gross National Debt Percent of GDP ($in Billions)

Year	**Gross Nat. Debt**	GDP	GNP/GDP
1990	$3,233	$5,802	55.7%
1991	$3,665	$5,986	61.1%
1992	$4,063	$6,319	64.3%
1993	$4,411	$6,642	66.4%
1994	$4,693	$7,054	66.6%
1995	$4,974	$7,401	67.2%
1996	$5,245	$7,813	67.1%
1997	$5,413	$8,318	65.1%
1998	$5,526	$8,781	62.9%
1999	$5,656	$9,269	61.0%
2000	$5,674	$9,873	57.3%
2001	$5,807	$10,082	57.4%
2002	$6,198	$10,446	59.3%
2003	$6,760	$10,988	61.5%
2004	$7,355	$11,735	62.7%
2005	$7,905	$12,487	63.3%
2006	$8,451	$13,254	63.8%
2007	$8,951	$13,841	64.7%
2008	$10,011	$14,441	70.1%
2009	$11,898	$14,256	83.3%
2010	$13,551	$14,660	92.0%
2011	$14,781	$15,094	97.9%
2012	$16,059	$15,797	101.7
2013	$16,732	$16,800	99.6
2014	$17,810	$17,348	102.7
2015	$18,138	$17,947	101.1
2016	$19,560	$18,569	105.3

Payment of interest on the debt to a country's own citizens is a redistribution of income and therefore does not directly decrease total demand. However, 45 percent of the net public debt or $6,281 billion is owed to foreign banks, individuals, businesses and governments. As the portion of the debt held by foreigners' increases, greater amounts of interest are paid out each year to foreign citizens. Payment of interest on debt held by foreigners sends money out of this country, which could contribute to a reduction in aggregate demand sometime in the future.

Will the Federal Government go bankrupt if it continues to increase its debt? There is very little risk of this happening because the Federal Government can increase taxes to pay the debt. However, there are some problems that continue as a result of a large net national debt. The first burden of the debt is that a larger portion of the taxes paid by future generations of Americans will be used to pay interest on the debt. These tax dollars could be put to a much better use, such as investments in infrastructure and education.

A second burden of the huge net national debt is its effect on private investment. This is defined by economists as the crowding-out effect. According to this theory, a growing net national debt will decrease private investment and reduce the growth rate of private capital stock. As the growth rate of worker productivity declines because of a decrease in the growth rate of capital, the growth rate per capita GDP (gross domestic product divided by the labor force), will decline. Therefore, a growing net national debt has the potential to retard the growth rate of a nation's future standard of living.

The Social Security Trust Fund

Also, a political hot button is the Social Security Trust Fund. The major portion of the $5,387 billion in the intra-governmental holdings or about $2,797 billion belongs to the Social Security Trust Fund. However, the trust fund is only an accounting entry backed by non-marketable bonds issued by the Federal Government. The actual cash is used by the Federal Government for general expenditures or paying down the net national debt. For example, in fiscal year 2016 the budget results released by the Treasury Department showed a federal government deficit of $1,049 billion. In addition, there was an increase in the intra-government accounts of $373 billion. Therefore, when the change in Social Security and other government trust funds are added to the Federal Government's deficit of $1,049 billion the combined deficit is $1,422 billion. The increase in the Federal Government Debt from $18,138 billion in 2015 to $19,560 billion in 2016 and the reasons for the increase is demonstrated in Table 13-6.[1]

Table 13-6

Change in Federal Debt

Federal Government Debt ($ in Billions)

Year	Held by Public	Held by Government	Total Debt
2016	$14,173	$5,387	$19,560
2015	$13,124	$5,014	$18,138
Change	$ 1,049	$ 373	$ 1,422

Changes in Gross Federal Debt 2016 v. 2015

Description	Increase in Debt
Federal Government Deficit	$ 587
Past Years Restoration, Principal and Interest	$ 462
Social Security Trust Fund	$ 34
Civil Service Retirement Fund	$ 155
Military Retirement Fund	$ 68
Medicare Trust Funds	$ (6)
Other Federal Trust funds	$ 122
Total Changes in Gross National Debt	$ 1,422

Source: GAO United States Government Accountability Office Report to the Secretary of the Treasury, Nov. 2016 Page 29.

Note: The fiscal year 2016 increase in debt held by the public of $1,049 billion was greater than the reported fiscal year 2016 federal deficit of $587 billion primarily because of the restoration of principal and interest, as well as increases in the government's cash balance and federal direct student loans.

The problem with the Social Security Trust Fund is that if sometime in the future Social Security revenues are less than expenses, (estimated by the Social Security Administration to occur in 2017) the only source of paying the difference between receipts and benefits is to exchange non-marketable debt with marketable debt or in other words to increase the net national debt. Also, Congress lowered the FICA tax in 2012 to stimulate the economy. The reduction in payroll taxes resulted in a deficit in the Social Security Trust Fund in 2012. The FICA payroll tax rate was restored to its 2011 level for 2013.

The Burden of the Twin Deficits

The international current account deficit and the net federal deficit taken together are linked to the international financial markets. The current account deficit must be offset by capital inflows from foreign citizens and foreigners finance a large part of the net national debt. A simple source and uses of fund's statement can be used to show the relationship of these twin deficits to the financial markets.

International Financial Markets - Sources and Uses of Funds

Sources of Funds	Uses of Funds
Domestic Savings	Investments
Foreign Capital Inflow	Government Budget Deficit

A nation's economy can compensate for an increase in government budget deficits by reducing private investment, increasing the rate of savings, and increasing net capital inflows. Net capital inflows are created by net imports. Critics of the federal government's fiscal policy during the last 20 years, charge that the mismanagement of the budgeting process has left the nation burdened with debts owed to foreign lenders. This has caused export industries to lose market share in an increasingly competitive global economy and has reduced aggregate business investment as a result of the crowding-out effect.

EFFORTS TO REDUCE THE FEDERAL DEFICIT

By 1984, the federal budgetary process was in such bad shape that Herbert Stein, President Nixon's Chairman of the Council of Economic Advisors, wrote an article that was published in the December issue of the Economists. In that article, Stein states that, "We have no long-run budget policy." In response to this and many other criticisms, Congress has passed three bills designed to reduce or eliminate the deficit.

The Gramm-Rudman-Hollings Act of 1985

This law established a declining set of deficit targets, beginning with a deficit target of $144 billion for fiscal year 1987 and to eliminate the deficit by fiscal 1991. An exception was written into the law allowing the deficit ceiling to be waived in the event that real gross national product grew at an annual rate of 1 percent or less, for two consecutive quarters. The deficit targets were revised in 1987, which delayed balancing of the budget until 1993. The feature that was supposed to give this law some real ability to control expenditures was a provision for making mandatory spending cuts if Congress failed to provide a budget that would be within $10 billion of the Act's target. However, the targets developed by the Gramm-Rudman-Hollings Act were not met as the federal deficit was $221 billion in fiscal year 1990, compared to a target of $100 billion.

One of the major reasons that this act failed to meet its deficit reduction targets was that entitlements such as social security, Medicare, and aid to dependent families, were exempted from its cost reduction provisions. Alice Rivlin, who was President Clinton's budget director, wrote in the October 3, 1989, issue of the Wall Street Journal, that the Gramm-Rudman-Hollins Act was a "well intentioned experiment that failed."

The Budget Deficit Reduction Act of 1990

The growth of the deficit in fiscal year 1990 resulted in a new reform effort. This was the Budget Deficit Reduction Act of November, 1990. The act consisted of a negotiated package of spending cuts (primarily defense) and tax increases that were to total $500 billion for the five years from fiscal 1991 through fiscal 1995. In addition, this act included a new approach to automatic enforcement, a "pay-as-you-go" mechanism. Under this provision, spending was divided into three broad categories: defense, domestic, and international. In theory, if any new legislation pushed spending above a set ceiling for any category, all the programs in the category would be cut proportionately to bring the category back into balance.

On September 30, 1990, President Bush explained the new law to the public by stating that: "The bipartisan leaders and I have reached agreement on the federal budget. Over a period of five years, the deficit would be reduced by $500 million." However, the budget deficit continued to increase as spending increased faster than revenue, even with the new taxes that were enacted under the law. In fiscal year 1991, the federal deficit rose to $270 billion, in fiscal 1992 to $290 billion and was over $255 billion in fiscal 1993.

The Omnibus Budget Reconciliation Act of 1993

In August of 1993, Congress passed, by a one vote margin, a new deficit reduction law. The new law called for some spending cuts because of a proposed reduction in the federal civilian work force. The federal work force was reduced from an average of 2.989 million in fiscal year 1992 to 2.858 million in June of 1994, a decrease of over 130 thousand workers. However, the bulk of the savings from this staff reduction was used to fund the Clinton administration's 1994 crime bill. The revenue raising provisions of the bill called for marginal tax increases on the "wealthy" by raising the top rates, from 31 percent of adjusted gross income to 36 percent, for all married couples earning more than $140,000 per year. The 1990 bill increased the top rates from 28 percent to 31 percent. Also, the gasoline tax was raised by 4.3 cents per gallon following a raise of 5 cents per gallon in 1990.

The tax increase provisions of this bill were sold to the public as a way to make the rich pay their "fair share." However, the wealthy did not become rich because they are stupid. Rich people usually employ tax lawyers and accountants who advise them on how to pay a minimum of taxes legally. For example, the total income-tax receipts in 1991, the first year after the 1990 budget act was signed, actually fell.

U.S. Treasury figures on income-tax receipts in 1991 show that the wealthy (defined here as people who earn $200,000 a year or more) paid $106.1 billion in income taxes in 1990, but in 1991, after the tax increase, paid $99.6 billion. The tax revenues received in 1991 from this group amounted to a reduction of $7.1 billion over the taxes received in 1990. This is because the wealthy found tax shelters in Municipal Bonds stopped investing in business expansion and curtailed other activities that would increase their tax burden.

Therefore, the only addition to federal tax revenues that resulted from the Budget Reduction Act of 1993 were from the 4.3 percent increase in the tax on gasoline and additional taxes on social security payments from our so called wealthy senior citizens that earn over $34,000 per year.

The debate over the gross national debt will continue well into the twenty-first century. Some debt is necessary for it provides an investment instrument for millions of Americans. Therefore, the question is not whether the debt should exist, but how much should be outstanding at any period, and also, how much of a burden should be placed on future taxpayers?

NOTES:

Chapter 13
National Debt and International Trade Deficits

1. GAO United States Government Accountability Office Report to the Secretary of the Treasury, November 2009, Pages 1-25.
2. Hyman, David, <u>Economics, Third Edition</u>, Irwin Business Publications, Burr Ridge, IL, 1994, p. 809.

CHAPTER 14

ECONOMICS AND PUBLIC CHOICE

"In order to get better government policy, we'd better look not to electing better people, but to changing the structure of the rules which constrain them." --James Buchanan

THE NATION-STATE TO THE FISCAL STATE

By the late nineteenth century, the nation-state that had been in existence since the sixteenth century, was being made over into an economic agency. This trend has been referred to by economists, including Joseph Schumpeter, as the evolution from the nation-state to the "fiscal state." The job of the leaders of the nation-state was seen as maintaining the climate for economic growth, keeping taxes low and encouraging savings. The great depression gave rise to the belief that the national government should control its country's economic environment.

Since World War II, most developed countries have come to believe that there are no economic limits to what government can tax or borrow and, therefore, no economic limit to what government can spend. Schumpeter pointed out that as long as governments have been around, the budget process has begun with an assessment of revenues. Expenditures would be allocated to causes based on available resources. Since the supply of "good causes" was inexhaustible, and the demand for spending was therefore infinite, the budget process consisted of deciding where to say no. As long as revenues were considered as a constraint, it was difficult for a government to act as either a social or an economic agent.[1]

Following World War II, most developed countries had adopted the financial theories of John Maynard Keynes. However, what was lacking from Keynes's theory was the role that would be played by government. Keynes assumed that a wise and efficient government, would faithfully apply sound fiscal policy. However, fiscal policy must be applied by people, in this case politicians and government bureaucrats. Economic theory can often become dangerous in the hands of politicians, who quite often assume that there are no limits to the revenues that government can obtain. In the hands of modern day politicians, government has become the master of the individual in society. By using taxes and expenditures, government can redistribute society's income. However, there is a serious question as to whether modern governments have succeeded in bringing about a meaningful redistribution of income. Vilfredo Pareto (1848-1923) the Swiss sociologist developed a law concerning income distribution. Pareto's Law stated that income distribution between major classes in society is determined by two factors: the culture of the society, and the level of productivity within the economy. According to Pareto, the more productive an economy was, the greater would be the equality of income. Taxes, Pareto argues, cannot change the inequality of income.[2]

THE PUBLIC CHOICE SCHOOL OF ECONOMICS

Keynesian economics assumes an efficient and benevolent government to carry out fiscal policy. However, governments in most developed countries, have become such heavy spenders that they can no longer use fiscal policy to counteract the effects of recession. In the United States, the federal government reached the limit of its ability to tax and borrow in the 1980's. This made fiscal policy practically useless during the recession of the early 1990's. Worst of all, the fiscal state has become a "pork-barrel state." If the budget process starts with the determination of expenditures rather than a realistic forecast of revenues, there is no fiscal discipline; government spending becomes the means for politicians to obtain votes. Politicians, therefore, run on platforms designed to convince local voters that they will extract a larger part of the federal budget for spending projects in their districts, then their opponents. In the fiscal state, the looting of the federal treasury is done by politicians to ensure their own election.

The pork-barrel state thus increasingly undermines the foundations of a free society. The elected representatives use the taxes of their constituents to enrich special-interest groups, who in turn, are heavy contributors to the elected official's campaign fund. Joseph Schumpeter warned in 1918 that the fiscal state would in the end undermine government's ability to govern. Eighteen years later, Keynes hailed the fiscal state as the great liberator of a depressed economy. Keynes argued, that government, no longer limited by restraints on expenditures, could govern effectively by manipulating government spending and taxation. However, in the 1990's, it is becoming quite clear that Schumpeter might have been right.

Economic Rent Seeking

One of the key elements of the Public Choice theory is economic rent seeking. Economists define economic rent, as any payment to a factor of production in excess of its opportunity cost. An example is the huge salaries that sport figures earn. Major league athletes usually earn much more than they could earn using the same time in, for example, teaching a course in economics.

Entrepreneurs are constantly attempting to earn such profits by lowering unit costs, introducing new products or creating brand images in the minds of consumers. When they are successful the income that they earn may be substantially higher than their competitors. However, economic profit that is earned as a result of private market activity is not the only category of economic rents. Many business managers and workers, through labor unions, often turn to government in search of economic rents rather than trying to gain a competitive advantage through the marketplace. An additional profit earned, because of a government program that raises prices or serves to reduce unit costs, is worth just as much as profit earned through the marketplace. Often profit earned from developing a competitive advantage in the marketplace is short term. This is because the competition may develop a new process or a new product that reduces unit cost or better satisfies customer needs. Government regulations, on the other hand, cannot only create opportunities to earn economic rents, but often shield those opportunities from competitors.

Political rent seeking is often referred to by economists as the act of obtaining and defending economic rent through government action. Government restrictions on market activity are often found in the areas of price controls and restrictions on competition. An example of price controls is the case of milk price supports. This occurs when the government places a floor on the market price of milk. If the price of milk falls below the floor price, the federal government purchases the excess milk in order to maintain the targeted price. Public choice economists see this policy as a classic case of political rent seeking. This is because a large portion of the benefits of price supports goes to farmers who are not in need of the supports. However, politicians who are in search of votes, would rather support a bill that has the backing from a large group of farmers instead of only the farmers that actually need assistance.

Government restrictions on competition are another way of generating rents. For example, tariffs and import quotas shield domestic firms from foreign competition. By eliminating foreign competition, firms are able to raise prices above the competitive market level. There are also examples of rent seeking within the domestic economy. For instance, licensing fees and professional examinations restrict the number of competitors who can enter such fields as public accountants, medicine and law.

The theory that government policies do not always promote efficiency and fairness is not a new one. Economists have long been aware of the law of unintended consequences. However, political choice theorists go beyond the tendency of government policies to have effects that are vastly different from their original intentions. Political choice economists argue that the element of rent seeking in the formulation of government policy suggests that there is a systematic tendency for government programs to cause rather than cure economic efficiencies.[3]

James Buchanan, Fiscal Responsibility and Public Choice

As early as the 1970's, it had become apparent that the use of fiscal policy to counteract recession and inflation, did not always work. Fiscal policy to stimulate an economy and avoid a recession was used by President Johnson in the mid 1960's. However, fiscal policy was not effective in fighting the inflation of the 1970's. Also, as a result of the huge budget deficits of the 1980's, fiscal policy lost its ability to combat a recession. A new school of economic theory was needed to explain why fiscal policy, the main tool of Keynesian economics, no longer worked. This new theory was developed by James M. Buchanan, who currently is a professor with George Mason University. In 1986, Buchanan won the Nobel Memorial Prize in Economics, for his work in what became known as "The Public Choice Theory." The public choice theory is a study of how people use the institutions of government to promote private ends. The public choice school attempts to explain some of the modern day economic and political problems, for example:

- Why does the United States suffer from continuing budget deficits?

- Why do special interest groups proliferate?

- Why do bureaucracies continue to expand despite presidential promises to trim them?

A basic principle of public choice theory is that people act in the same way in both public and private roles. In analyzing people's private choices, economists have long assumed that people act in rational pursuit of self-interest. As consumers, they maximize their utility; as entrepreneurs, they maximize profit. Therefore, public choice theorists assume that the actions of people, in public roles, are guided by self-interest as well.

The Problem of Budget Deficits

Buchanan, does not show politicians simply as economic villains. He searches for the reasons that encourage them to act hypocritically. Buchanan argues that it is the budgeting system that leads to government deficits. Buchanan uses the theories of Jeremy Bentham to explain the spending programs initiated by Congress. Politicians want to please their constituents. People, according to Bentham, would prefer pleasure to pain. Government spending programs bring visible pleasure to some groups of people, and taxes are painful. Therefore, politicians assume that constituents would prefer pleasure to pain or high spending and low taxes to balanced budgets. It does not take a financial wizard to conclude that this will translate into budget deficits.

Critics of the public choice school argue that if persistent budget deficits hurt the economy, people will begin to feel the pain and demand a balanced budget. Buchanan answers these critics by explaining that budget deficits do hurt, but the pain is not direct. Reductions in spending programs have an immediate effect. However, even though the result of reduced spending is a healthier economy, the benefits of fiscal responsibility, are long-term. Budget deficits are created by lowering taxes and raising government spending. Both actions by government tend to please taxpayers and beneficiaries. Deficits may reduce the economy's ability to grow, but the effects are indirect. Deficits require people to imagine the future and to determine how they will be affected in the long run.

Buchanan argues that deficit spending ignores the future, and it harms future generations. He even raises a moral question; are deficits a form of taxation without representation? Congressmen today enhance their constituents' present welfare, as well as their own re-election probability, by jeopardizing the welfare of their grandchildren. The unborn cannot vote. Yet congress, by creating large deficits, is presenting each of them with a future financial liability.[4]

The Power of Special Interest Groups

Elected representatives often have interests of their own that do not match those of the voters that elected them. For a politician, re-election is the highest priority. However, getting elected costs money. Therefore, a representative must become proficient at raising campaign funds. Lobbyists for favor-seeking special-interest groups offer the richest sources of contributions for political candidates. Campaign contributions do not buy votes directly, but they buy time on representatives' crowded schedules. Often the side that receives the most time to present its viewpoint, is the side that wins the legislative battle.

In order to present their views to congress, special-interest groups hire people or firms to lobby for them. Lobbying, by definition, is any method used to communicate with elected officials for the purpose of educating or persuading them toward the views of a special-interest group. In order for an individual voter to communicate with their elected officials, they must send to them letters or telegrams, take out newspaper ads or telephone their office directly. Few voters feel that they have enough at stake in any one issue to justify the effort of any of these means of communication. However, groups of people with common interest can share the costs of making their views known to their representatives. They can hire full-time lobbyists to present their views to state and federal legislatures. As a result, their influence may be much greater than would be possible if each member acted individually.[5]

The Expansion of Government Bureaucracies

The actual work of government, at all levels, is accomplished in the multitude of departments, agencies and bureaus that are collectively known as "The Bureaucracy." Government bureaus bear some resemblance to private firms. Both bureaus and firms use the hierarchical principle of management. However, despite the many similarities, bureaus are different from private companies. One of the major differences is the self-interest of the bureaucrats. Government managers are not judged on the basis of their contribution to profit or the building of market share for the firms' products. Bureaucrats are judged, and paid, based on the size of their organization. Therefore, the major interest of the heads of government bureaus is the expansion of their organizations.

In a government bureau, the value of a job to the organization is determined by a staff of personnel specialists. As of June, 1994, the federal government had almost 2.9 million workers. The basic pay scale for government workers is broken down into 18 different pay categories with 10 different pay steps in each category. This pay scale does not even include the executive service of the federal government, which has its own pay scale. This type of organization, by its very size and complexity alone, makes it impossible to accurately evaluate each job. Therefore, job grades in the federal government are, for the most part, determined by the size of the organization or the size of the staff, not on the complexity of the job.

Salary, perquisites such as office size, type of furniture, travel budgets, prestige and most promotions, all tend to increase as the bureau or staff that a manager oversees, increases. Thus, agency directors actively lobby congress and the administration for increases in their budgets and responsibilities. It is rare to see an agency argue that some function it now performs is not required. It is virtually unknown for an agency to return unspent funds to the treasury. Most agencies feel that if they do not spend all of the funds that are allocated to them, their next year's budget will be reduced. Therefore, there is no incentive to spend less than the budget allotment and every incentive to constantly lobby congress for additional funds. A consequence of the way agencies are managed is that they often grow larger than congress originally intended. Congress originally sets up an agency in response to lobbying pressure from an interested group of voters. However, after the agency has been set up, pressure for expansion comes from both interested voters and the agency itself.[6]

Economics and Public Choice

Many economists regard the public choice school with some skepticism. However, most economists admit that this theory offers at least one important lesson. The lesson is that the public should not assume that government takes economically prudent steps in the face of political opposition. Modern economic textbooks point out that market imperfections such as monopolies and the uneven distribution of income, may be cured by government action. Public choice theorists ask the question: will the government actually do its theoretical duty? Just as the market may have imperfections, government is not perfect. Adam Smith told us that people act in their own self-interest. Government employees are people too. Why then should we expect a government employee to be any different than the rest of us?

NOTES:

Chapter 14
Economics and Public Choice

1. Drucker, Peter, Post Capitalist Society, Harper Business, New York, N.Y., 1993, p. 126.
2. Drucker, p. 131.
3. Dolan, Edwin G. & Lindsey, David E., Economics, Seventh Edition, The Dryden Press, Orlando, FL, 1994, p. 460.
4. Buchholz, Todd G., New Ideas From Dead Economists, Penguin Books, New York, N.Y. 1989, p. 252.
5. Dolan & Lindsey, p. 710
6. Dolan & Lindsey, p. 715.

CHAPTER 15

ECONOMIC GROWTH AND EMPLOYMENT

"In a Global Economy, a worker has two things to offer; skills or the willingness to work for low wages." —Lester Thurow

MEASURING ECONOMIC GROWTH

In a global economy, the basic goals of consumers are often similar. These goals are, survival, growth, and prosperity. What makes countries different, from an economic point of view, is the probability of the attainment of each of these basic goals. In many of the world's developed countries, the goals of growth and prosperity are obtainable and measurable. In almost all of the undeveloped countries, the goal is often only survival, and often that goal is not achieved.

Economists use two measures of growth, real national income and per capita real national income. The term real means that gross national income has been adjusted for the effects of inflation using the country's gross domestic product deflator. As more goods and services are produced, the real income of a nation increases, and people are usually able to consume more. Per capita real national income is a term used by economists to describe the ratio between a country's real national income and its population. The ratio is calculated as follows:

$$\frac{\text{Real national income}}{\text{Total Population}} = \text{Per capita real national income}$$

Based on this formula, a country could experience growth in its real gross domestic product, but if the population is growing at an even faster rate, output per person actually will fall. If economic growth is defined as a rising real per capita national income, then a nation's output of goods and services must increase faster than its population.

Governments can facilitate economic growth in many different ways. If a country is undeveloped, its government must first establish a set of laws that provide basic stability. In order to increase a country's total output, it must increase its productive capability. To increase the productivity of its assets a country must increase its capital investment either through its internal savings or foreign investment. Therefore, a stable government is the first requirement for increasing a country's national income.

Governments can also facilitate the growth in real per capita national income through the use of macroeconomic policy. However, to increase a country's real per capita income, in the long-run, macroeconomic policy must be directed at increasing production, i.e., increasing aggregate supply. In order to increase the supply of goods and services, government investment must be directed toward improving the performance of the factors of production, i.e., labor, land, capital, and technology.

Labor

Economic growth depends on the size and quality of the labor force. Education and training are the key success factors in the quality of a nation's labor force. Therefore, government programs directed at improving education and training will result in increased productivity and, in turn, increased per capital output.

Capital

To produce goods efficiently, capital must be combined with labor. The ability of a country to invest in capital goods is tied to its ability to generate domestic savings. A lack of current savings can be offset by borrowing, but the availability of borrowing is limited by the prospects of a country's future potential to save. However, the lower the standard of living in a country, the harder it is for its people to forgo current consumption in order to save. Governments can facilitate capital investment with a tax system that rewards personal savings and by direct investment in their county's infrastructure, i.e., roads, bridges, and telecommunication systems.

Land

Capital and labor can be combined with land to produce goods and services. Abundant natural resources can contribute to economic growth, but natural resources alone do not generate growth. Government can help manage natural resources so that there is a maximum amount of value that is added to the resources through the production process. A country is usually better off if it can increase the value of its natural resources rather than selling the resource to other countries in its natural state. For example, government could prevent the sale of raw timber to foreigners and only permit the export of finished wood products.

Technology

Advances in technology allow the production of more output from a given amount of resources. This means that technological progress accelerates economic growth for any given rate of increase in the labor force and the stock of capital. However, technological change depends on the scientific community. The more educated a population, the greater it's potential for technological advances. Education gives industrial countries a substantial advantage over developing countries in creating new products and in improving the manufacturing process. Government can assist in technological development by directly investing in research and development. The greater the investment made for research and development, by a country, the better its chances for technological advancement.

The above analysis of the factors of production provides a foundation for the next step in the examination of world growth and prosperity. Therefore, this model will be used to determine the probability of growth in real per capita national income in the undeveloped countries, the ex-communist countries, and the industrialized countries of the world.

THE EMPLOYMENT ACT OF 1946

The Full Employment Act of 1946 sought to strengthen the economic gains to the U.S. economy that had resulted from massive government spending during World War II (1939—1945). Applying the theory of John Maynard Keynes, who argued that intensive government spending was necessary to end economic depression, President Harry S. Truman (1945–1953) proposed a 21-point program in 1945 to boost the U.S. economy. The plan called for full employment legislation, an increased minimum wage, and better unemployment and social security benefits as well as housing assistance. Truman believed the bill would ensure that the country would not slip back into depression because it allowed the initiation of remedial action, such as tax cuts and spending programs if economic indicators shifted downward. In January of 1945 four senators, Robert F. Wagner of New York, James E. Murray of Montana, Elbert Thomas of Utah and Joseph O'Mahoney of Wyoming, sponsored a bill that was designed to guarantee full employment. However, because of strong reaction by business interest, the bill as originally written could not be passed.

Full employment was therefore reduced to a goal of high employment. The Employment Act was finally passed by congress and signed by President Truman in 1946. The bill stated that it now was the recognized responsibility of the federal government to provide an environment where those able, willing, and seeking to work, could find employment. In addition, the Employment Act of 1946 created the Council of Economic Advisors to consult with the president on measures to enhance employment and economic policy. The passage of the Employment Act of 1946, with its provision for a council of economic advisors, was very important to the history of economics. It established economics firmly in the center of modern American political theory.

MEASURING EMPLOYMENT

To understand the goals of the Full Employment Act of 1946 it is necessary to analyze what the terms employment and unemployment mean and how they are measured. Data on employment and unemployment is calculated and released monthly by the U.S. Bureau of Labor Statistics in the Employment Situation Summary. The release contains data from two separate surveys: The Household Survey and the Establishment Survey. The Household Survey is a monthly sample survey of approximately 60,000 households. The most publicized data from the Household Survey is each month's unemployment rate. The unemployment rate is the percentage of the U.S. labor force that is unemployed. It is calculated by dividing the number of unemployed individuals by the total civilian work force. An individual is counted as unemployed if they are over the age of 16 and are actively looking for a job, but cannot find one. Students, those individuals who choose to not work, and retirees are not in the labor force, and therefore are not counted in the unemployment rate. Table 15-1 details the employment and unemployment statistics for April 2017. According to the Bureau of Labor Statistics the civilian labor force was 160,213 million for April. Also, there were 7.1 million persons unemployed which resulted in an unemployment rate of 4.4 percent.

Who Is Unemployed?

Unemployment varies significantly among groups of individuals and geographic sectors of the economy. Table 15-2 shows the unemployment rates for a number of groups of individuals, with unemployment ranging from 4.0 percent for adult women to 14.7 percent for teenagers.

Table 15-2 shows changes in the unemployment rate in each of the reported groups from April 2017 compared to April 2016. For April 2017, the largest number of unemployed was teenagers at 14.7 percent and African Americans 7.9 percent. There are also large differences between the level of education obtained and the rate of unemployment. For the month of April 2017, the unemployment rate among those with less than a high school diploma was 6.5 percent and only 2.4 percent for those with a Bachelor's degree or higher.

Table 15-1: Calculation of the Unemployment Rate – April 2017: Numbers in Thousands. Household Survey

Population	Thousands	Description
Total civilian members of population	254,588	Including those under 16, the military and persons in institutions
Those not in the Labor force	94,376	Retired, students, and individuals choosing not to work
= Labor force	160,212	Total population minus those not in the labor force
Minus Persons Employed	153,156	Individuals with jobs
Equals Unemployed	7,056	Individuals without a job actively seeking one
Unemployment Rate =	Unemployed / Labor Force	$\frac{7,056}{160,212} = 4.4\%$

Source: Table A. Major Indicators of labor market activity, seasonally adjusted data April 2017.

The participation rate shown in Table 19-2 is calculated by dividing the civilian labor force for each category by the total population in that group. It is an indication of the percent of the total civilians in that category that are participating in the labor force. For example, for the total civilian workforce the participation rate for April, 2017 (62.9 percent) was calculated by dividing the civilian work force (160,212) by the total civilian population (254,588).

Table 15-2 Unemployment Rates by Group

Description of	Unemployment	Rate	%

Group	April 2016	April 2017	Change
Adult Men	4.6	4.0	-.6
Adult Women	4.5	4.1	-.4
Teenagers	16.0	14.7	-1.3
White Workers	4.3	3.8	-.5
African American	8.8	7.9	-.9
Hispanics	6.1	5.2	-.9
All Workers	5.0	4.4	-.6

Total 25 Years or Older Description of Group	Participation Rate %	Unemployment Rate % Dec. 11
Less than a high school diploma	44.7	6.5
High School graduate no college	57.7	4.6
Some college or Associate Degree	65.8	3.7
Bachelor's degree or higher	74.0	2.4
Total Civilian Work Force	62.9	4.4

Source: Household Survey Table A-4 Employment status of the civilian population 25 years and over by educational attainment, April 2017, seasonally adjusted.

The above table indicates that there is a wide disparity between the level of education in both the participation rate and the unemployment rate of these groups. For example, for those civilians with a bachelor's degree or above there is a low rate of unemployment at 2.4 percent while over 6.5 percent of those who have less than a high school diploma are not employed and to make matters worse only 44.7 percent of this population actually participates in the job market. In addition, the civilian work force that is under 20 years of age (teenagers) had the highest unemployment rate mainly because they have not yet obtained the necessary skills to meet employer demands.

This would indicate that there is a strong correlation between those that are employed and the education and skills that they bring to the job market. Another way to explain the high unemployment rate in a growing economy is that there is a mismatch between the skills required in the labor market (the demand for labor) and the skills that are available in the labor market (supply of labor). This is an indication that our schools, especially in the K-12 grades are not turning out students with the skills needed to participate in the labor market. This is a long-term problem that cannot be solved by short-term fiscal or monetary policy changes. What is needed is a plan to increase the educational obtainment of America's workers now and in the future.

Unemployment Rate Change, April 2017 vs. April 2016

The unemployment rate for April 2017 was 4.4 percent compared to 5.0 percent for April 2016. Although the unemployment rate decreased by .6 percent a portion of the reduction was caused by an increase in those that were not looking for work.

Table 15-3 Analysis of the Employment data for Dec. 2015

Description	April 2016	April 2017	Change
Civilian Labor Force	158,938	160,213	1,275
Participation Rate	62.8	62.9	.1
Employed	151,028	153,156,	2,128
Unemployed	7,910	7,056	-854
Not in Labor Force	94,031	94,375	344
Unemployment Rate	5.0	4.4	-.6

The unemployment rate for April 2017 was .6 percent lower than April 2016. This is an indication that employment situation improved from the previous year. However, while the unemployment was reduced to 4.4 percent the number of persons who gave up looking for work (those not in the labor force) increased by 344 thousand from April 2016 to April 2017. If the change in the number of those persons not looking for work were added to both sides of the equation, the unemployment rate would have been 4.6 percent for April 2017. This is an indication that the real employment situation has improved since April 2016 as the number of those employed increased at a faster rate than the number of people not in the labor force.

Table 15-3-B Unemployment rate including Persons Not Looking for Work

Description	April 2016	April 2017	Change
Labor Force	158,938	160.212	1,274
Persons Not Looking	94,031	94,375	344
Unemployed	7,910	7,056	854
Adjustments			
Unemployment	(7,056+344))	7,400	

Labor Force	(160,212+344)	160,556	4.6%

The December employment data also shows a positive trend as more part-time workers found full-time employment. For example, below is the change in the amount of full-time versus part-time workers for April 2017 compared to March 2017.

Description	March 2017	April 2015	Change
Employed Full-time	126,724	127,184	460
Employed Part-time	26,276	25,972	-304
	-----------	-----------	-------
Total Employment	153,000	153,156	156

The Establishment Survey - Employment by Industry

Table 19-4 shows the employment and data for the month of April 2017, the change from December 2007 through April 2017 and the increase in jobs from March 2017 through April 2017. The data is from the Establishment Survey.

The Establishment Survey is derived from a monthly sample survey of about 160,000 businesses and government agencies. The Establishment Survey breaks down employment and unemployment numbers by major industry classifications. The industry breakdown helps the Bureau of Labor Standard to better understand where the bulk of unemployment comes from. For example, Table 19-4 shows that the gain of jobs for the Month of April 2017 was 211 thousand. Employment in the private sector increased by 194 thousand jobs while employment in the government increased by 17 thousand jobs.

Table 15-4 also contains employment data for December 2007 which the National Bureau of Economic Research determined was the start of the last recession. From the start of the recession through April 2017 the economy experienced a gain of 7,911 thousand jobs. There were still some industries that experienced job losses, the largest job losses were concentrated in three industries, construction, manufacturing and the information industries. The construction and manufacturing industries showed small gains from March 2017 to April 2017, but they have a long way to go to reach their 2007 levels. The largest gains in jobs were in professional and business services, education and health services and leasing and hospitality.

Unemployed workers often do not have the income to support themselves or their families. The stress of being unemployed is reflected through increases in alcohol and drug abuse, marital problems, and criminal activity among those who are unemployed. State and federal governments reduce the personal financial cost of being unemployed through the unemployment compensation provided too many unemployed workers.

The Costs of Unemployment

Government spending is funded mostly from tax revenues. Therefore, unemployment compensation spreads out the cost of being unemployed among taxpayers, instead of having the entire burden fall on the unemployed worker. Also, the availability of unemployment compensation reduces the pressure on an unemployed worker to accept any job offer and may actually tend to slightly raise the jobless rate in the short-term.

Table 15-4
Industry Payroll Employment (in Thousands)

Industry	Dec. 2007	April 2017	Dec. 2007 To April 2017	March 2017 vs. April 2017
Mining and Logging	743	704	-39	10
Construction	7,523	6,877	-646	5
Manufacturing	13,777	12,396	-1,381	6
Trade, Transportation and Utilities	26,725	27,390	665	19
Information	3,025	2,735	-290	-7
Financial Activities	8,243	8,422	179	19
Professional and Business Services	18,109	20,606	2,497	39
Education and Health Services	18,570	23,007	4,437	41
Leasing and Hospitality	13,551	15,856	2,305	55
Other Services	5,517	5,730	213	7
Government Services	22,369	22,340	-29	17
Total Employed	138,152	146,063	7,911	211

Source: Table B1. Employment, Hours and Earnings: From the Current Employment Statistics Survey, April, 2017

The Costs of Unemployment

Government spending is funded mostly from tax revenues. Therefore, unemployment compensation spreads out the cost of being unemployed among taxpayers, instead of having the entire burden fall on the unemployed worker. Also, the availability of unemployment compensation reduces the pressure on an unemployed worker to accept any job offer and may actually tend to slightly raise the jobless rate in the short-term.

Basic Economics

Types of Unemployment

Economists use the term the Natural Rate of Unemployment to explain why the unemployment rate is always greater than zero. The natural rate of unemployment is an equilibrium in which the volumes of job-seeking by workers and worker-seeking by employers reach a balance controlled by fundamental determinants of the relative prices of the two activities. In addition, policymakers have adopted the view that the natural rate of unemployment varies over time. For example, during the period from 1960 through 1989, the natural rate of unemployment was considered to be between 5 and 6 percent. However, during the 1990's when unemployment fell to rates as low as 3.9 percent, many economists revised their estimates at between 4 and 5 percent. In the twenty-first century, many economists consider the historical natural rate of unemployment to again be between 5 and 6 percent or even higher.

There are three types of unemployment; each describes the particular circumstances of the individual who is not employed. Frictional unemployment is temporary unemployment arising from the normal job search process. Frictional unemployment refers to those people who are seeking better or more convenient jobs. Frictional unemployment always exists in any economy and prevents the unemployment rate from being zero.

Structural unemployment is the result of changes in the economy caused by technological progress and shifts in the demand for goods and services. Structural changes eliminate some jobs in certain industries, such as the apparels industry in the U.S. which has lost many jobs to China, and create new jobs in faster growing areas such as professional and business services. Persons who are structurally unemployed do not have marketable job skills and may face prolonged periods of unemployment, as they must often be retrained or relocate in order to find employment.

Cyclical unemployment is caused by a drop in economic activity such as an inventory reduction by U.S. auto manufacturers due to a reduction in sales. If this kind of unemployment hits many industries at the same time it causes an overall inventory reduction which leads to an economic downturn. Once the economy recovers, many of these companies seek to rehire the employees that were laid off. At the level of unemployment that economists consider to be the lowest possible, the normal rate of unemployment, the only unemployment that exists is due to friction in the labor market and structural changes in the economy.[1]

Controversy – Which measure of employment is more accurate?

There has been much political discussion about the failure of the number of employed to increase as real GDP increased by over 3 percent in 2006 and by 2.6 percent in 2007. Part of the explanation could be the increase in productivity that the economy experienced in both 2006 and 2007. The recession of 2008 changed the argument of job growth to one of job losses as the number of unemployed increased steadily throughout the year. For April 2017, the household survey showed total employment of 153,156 million while the payroll survey showed 146,036 million a difference of 7,120 million. Also, the household survey showed a gain in jobs from March 2017 through April 2017 of only 156 thousand while the payroll survey showed a gain of employment of 211 thousand jobs for the same period. This difference is an indication that there may be another variable which is the data itself. The major reason for the difference results of the two surveys is that the household and payroll surveys use different definitions of employment and distinct survey and estimation methods. Some of the major differences between the two surveys are shown in Table 15-5.[2]

The Bureau of Labor Statistics is hard at work trying to reconcile the two surveys and both surveys are needed for a complete picture of the labor market. In the meantime, the two political parties will probably use the survey that best supports their position.

For the month of April 2017, the Republicans might use the establishment survey to show job gains of 211 thousand and that employment has increased due to their policy changes. Meanwhile the Democrats might use the household survey showing a gain of only 156 thousand jobs for the same month to argue that the administration's policies are not leading to any significant job growth. Interestingly enough, the surveys from the Bureau of Labor Statistics often support both positions.

Table 15-5: Trends in Payroll and Household Survey Employment Survey Methods

Comparison By:	Household Survey (CPS)	Payroll Survey (CES)
Universe	Civilian non-institutional population age 16 and over	Non-farm wage and salary jobs
Type of Survey	Monthly sample survey of approximately 60,000 households	Monthly sample survey of about 160,000 businesses and government agencies
Major Outputs	Labor force, employment, unemployment, and associated rates with significant demographic detail	Employment hours, and earnings with significant industry and geographic detail
Reference period	Calendar week that includes the 12th of the month	Employer pay period that includes the 12th of the month
Employment concept	Estimate of employed persons (multiple job holders are included once	Estimate of Jobs (multiple job holders counted for each job)

NOTES:

Chapter 15
Economic Growth and Employment

1. Colander, David, C., <u>Macroeconomics,</u> Irwin Business Publications, Burr Ridge, IL, 1994. p. 471.
2. Colander, p. 478.

3. Data for Tables 15-1 through 15-4 was provided by U.S. Department of Labor, Bureau of Labor Statistics, from the Current Population Survey, April 2017.

CHAPTER 16

MONEY AND THE FEDERAL RESERVE SYSTEM

No matter who you are, making informed decisions about what to do with your money, will help build a more stable financial future for you and your family -- Alan Greenspan

WHAT IS MONEY?

Money according to Adam Smith is a commodity or token that everyone will accept in exchange for the things they have to sell. In any society, money is the asset, commodity or token that serves as a medium of exchange. Different societies throughout history have quite different money systems. The major historical types of money were Commodity moneys, Fiat money, and Fiduciary money.

Commodity moneys have value in non-monetary uses equivalent to the monetary value of the commodity. Historically, copper, gold and silver coins have been the most used in European and East Asian societies. An example is the gold and silver coins that have values roughly equal to the price the metal would command if it were used to create jewelry. Fiat money is a monetary standard that people are required by law to accept as a medium of exchange or a standard of deferred payment. It is money because the government that issued the money (usually paper money) says that it is and guarantees its use for payment of goods and services. Bank money is also called fiduciary money because it is based on the trust people have that the bank will honor its obligation and pay as promised. Fiduciary money may be based on promises to pay in commodity money such as gold coins or in fiat money such as U.S. dollars. Modern monetary systems are largely based on fiduciary money. The two major kinds of fiduciary money are bank notes and checking accounts. Bank notes were widely used in the in Europe and America during the nineteenth century. Bank notes in The United States were replaced by Treasury notes after the Civil War. Today in most modern societies checks are used as money. Therefore, the Federal Reserve includes checking accounts and travelers checks in its M1 definition of money.

The Functions of Money

Money has three functions in the economy: It is a medium of exchange, a unit of account, and a store of value. These three functions distinguish money from other assets. A medium of exchange is an item that buyers give to sellers when they purchase goods and services. When you buy a football at a sporting goods store, the store gives you the brand new football, and you give the store money in the form of fiat money, U.S. bills and coins or fiduciary money, bank checks or bank debit cards. The transfer of money from buyer to seller allows the transaction to take place. When you walk into a store you are confident they will accept your money for the football because money is commonly accepted as a medium of exchange.

A unit of account is the yardstick people use to post prices and record debts. When you go shopping you observe that a Wilson NFL football costs $25 and a hamburger at McDonald's costs $2. Similarly, if you take out a loan from a bank, the size of your future loan repayments will be measured in dollars, not in a quantity of other goods. When we want to measure and record economic value, we use money as a unit of account.

A store of value is an item that people can use to transfer purchasing power from the present to the future. When a seller accepts money today in exchange for a good or service, that seller can hold the money and become a buyer of another good or service at another time. A person can also transfer purchasing power from the present to the future by buying and holding stocks, bonds and real estate. The term wealth is used to refer to the total of all stores of value, including both money and non-monetary assets. Economists use the term liquidity to describe the ease with which an asset can be converted into the economy's medium of exchange. Because money, either coin paper or checking deposits, is the economy's medium of exchange, it is the most liquid asset available. When people decide in what form to hold their wealth, they have to balance the liquidity of each possible asset against the asset's usefulness as a store of value. Money is the most liquid asset, but it is far from perfect as a store of value. When prices rise the value of money falls, for example, when goods and services become more expensive, each dollar can buy less. This link between the price level and the value of money is important for understanding how money affects the economy and why interest is paid to investors for the use of their money.[1]

Interest is the price that borrowers pay for the use of someone else's money. Interest on a loan of money such as a bank loan or a sale of a corporate or government bond is based on three conditions: Liquidity, market risk and default risk. Liquidity is the price that the lender demands for temporarily giving up the current opportunity to buy a good or service with money. Market risk is the probability that interest rates in the market for a comparable security will increase due to an increase in inflation. Increased rates of inflation will lead to higher prices for goods and service resulting in a reduction in the value (price) of the security. If the owner of the security needs to redeem it prior to maturity they may have to accept a reduction in the face value of that security. Default risk is based on the probability that the borrower will not repay the loan or bond when it matures. Interest is therefore determined by adding together the liquidity value, the market risk and the lender's default risk of a bank loan on a security. This is why a U.S. government issued security with a short-term maturity such as a 90-day Treasury Bill has a lower rate of interest than a 10 Year Government Bond.

The Federal Reserve Definitions of Money

The quantity of money circulating in the economy is referred to by the Federal Reserve as the money supply. There is more than one definition of the money supply; the most obvious is currency, the paper bills and coins in the hands of the public and the vaults of banks. However, currency is not the only asset that can be used to buy goods and services. Almost all stores accept personal checks and bank debit cards which act as electronic checks. Wealth held in a checking account is almost as convenient for buying things as wealth held in a consumer's wallet. Therefore, checking account deposits and traveler's checks are included in the definition of money. Also, savings accounts can easily be converted into cash without loss of principle along with deposits in money market accounts such as negotiable orders of withdrawal (NOW) accounts.[2]

In a complex economy, such as that of the United States, it is not easy to distinguish between what is called money and assets that cannot. The coins in an individual's pocket are clearly part of the money supply and the Golden Gate Bridge in San Francisco clearly is not, but there are many alternatives between these extremes for which the choice is less clear. Therefore, the Federal Reserve has developed definitions of money and the money stock based on the liquidity of the assets considered. Table 16-1 shows the items included in the money supply developed by the Federal Reserve.

In 2015 the money supply increased by $667.4 billion or 5.7 percent over 2014. M1 increased by $184.6 billion or 6.4 percent and M2 increased by 482.8 billion or 5.5 percent over 2014. The largest increase was in demand deposits and savings deposits at commercial banks. This large increase is an indication that the Federal Reserve System continued to make large deposits at commercial banks to purchase government securities

The Federal Reserve Defines the M1 and M2 Money Supply as follows:

M1: The sum of currency held outside of depository institutions, Federal Reserve Banks, and the U.S. Treasury; travelers checks; and demand and other checkable deposits issued by financial institutions (except demand deposits due to the Treasury and depository institutions), minus cash items in the process of collections and Federal Reserve float.

M2: M1 plus savings deposits (including money market deposit accounts) and small denomination (under $100,000) time deposits issued by financial institutions, and shares in retail money market mutual funds (funds with initial investment of under $50,000), net of retirement accounts.

Table 16-1

Money Stock Measures – December 2016 vs. 2015

Money Market Measure	Dec. 2015 $ in billions	Dec. 2016 $ in billions	Change 2016 vs. 2015
M1	$	$	$
Currency in Circulation	3,338.6	1,419.7	81.1
Travelers Checks	2.5	12.2	-.3
Demand Deposits at Commercial Banks	1,228.4	1,353.4	125.0
Other Checkable Deposits	513.9	551.5	37.6
Total M1	**3,083.4**	**3,326.8**	**243.4**
M2 = M1 Plus			
Savings Deposits	8,179.9	8,827.1	647.2
Small Denominations Time Deposits	408.5	347.0	-61.5
Money Market Funds	639.4	680.0	40.6
Total M2 Additions	**9,227.8**	**9,854.1**	**626.3**
Total M2	**12,311.2**	**13,180.9**	**869.7**

HOW BANKS CREATE MONEY

Based on the above information you can see that the Federal Reserve has several definitions of money which include bank demand, savings and time deposits. Changes in the quantity of money originate with actions of the Federal Reserve System, depository institutions, or the public. The actual process of money creation takes place primarily in commercial banks. Checkable liabilities of banks are considered to be money. These bank liabilities are customers' accounts. They increase when customers deposit currency and checks and when the proceeds of loans made by the banks are credited to borrower's accounts. Many years ago, bankers discovered that they could make loans merely by giving their promises to pay, a bank note, in some acceptable commodity such as gold, to borrowers. In this way, banks began to create money. More notes could be issued than the gold that they held in their vaults because only a portion of the notes outstanding would be presented for payment at any one time.

Transaction deposits are the modern counterpart of bank notes. It was a small step from printing notes to making book entries crediting deposits of borrowers, which the borrowers in turn could spend by writing checks, thereby effectively printing their own money. The modern bank must be prepared to convert deposit money into currency for those depositors who request currency. In addition, the bank must make remittance on checks written by depositors and presented for payment by other banks. Finally, it must maintain legally required reserves, in the form of vault cash and/or balances at its Federal Reserve Bank. This is called the reserve requirement and is explained in a previous chapter. The Federal Reserve, through its ability to vary both the total volume of reserves and the required ratio of reserves to deposit liabilities, influences banks' decisions with respect to their assets and deposits. One of the major responsibilities of the Federal Reserve System is to provide the total amount of reserves consistent with the monetary needs of the economy at reasonably stable prices.

As an example of how banks create money, let's assume that expansion of the money stock M1 is desired by the Federal Reserve System. One way the central bank can initiate such an expansion is through purchases of securities in the open market for $10,000. Payment for the securities adds to bank reserves. The purchase is made from a government securities dealer and is deposited in the dealer's bank account, for example, at NY Bank A. At the same time, Bank A's reserve account at the Federal Reserve is credited for the amount of the securities purchase. The Federal Reserve System has added $10,000 of securities to its assets, which it has paid for, in effect, by creating a liability on itself in the form of bank reserve balances.

Commercial Banks are required to hold reserves equal to only a fraction of their deposits. Reserves in excess of this amount may be used to increase earning assets; loans and investments. Under current regulations, banks are required to keep 10 percent in reserves against their transaction accounts. If NY Bank A receives a $10,000 deposit and the reserve requirement is 10%, they need to retain only $1,000. The remaining $9,000 is excess reserves. This amount can be loaned or invested. What banks do when they make loans is to accept promissory notes in exchange for credits to the borrowers' transaction accounts. Loans (assets) and deposits (liabilities) both rise by $9,000. Reserves are unchanged by the loan transaction. But the deposit credits constitute new additions to the total deposits of the banking system. If the bank holding the $9,000 of deposits just created, in turn make loans equal to their excess reserves, then loans and deposits will rise by a further $8,100 ($9,000 x .90) in the second stage of expansion. This process can continue until deposits have risen to the point where all the reserves provided by the initial purchase of government securities by the Federal Reserve System are just sufficient to satisfy reserve requirements against the newly created deposits.

Carried through to theoretical limits, the initial $10,000 of reserves distributed within the banking system can give rise to an expansion of $90,000 in bank credit and supports a total of $100,000 in new deposits under a 10 percent reserve requirement. The deposit expansion multiplier for a given amount of new reserves is thus the reciprocal of the required reserve percentage (1/.10 = 10). The multiple expansions are possible because the banks as a group are like one large bank in which checks drawn against borrowers' deposits result in credits to accounts of other depositors, with no net change in the total reserves.[3]

However, a given increase in bank reserves is not necessarily accompanied by an expansion equal to the theoretical potential based on the required ratio of reserves to deposits. Wat happens to the quantity of money will vary, depending upon the reactions of banks and the public. A number of leakages may occur such as the public might choose to hold more money as currency and banks might not be able to turn all excess deposits into loans. For example, the relationship between currency in circulation and demand and savings deposits can be used as a proxy for the cash drain ratio. An estimate of the cash drain can be developed using the data in Table 16-1 and dividing currency in circulation by the total of demand and savings deposits ($1,506/$10,180 billion). This equation results in a cash drain ratio of about 14.8 percent. The deposit expansion multiplier formula then can be restated as follows:

$$DEM = \frac{1}{RR + \text{Cash Drain}} \quad \frac{1}{.10 + .148} = 4.0$$

This reduces the deposit expansion multiplier from 10 to 4.0 percent. If the banking system's holdings of excess reserves is considered the multiplier would be reduced even further.

BALANCE SHEET OF THE FEDERAL RESERVE SYSTEM

Each week, the Federal Reserve posts its current release H.4.1. This release is titled Factors Affecting Reserve Balances and shows the current numbers from what is commonly called the Federal Reserve Balance Sheet. The one power that the Fed unquestionably possesses is the ability to create money. It traditionally did so by buying Treasury securities from the public, crediting the sellers' banks with newly created Federal Reserve deposits (a "liability" from the Fed's point of view), and adding the securities purchased to the Fed's asset holdings. Those newly created Federal Reserve deposits are essentially electronic credits that the banks could use to receive delivery of cash from the Federal Reserve.

Table 16-2 details the Federal Reserve Balance Sheets for 2016 and 2015. The assets of the Federal Reserve for 2016 totaled 4,511,369 billion compared to $4,531,984 for 2015 and decrease of $20.615 billion or .45 percent. The largest increase was in Mortgage backed securities of $6,153.

Table 16-2
Federal Reserve Balance Dec. 2016 vs. Dec. 2015

Federal Reserve Assets ($ Millions)	Dec 30 2015	Dec. 30 2016	Change 2016 vs. 2015
Treasury Securities	$2,461,554	2,463,591	2,037
Federal Agency Debt	32,944	16,180	-16,764
Mortgage Backed Securities	1,747,467	1,753,620	6,153
Securities Held	4,241,965	4,233,391	-8,574
Repurchase Agreements	0	0	0
Loans			
Discount Window	553	15	-538
Term Asset-Backed Securities Loan Facility	0	0	0
Other Credit	82	29	-53
Total Loans	635	44	-591
Maiden Lane LLC	1,717	1,707	-10
Other Federal Reserve Assets	30,272	29,061	-1,211
Miscellaneous Assets	257,395	247,166	-10,229
Total Assets	4,531,984	4,511,369	-20,615
Currency in Circulation	1,426,176	1,506,076	79,900
Reverse Repurchase Agree.	498,519	540,549	42,030
None Reserve Deps. with Fed	351,987	465,071	113,084
Other Liabilities and Capital	46,621	47,118	497
Reserve Balances	2,208,681	1,952,555	1-256,126
Total Liabilities and Capital	$4,531,984	4,511,369	-20,615

Another measure that the Fed employed to allow this ballooning of its assets was to start paying banks an interest rate on reserves equal to its target for the fed funds rate itself, essentially eliminating any incentive for the banks to lend fed funds and encouraging banks instead to simply let excess reserves accumulate. As of December 38, 2016, banks were sitting on about $465 billion in none reserve deposits with the Fed, doing absolutely nothing with them. The Fed was in effect lending those funds in place of the banks. As of December 28, 2016, the Federal Reserve held $1,953 billion in reserve deposits a decrease over 2015 of $256 billion.

Description of the Federal Reserve Balance Sheet Loan Assets

The key loan asset items on the Federal Reserve Balance Sheet, with descriptions provided by the Federal Reserve Release H-4, are listed below:
1. Repurchase and Reverse Repurchase Agreements: The Fed uses repurchase agreements, also called "RPs" or "repos", to make collateralized loans to primary dealers. In a reverse repo or "RRP", the Fed borrows money from primary dealers. The Fed uses these two types of transactions to offset temporary swings in bank reserves; a repo temporarily adds reserve balances to the banking system, while reverse repos temporarily drains balances from the system. Repos and reverse repos are conducted with primary dealers via auction. In a repo, dealers bid on borrowing money versus various types of general collateral. In a reverse repo, dealers offer interest rates at which they would lend money to the Fed versus the Fed's Treasury general collateral, typically Treasury bills.
2. The Asset-Backed Commercial Paper Money Market Mutual Fund Liquidity Facility: is a lending facility that provides funding to U.S. depository institutions and bank holding companies to finance their purchases of high-quality asset-backed commercial paper (ABCP) from money market mutual funds under certain conditions. The program is intended to assist money funds that hold such paper in meeting demands for redemptions by investors and to foster liquidity in the ABCP market and money markets more generally.
3. Maiden Lane LLC: On June 26, 2008, the Federal Reserve Bank of New York (FRBNY) extended credit to Maiden Lane LLC under the authority of section 13(3) of the Federal Reserve Act. This limited

liability company was formed to acquire certain assets of Bear Stearns and to manage those assets through time to maximize repayment of the credit extended and to minimize disruption to financial markets. Payments by Maiden Lane LLC from the proceeds of the net portfolio holdings will be made in the following order: operating expenses of the LLC, principal due to the FRBNY, interest due to the FRBNY, principal due to JPMorgan Chase & Co., and interest due to JPMorgan Chase & Co. Any remaining funds will be paid to the FRBNY.8

Quantitative Easing I, II and III

This is a government monetary policy recently used by The Federal Reserve Banks to increase the money supply by buying government securities or other securities from the market. Quantitative easing increases the money supply by flooding financial Institutions (Brokerage firms and Commercial Banks) with capital in an effort to promote increased lending and liquidity.

The Federal Reserve increased its holdings of Securities by $769 billion from December 2009 through December 2011. Federal Reserve Chairman Ben Bernanke Stated in November 3, 2010 that the Fed planned to again increase its holdings of securities and increasing the money supply by about $600 billion during the first half of 2010. The Federal Reserve continued to expand the money supply by purchasing about 85 billion in government securities each month through 2013. For 2014 Janet Yellen, the new Federal Reserve Chairman, planned to reduce the buying of Fed securities to about 65 billion per month and slowly phase out the purchasing of Fed securities sometime in 2016.

The Feds Explanation on the Purchases of Treasury Securities

On November 3, 2010, the Federal Open Market Committee (FOMC) decided to expand the Federal Reserve's holdings of securities in the System Open Market Account (SOMA) to promote a stronger pace of economic recovery and to help ensure that inflation, over time, is at levels consistent with its mandate. In particular, the FOMC directed the Open Market Trading Desk (the Desk) at the Federal Reserve Bank of New York to purchase an additional $600 billion of longer term Treasury securities by the end of the second quarter of 2011.

The FOMC also directed the Desk to continue to reinvest principal payments from agency debt and agency mortgage-backed securities into longer-term Treasury securities. Based on current estimates, the Desk expects to reinvest $250 to $300 billion over the same period, though the realized amount of reinvestment will depend on the evolution of actual principal payments. Taken together, the Desk anticipated conducting $850 to $900 billion of purchases of longer-term Treasury securities through the end of the second quarter. This would result in an average purchase pace of roughly $110 billion per month.[8] For 2014 The Fed continued to purchase securities and expanding their balance sheet by $466.6 billion over 2013.

An Opposing View of QE II and III From Larry Kudlow

Fed head Ben Bernanke and the FOMC dropped a new policy bomb at their meeting this week. Now they say inflation is too low. That's the real problem. And the solution, punch up the money supply and punch down the dollar.

The Fed actually has opened the door even wider for more money-creating, balance-sheet expanding, Treasury-bond-buying actions at its next scheduled meeting, which will come the day after the midterm elections on November 3, 2010. That's when QE2 may sail. "Quantitative easing" is what they call it. I call it dollar whack-a-mole.

One of the cornerstones of economic growth in a free-market model is domestic price stability and a stable, reliable dollar. This is crucial for confidence and capital formation. In fact Nobel Prize winning economists Robert Mundell always argued for low tax rates to spur growth and a steady dollar linked to gold to ensure price stability.

But now we are moving deeper into monetary Keynesian fine-tuning to control the economy. That, plus an overspending Keynesian fiscal policy, may be combined with higher tax rates and an ever-weakening dollar. It's totally wrong. It's exactly the reverse of Mundell's thesis. Sinking the greenback and pumping more money into the system while raising tax rates and overspending is, over time, a prescription for stagflation: too much money chasing too few goods.

Now think of this: With all the Fed's pump-priming since late 2008, there is still $1 trillion of excess bank reserves sitting on deposit at the central bank. This massive cash hoard suggests that liquidity is not the problem for the financial system or the economy. And putting another $1 trillion into excess reserves only doubles the problem.

A much better idea would be a fiscal freeze on spending, tax rates, and regulations. This is apparently what the tea-party driven Republican congressional leaders intend for their election platform.
Such a freeze would go a long way toward reducing the massive overhang of uncertainty that has plagued the economy and stifled the animal spirits. The Fed can print money, but it can't print new jobs or growth. On the other hand, a rollback of the big-government obstacles to growth would get folks to put money to work.[9]

NOTES:

Chapter 16
Money and the Federal Reserve System

1. Mankiw, Gregory, N., Principles of Economics, The Dryden Press, Orlando, FL, 1998, p. 593.
2. Mankiw, p. 595.
3. Federal Reserve of Chicago, Modern Money Mechanics, Chicago, IL, P. 1-6.
4. Colander, David, C., Macroeconomics, Irwin Business Publications, Burr Ridge, IL, 1994. p. 471.
5. Colander, p. 478.
6. Heilbroner, Robert, Making of Economic Society, 9th Edition, Englewood Cliffs, N.J., Prentice Hall, 1993, p. 229.
7. Federal Reserve Bank of New York, Statement Regarding the Purchase of Treasury Securities, November 3, 2013.
8. Federal Reserve Release H-4. December 30, 2015.
9. Kudlow, Larry, Destroying King Dollar Is Not the Solution Townhall.com, September 24, 2012.

CHAPTER 17

ECONOMICS IN THE TWENTY FIRST CENTURY – THE GEORGE W. BUSH ADMINISTRATION

A government big enough to give you everything you want, is strong enough to take everything you have. - **Thomas Jefferson**

On November 7, 2000, American voters went to the poles to elect a new president. The contest was between Al Gore, Vice President for eight years under Bill Clinton and George W. Bush the Governor of Texas and eldest son of former president George H.W. Bush. Stripped of many normally winning Republican issue (the cold war, crime, the economy), Bush took a lesson from the 1996 election, and proceeded to run on historically Democratic issues (education, health care, and social security). Bush did continue to pursue one Republican strategy with a proposal to lower individual tax rates. Bush's background was different than the typical candidate for national office as he had an extensive business background and a Master's Degree in Business Administration from Harvard University.

The certified results of the election on November 7 were that George W. Bush won the presidency with the closest vote in the history of America elections. However, the actions of the next 35 days resembled more a soap opera than an orderly transition of power. Shortly before 8 p.m. all of the major television networks estimated that Vice President Gore had beaten Governor Bush in the key state of Florida. But as the night went on and results came in from the state's heavily republican Panhandle region, the networks were forced to retract that estimate.

As the night wore on it became clear that the victor in Florida would win the electoral votes necessary to claim the presidency. In the morning of November 8th, a series of early-morning events set the stage for a protracted presidential battle. First, at about 2:15 a.m., the major networks called Florida and the election for Bush. Al Gore, hearing that he probably will lose Florida by about 50,000 votes called Texas Governor Bush and conceded the election. But 45 minutes later, while Gore was en route to a rally in Nashville to give a concession address, aides reach him and tell him that Bush's lead in Florida has shrunk dramatically. Gore than called Bush to rescind his concession.

On December 8th, divided 4 to 3, the Florida Supreme Court ordered manual recounts in all counties with significant numbers of presidential under votes (ballots where no selection for president was made). The Bush lawyers reacted by appealing the decision to the U.S. Supreme Court and sought an injunction to stop the hand counts. Bush's lawyers argued that the Florida Supreme Court overstepped its bounds by ordering a manual recount.

On December 12th, the U.S. Supreme Court ended the debacle handing down a 5 to 4 decision that settled the matter and effectively declared George W. Bush to be the 43rd president of the United States.

On December 12, 2000 George W. Bush was officially declared to be the new president of the United States. The election of 2000 was one of the closest in the history of the United States. George W. Bush won the election with an Electoral College vote of 271 to Al Gore's 266 but lost the popular vote by 541 thousand. However, Bush was not the only president to lose the popular vote and win the election, two other presidents were elected by receiving a majority of the electoral votes and losing the popular vote. The other two presidents were Rutherford Hayes in 1876 and Benjamin Harrison in 1888.

THE FIRST YEAR OF THE NEW CENTURY

During his first six months in office President Bush concentrated in three areas: Tax reduction, an energy policy and education reform legislation. The progress during 2001 was as follows:

Tax Reform

The Tax Reform and Rebate Act of 2001 was signed into law on June 6, 2001. The new tax law cut individual income taxes by $1.35 trillion over ten years. "Across-the board tax relief does not happen very much in Washington, D.C., in fact it has happened only twice: President Kennedy's tax cut in the 60s and President Reagan's tax cut in the 80's," Bush said. "And now it's happened for a third time. And it's about time."

The new law reduces the lowest rate from 15 to 10 percent, and the highest rate form 39.6 percent to 35 percent. Some of the law's provisions are delayed several years, but eventually will double the child tax credit from $500 to $1,000, reduce the tax penalty on married couples and fully repeal the tax on estates. One provision of the law, to cut the lowest rate on personal income taxes to 10 percent was made retroactive to January 1, 2001, and taxpayers were sent a rebate check to cover that cutback. The rebate checks were sent to all those who filed a tax return for the year 2000. Singles received $300, single parents received $500 and married couples received $600 provided that they had at least $12,000 in taxable income. For example, the rate was reduced from 15 percent to 10 percent. If a married couple had $12,000 of taxable income they would receive $600 based on a calculation of (5% times $12,000) or $600.

Education Reform

On January 8, 2002, President Bush signed into law the "No Child Left Behind Law of 2001. The Act, which embodies the administration's education reform plan sent to Congress on January 23, 2001, was the most sweeping reform of the Elementary and Secondary Education Act since ESEA was enacted in 1965. It redefines the federal role in kindergarten through grade 12 education and will help close the achievement gap between disadvantaged and minority students and their peers. The new law is based on four basic principles: increased accountability for results, more choices for parents and students, greater flexibility for states, school districts and schools and putting reading first.

The NCLB Act will strengthen Title I accountability by requiring States to implement statewide accountability systems covering all public schools and students. These systems must be based on challenging State standards in reading and mathematics, annual testing for all students in grades 3-8, and annual statewide progress objectives ensuring that all groups of students reach proficiency within 12 years. School districts and schools that fail to make adequate yearly progress toward statewide proficiency goals will, over time, be subject to improvement, corrective action, and restructuring measures aimed at getting them back on course to meet State standards.

The NCLB Act significantly increases the choices available to the parents of students attending Title I schools that fail to meet State standards, including immediate relief beginning with the 2002-03 school year. Local Education Agencies (LEAs) must give students attending schools identified for improvement, corrective action, or restructuring the opportunity to attend a better public school, which may include a public charter school, within the school district. The district must provide transportation to the new school, and must use at least 5 percent of its Title I funds for this purpose, if needed. For those attending persistently failing schools' LEAs must permit low-income students to use Title I funds to obtain supplemental education services from the public-or-private-sector provider selected by the students and their parents. In addition to helping ensure that no child loses the opportunity for a quality education, the choice and supplemental service requirements provide a substantial incentive for low-performing schools to improve.

The NCLB Act gives States and school districts unprecedented flexibility in the use of Federal education funds in exchange for strong accountability for results. New flexibility provisions in the NCLB Act include authority for States and LEAs to transfer up to 50 percent of the funding they receive under 4 major State grant programs to any one of the programs, or to Title I. The covered programs include Teacher Quality State Grants, Educational Technology, Innovative Programs, and Safe and Drug-Free Schools

The new Reading First initiative would significantly increase the Federal investment in scientifically based reading instruction programs in the early grades. One major benefit of this approach would be reduced identification of children for special education services due to a lack of appropriate reading instruction in their early years. The new Reading First State Grant program will make 6-year grants to States, which will make competitive sub grants to local communities. Local recipients will administer screening and diagnostic assessments to determine which students in grades K-3 are at risk of reading failure, and provide professional development for K-3 teachers in the essential components of reading instruction.

Other changes will support State and local efforts to keep our schools safe and drug-free, while at the same time ensuring that students, particularly those who have been victims of violent crimes on school grounds, are not trapped in persistently dangerous schools. States must report school safety statistics to the public on a school-by-school basis, and LEAs must use Federal Safe and Drug-Free Schools and Communities funding to implement drug and violence prevention programs of demonstrated effectiveness.[1]

While the NCLB Act looks good on paper, many parts of the plan may conflict with the edicts of political correctness and policies of social advancement within the existing school systems. Therefore, the real value of the Act will be in the implementation by the States and Local School Districts.

The Energy Plan

On May 16th President Bush released an energy strategy with an eye toward the long term. "We face a shortage of energy," Bush said the next afternoon in Iowa. "It is real. It is not the imagination of anybody in my administration, it's a real problem." The new plan, according to Bush, would encourage new, environmentally friendly exploration for new sources of oil and natural gas, while encouraging conservation efforts and developing other sources of energy as well. The major parts of the plan are as follows:

Executive orders and agency reviews aimed at easing regulations the industry says slow the siting and licensing of power plants and gas refineries

A review of the Clinton administration's interpretation of "new sources review rules" that the coal industry and refiners say discourage them from making technological and other improvements because they run the risk of tougher environmental rules.

Opening parts of the Arctic National Wildlife refuge to oil and gas exploration, and encouraging the Interior and other departments to look at opening other federal lands now off-limits to energy exploration.

A ten-billion-dollar investment, over ten years, for tax incentives including hybrid vehicle purchases, methane gas development, and solar power cell installation.

The energy bill created the most controversy in Congress of the three bills. The Democrats arguing over conserving energy as the best way to handle energy shortages and Republicans arguing that increased energy supply is equally important in solving the countries long-term energy problems.

AMERICA'S NEW WAR

The front cover of Newsweek's September 24th 2001 issue showed three firemen raising the American flag over "ground zero." Ground zero is usually a term used to describe a war zone, however, in this case it was the location of the World Trade Center in New York City. The caption on the front page read "God Bless America." The picture, taken by Thomas E. Franklin, simultaneously showed the tragedy that had just occurred in New York City and the heroics displayed by its government workers and average citizens. On September 11, 2001 two large jet airplanes crashed into the twin towers of the world trade center and one jet crashed into the Pentagon in Washington DC and instantaneously changed the lives of the people of and entire country and perhaps the entire free world.

While the final toll of the victims in the World Trade Center will possible never be known, it is estimated by the City of New York that about 3,000 people were either dead or missing including over 300 city firefighters and 40 policemen. In total, this was the worst act of aggression ever committed on American soil.

AMERICA STRIKES BACK

On October 7, 2001 President Bush addressed the nation from the Treaty Room of the White House. Bush outlined in this speech the beginning of air strikes on Afghanistan.

"On my orders, the United States military has begun strikes against al Qaeda terrorists training camps and military installations of the Taliban regime in Afghanistan. We are joined in this operation by our staunch friend, Great Britain. Other close friends, including Canada, Australia, Germany and France, have pledged forces as the operation unfolds. More than 40 countries in the Middle East, Africa, and across Asia have granted air transit or landing rights. Many more have shared intelligence. We are supported by the collective will of the world."

THE RECESSION OF 2001

The American economy and especially the stock market do not like surprises. Consequently, on September 12, 2001 the stock market showed an across the board decline with the Dow Jones Index dropping over 600 points. The shock of the attack on September 11 sent the airline travel and vacation industry into a tailspin. On December 21, the Bureau of Economic Analysis in a news release indicated that a recession was at hand as it reported real gross domestic product decreased at an annual rate of 1.3 percent in the third quarter of 2001. In November of 2001 the National Bureau of Economic Research's Business Cycle Dating Committee said the U.S. economy had entered a recession in March of 2001 after a 10-year expansion. According to their Web site the NBER defines a recession as "A significant decline in activity spread across the economy, lasting more than a few months, visible in industrial production, employment, real income and wholesale-retail trade."

The President, Congress, and the Federal Reserve were working to avoid a recession or at least to lessen its effect. Since the beginning 2001 the Federal Reserve had lowered the target rate on fed funds twelve times with the rate by year-end 2002 standing at 1.25 percent. But many analysts are worried that the rate cuts won't do enough to encourage American consumers to pick up their spending again now that their confidence has been hurt by the September 11 attacks. One of the major problems with the economy is that companies simply spent too much money on new technologies and equipment in the 1990s. When demand for new products dried up in 2000, manufacturers stopped making new goods until their backlog could be sold off. With many manufacturers experiencing what the Fed calls "low capacity utilization" no amount of cheap credit is going to persuade companies to borrow to buy more equipment until they know somebody is going to buy what they produce

In August of 2002, The Bureau of Economic Analysis released its revised estimates of GDP for 2001. The revised data showed a reduction in Real Gross Domestic Product for each of the first three quarters of 2001. Also, the annual growth in Real GDP was revised downward from 1.3 percent to 0.3 percent. According to the revised estimates, GDP reached a peak in the fourth quarter of 2000 and decreased 0.6 percent in the first quarter of 2001, 1.6 percent in the second quarter, and 0.3 percent in the third quarter. The revised data indicates that by all economic definitions, there was a mild recession in 2001. The major reason for the recession was a reduction in gross private domestic investment of 10.7 percent versus 2000. The entire reduction was due to a decrease in business spending on new factories, business equipment and software during 2001.

For 2002, the economy showed modest growth as real GDP increased at an annual rate of 5.0 percent in the first quarter, 1.3 in the second quarter, and 4.0 for the third quarter and 1.4 percent for the fourth quarter. For the entire year, real GDP grow at a rate of 2.4 percent. The Federal Reserve, at its August meeting, was still predicting growth rates for GDP in the 3 percent range for 2003, but to hedge their bets the Fed decreased the federal funds rate by 50 basis points to 1.25 percent at their November 2002 meeting.

THE NOVEMBER 2002 ELECTIONS

On November 5th, 2002 Americans went to the polls and voted in record numbers. The results of the election was that Republicans maintained control of the House of Representatives and gained control of the Senate. Not since 1902 has a first-time Republican president seen his party win both the House and the Senate in a midterm election. Senator Trent Lott, the new Senate majority leader, commented on the election results by saying Republicans had been "fired up about the campaign, particularly with President Bush on the trail to provide support." But even Senator Lott acknowledged that the scope of the victory "did exceed our hopes and expectations."

For at least 2 more years, Republicans will control all three branches of government allowing them to shape the political battles to come. Already, President Bush's advisors have been at work on a possible set of new tax cuts whose centerpiece would be the permanent extension of his 10-year reduction of income taxes, including reducing or eliminating both the marriage tax and the inheritance tax. In addition, in November of 2002, President Bush signed a new law creating the Department of Homeland Security.

MAJOR LEGISLATION ENACTED IN 2003

Medicare Prescription Drug, Improvement and Modernization Act

President Bush signed this Act in December of 2003, which he referred to as "the greatest advance in health care coverage for America's seniors since the founding of Medicare." The Act provided a prescription drug plan for seniors starting in 2006. Other provisions of this Act increased payments to Medicare providers, provided new preventive health care benefits to seniors, established health care savings accounts, and curtailed the number of employers expected to drop retire health care coverage by providing a subsidy to firms with a retirement health plan certified to be at least the equivalent of the standard Medicare drug plan. The plan was criticized by conservatives for being too expensive and by liberals by not providing enough benefits. However, the American Association of Retired People (AARP) advocated passage of the plan as a good start in providing at least some prescription drug benefits to seniors.

Jobs and Growth Tax Relief Reconciliation Act of 2003

This Act was signed into law on May 28th 2003. The major purpose of the act was to stimulate economic activity especially business investment. The major provisions of the Act were to decrease temporarily the tax rates on stock dividends and capital gains, to increase temporarily incentives to speed up investment in capital equipment by allowing faster depreciation write-offs and to accelerate many of the individual income tax reductions provided in the 2001 tax cuts.

While it is difficult to determine the exact effect of the tax cuts on business investment in 2003 the direction of change is predictable. The third quarter of 2003 showed an increase in GDP of 8.2 percent, followed by a 4.1 percent in the fourth quarter. The largest percent increase, 12.8 percent in the third quarter and 15.1 percent in the fourth quarter, was in nonresidential investment in business equipment and software. For all of 2003, GDP increased by 3.1 percent with consumer expenditures increasing by 3.1 percent and gross private domestic investment by 4.3 percent. With the better than expected growth rates for 2003, GDP grew in the 4 to 5 percent range for 2004 and many economists are forecasting a growth of over 3 percent for 2007.

GULF WAR II

After the War in Afghanistan, the attention of the U.S. government turned to Iraq and the violations of the U.N. peace agreement with that country. In his address to the United Nations on September 12, 2002, President Bush said: "The history, the logic, and the facts lead to only one conclusion: Saddam Hussein's regime is a grave danger. To suggest otherwise is to hope against the evidence. To assume his regime's good faith is to bet the lives of millions and the peace of the world in a reckless gamble. And this is a risk we must not take." President Bush then challenged the U. N. to enforce its previous resolutions, against the Iraq.

On November 8, 2002, the 15 member United Nations Security Council voted to approve resolution 1441 which unanimously adopted strengthening the weapons inspection for Iraq and gave Baghdad "a final opportunity to comply with its disarmament obligations." The resolution stated that Iraq remains in material breach of the U.N. Security Council resolutions relating to Iraq's 1990 invasion of Kuwait and requires that Baghdad give UNMOVIC and IAEA a complete and accurate declaration of all aspects of its chemical, biological and nuclear weapons programs, ballistic missiles systems, as well as information on other chemical biological, and nuclear programs which are supposed to be for civilian purposes within 30 days. Finally, resolution 1441 warns Iraq that "it will face serious consequences" if it continues to violate its obligations as spelled out in the resolution.

Iraq did provide the U.N. with a description of its current chemical and biological weapons, but declared that they no longer had any of these weapons. The report was basically a rehash of old documents and did not satisfy even the most lenient members of the Security Council. The question then became what is the real role of the U.N. inspectors, to search for Iraq's weapons of mass destruction or to supervise their destruction? This question and the one of how long the inspectors should continue the search for WMD became the subject for debate among the members of the U.N. Security Council with France threatening to veto any further resolution to disarm Iraq by force. In the meantime, the United States and Britain had assembled an armed force of about 250 thousand troops in Kuwait and Qatar.

Finally, the patience of President Bush and Britain's Prime Minister Tony Blair had worn out. On March 17, 2003, the United States declared that the "diplomatic window has closed" for a peaceful resolution to the Iraq showdown and that President Bush would warn Saddam Hussein latter that day that the only way to avoid war was to leave the country. In a State Department news conference, Secretary of State Colin Powell said the crisis on Iraq was a "test the United Nations did not meet."

On Thursday March 20, 2003 Gulf War II started with the bombing of an Iraq building where the U.S. believed Iraq's president and some high-ranking officers were staying. After that attack, Saddam Hussein was not seen in public again and although there were some videotape messages seen on Iraqi television, it was never certain if he had survived the attack. By Friday a bombing attack from a coalition lead by the United States and Britain started and a ground force headed from Kuwait towards Iraq. After just three weeks of war, U.S. tanks rolled unmolested into the center of Iraq's capital city to a tumultuous welcome from jubilant residents. U.S. military leaders proclaimed an end to Saddam Hussein's control of Baghdad, stopping just short of declaring victory in the campaign to oust the Iraqi president and to destroy the Baath Party Regime.

Television cameras showed stunning images of American troops walking on the streets of Baghdad among residents celebrating the downfall of the Baath Party after more than two decades of police-state control. Just 24 hours earlier, it appeared that U.S. forces might be in for a prolonged bout, but most Iraqi resistance melted away after another night of relentless pounding by U.S. warplanes and artillery. The people of Baghdad poured into the streets in celebration, waiving at U.S. troops and tearing down posters and busts of the Iraqi president. In one scene Iraqis attacked a giant statue of Saddam Hussein with sledgehammers. With the help of U.S. Marines who ran a cable from their tank to the 20-foot tall statue, they pulled it down literally yanking the image of the fallen leader out of his boots.[5]

On May 1, 2003, President Bush from the deck of the aircraft carrier USS Abraham Lincoln declared a formal end to the major combat operations in Iraq. The U.S. lead coalition had again defeated the forces of Iraqi and this time had freed the people of Iraq. However, restoring the peace and creating a democratic government in a county that has no recent experience in such a government will be at best a most difficult task.

On September 13, 2003 U.S. and coalition forces operating in the dark of night found Saddam Hussein in a hole beneath the courtyard of a hut near Dawr, a village 10 miles from his hometown of Tikrit. Saddam stayed inside this chamber whenever he perceived a threat. Soldiers were seconds from firing into the hole, or tossing a grenade, when Saddam's upraised hands signaled that he was prepared to surrender. "I am Saddam Hussein. I am the president of Iraq and I am willing to negotiate." One of the solders with an American sense of humor called down to the man in the whole "President Bush sends his regards." President Bush later warned that the danger to Americans in Iraq from the Baath party dead-enders or renewed attacks by foreign fighters will continue. However, the capture of Saddam moves Iraq into a decidedly new phase of the war. Saddam Hussein was consequently tried in an Iraqi court and convicted of crimes against humanity. He was executed by hanging in early January of 2007.

The United States and Britain have the necessary industry but will need the cooperation of many other industrialized countries to complete this monumental task of creating a democracy in the heart of the Middle East. According to President Bush, almost 300,000 Iraqi soldiers and police officers are trained and ready to take over an ever increasing amount of the task to secure the country. The future will tell the world if they are ready for the task of governing their own country, but the balance of political power in both Great Britain and The United States may rest on the outcome.

THE 2004 PRESIDENTIAL ELECTION

President Bush took the oath of office for his second term as president on January 20, 2005. In his inaugural speech, he defined his second term as a fight for freedom in every nation. "The best hope for peace in our world is the expansion of freedom in the entire world." Bush continued by saying, "Across the generations we have proclaimed the imperative of self-government, because no one is fit to be a master, and no one deserves to be a slave. Advancing these ideals is the mission that created our Nation. It is the honorable achievement of our fathers. Now it is the urgent requirement of our nation's security and the calling of our time. Bush continued this theme with a bold new policy statement. "It is the policy of the United States to seek and support the growth of democratic movements and institutions in every nation and culture, with the ultimate goal of ending tyranny in our world."

Bush concluded his address by saying: "When the Declaration of Independence was first read in public and the Liberty Bell was sounded in celebration, a witness said, "it rang as if it meant something." "In our time, it means something still. America, in this young century, proclaims liberty throughout the entire world, and to all the inhabitants thereof. Renewed in our strength, tested but not weary, we are ready for the greatest achievements in the history of freedom."[4] However, the good feelings did not last long as the war in

Iraq dragged on with no end in sight, the President and the Republican Congress was gradually losing the support of many American voters.

THE ELECTIONS OF 2006

On November 6, 2006 voters went to the polls to show their approval or disapproval of the Republican Controlled Congress. In a rout, Democrats won a 51st seat in the Senate and regained total control of Congress after 12 years of near-domination by the Republican Party. One of the key points of voter displeasure was the perceived lack of progress in the war in Iraq. The shift dramatically altered the government's balance of power, leaving President George W. Bush without Republican congressional control to drive his legislative agenda. Democrats hailed the results and issued calls for bipartisanship even as they vowed to investigate administration policies and decisions.

As watershed elections go, this one rivaled the Republican takeover in 1994, which made Newt Gingrich speaker of the House, the first Republican to run the House since the 1950's under President Dwight Eisenhower's administration. This time the shift comes in the midst of an unpopular war, with a Congress scarred by scandal and just two years from a wide-open presidential contest.

Democrats had nine new senators on their side of the aisle as a result of Tuesday's balloting. Six of them defeated sitting Republican senators from Pennsylvania, Ohio, Missouri, Rhode Island, Montana and Virginia. The other three replaced retiring senators from Maryland, Minnesota and Vermont.

In the House, Rep. Nancy Pelosi Democrat from California became the first female Speaker of the House of Representatives. She called for harmony and said Democrats would not abuse their new status. She said she would be "the speaker of the House, not the speaker of the Democrats." She said Democrats would aggressively conduct oversight of the administration, but said any talk of impeachment of Bush "is off the table."

Positioning for the 2008 Presidential and Congressional elections had already begun. In Congress, Democrats were now the party in power and the American voters expect some positive results.

The issue of social security running out of money by 2018 was still not resolved. The democrats will most likely try to increase taxes on social security by increasing the taxable income level to about $200,000 per year. Also, the minimum wage will most likely be increased; however, the remaining question was the outcome of the war in Iraq.

IT'S THE ECONOMY STUPID

In the first quarter of 2008 many economists including Federal Reserve Chairman Ben Bernanke were worried that a recession was eminent in 2008 and perhaps had already started. To avoid a recession or to at least reduce the severity of one, Congress passed and President Bush signed a bill to provide over 100 million in tax rebates to American consumers and tax breaks amounting to about $ 50 million to American businesses. This was in addition to the economic stimulus that was being provided by the war in Iraq. The stimulus package has a political element as well as an economic rational. The new Democratic Led Congress did not want to see a recession during their first term and President Bush did not want to leave office with the country in a recession.

NOTES:

Chapter 25
The Twenty-First Century – The George W. Bush Administration

1. Department of Education, <u>No Child Left Behind Reauthorization of the Elementary and Secondary Education Act,</u> Washington, DC, January 8, 2002.
2. CNN.com, <u>September 11: Chronology of Terror,</u> September 12, 2001.
3. White House News Release, <u>Address to a Joint Session of Congress and the American People,</u> Washington, DC, September 20, 2001.
4. White House News Release, <u>Presidential Address to the Nation,</u> Washington, DC, October 7, 2001.

CHAPTER 18

THE TWENTY FIRST CENTURY: BARACK OBAMA AND DONALD TRUMP

"Nothing is easier or more pathetic than being a critic, because they're people who can't get the job done. But the future belongs for the dreamers, not the critics, the people who follow their heart no matter what the critics say." – Donald J. Trump.

THE ELECTIONS OF 2008

The 2008 presidential elections were held on November 4th. After a long primary campaign, Republican's choose John McCain a long-time Senator from Arizona and a Viet Nam War Hero and Democrats choose Barack Obama a young senator from Illinois. Young and charismatic but with little experience on the national level, Obama smashed through racial barriers and easily defeated John McCain to become the first African-American destined to sit in the Oval Office as America's 44th president. He was the first Democrat to receive more than 50 percent of the popular vote since Jimmy Carter in 1976.

The son of a Kenyan father and a white mother from Kansas, the 47-year-old Obama has had a startlingly rapid rise, from lawyer and community organizer to state legislator and U.S. senator, now just four years into his first term. He is the first senator elected to the White House since John F. Kennedy in 1960. After the longest and costliest campaign in U.S. history, Obama was propelled to victory by voters dismayed by eight years of George W. Bush's presidency and deeply anxious about rising unemployment and home foreclosures and a battered stock market that has erased trillions of dollars of savings for Americans. In the Congressional elections, Democrats fell short of the 60 votes they need to stop filibusters in the Senate and made more modest gains in the House than the leading prognosticators expected.

As president, Obama faces daunting problems. How to fix a financial system no one seems to fully understand. How to defeat terrorist enemies sheltered in the territory of our putative ally Pakistan. How to live up to the high expectations so visible in the cheering and tearful faces of his followers. Do President Obama and the Democrats have a mandate? Obama got a larger percentage than any other Democrat since 1964, and Democrats have congressional majorities comparable to those in Bill Clinton's first two years. But a Democratic policy of increased taxes on high earners seem ill-suited to a country facing a recession.

THE RECESSION OF 2008 AND 2009

The Business Cycle Dating Committee of the National Bureau of Economic Research met by conference call on Friday, November 28, 2008. The committee maintains a chronology of the beginning and ending dates (months and quarters) of U.S. recessions. The committee determined that a peak in economic activity occurred in the U.S. economy in December 2007. The peak marks the end of the expansion that began in November 2001 and the beginning of a recession. The expansion lasted 73 months; the previous expansion of the 1990s lasted 120 months.

A recession is a significant decline in economic activity spread across the economy, lasting more than a few months, normally visible in production, employment, real income, and other indicators. A recession begins when the economy reaches a peak of activity and ends when the economy reaches its trough. Between trough and peak, the economy is in an expansion. The committee viewed the payroll employment measure, which is based on a large survey of employers, as the most reliable comprehensive estimate of employment. This series reached a peak in December 2007 and has declined every month since then. Another common measure of a Recession is two consecutive quarters of negative growth in real GDP. This occurred in the third and fourth quarters of 2008.

The Troubled Asset Relief Program:

On October 2008, President Bush signed into law the Emergency Economic Stabilization Act of 2008. That legislation created the Troubled Asset Relief Program (TARP), which authorizes the Department of the Treasury to purchase or insure up to $700 billion of troubled assets. The term "troubled asset" is defined as:

(A) Residential or commercial mortgages and any securities, obligations, or other instruments that are based on or related to such mortgages, that in each case was originated or issued on or before March 14, 2008, the purchase of which the Secretary determines promotes financial market stability and;
(B) Any other financial instrument that the Secretary, after consultation with the Chairman of the Board of Governors of the Federal Reserve System, determines the purchase of which is necessary to promote financial market stability.

The legislation also requires the Congressional Budget Office (CBO) to prepare an assessment of each of those reports within 45 days of its issuance.

For the remainder of 2008, the Secretary of the Treasury had the authority to purchase $350 billion in assets. The Obama Administration has submitted a plan indicating its intent to use the remaining $350 billion; that funding will become available unless a joint resolution disapproving it is enacted. As of the end of December, 2008 the Treasury had spent $247 billion of the first $350 billion and had plans in place for most of the rest of that half of the funds. Currently the Treasury has had to borrow the full amount disbursed, thereby increasing debt held by the public by $247 billion. Disbursements and commitments so far fall into three categories: capital purchases, loans, and other actions.

1. Capital Purchases: Through June 30, 2009, the Treasury had purchased $203.19 billion in shares of preferred stock and warrants from about 214 U.S. financial institutions through its Capital Purchase

Program (CPP). The largest such transactions involve Citigroup, JP Morgan Chase, and Wells Fargo, at $25 billion each; Bank of America, at $15 billion; and Morgan Stanley and Goldman Sachs, at $10 billion each. Each financial institution that received such funds is required to pay a dividend equal to 5 percent of the government's investment in that institution for the first five years, and 9 percent thereafter. In addition, the Treasury has purchased $40 billion in preferred stock from the American International Group (AIG). That company is required to pay a dividend of 10 percent a year; the shares are redeemable by the company but have no set maturity date.

2. Automotive Industry Financing Program: As of June 30, 2009, $54.15 billion has been disbursed to this program. The Treasury has agreed to lend $18.4 billion to General Motors (GM) and Chrysler. The first loan disbursement of $4 billion was made to GM on December 31; another $4 billion was conveyed to Chrysler on January 2. The Treasury has also committed to disburse another $5.4 billion to GM on January 16 and an additional $4 billion at a later date contingent on the release of the second $350 billion of TARP funding. Finally, the Treasury is set to lend another $1 billion to GM to be used by the company to purchase equity in GMAC. The GM loans are accompanied by warrants, and the Chrysler loan is accompanied by an additional promissory note.

3. Other Actions: The Treasury, the Federal Reserve, and the Federal Deposit Insurance Corporation (FDIC) have, in combination, agreed to guarantee a $306 billion portfolio of assets owned by Citigroup. Through the TARP, the Treasury is responsible for up to $5 billion of potential losses on those securities. Furthermore, the Treasury is responsible for $20 billion in credit protection (against debtors that do not pay because of insolvency or protracted default) for the Federal Reserve's Term Asset-Backed Securities Loan Facility.

The Financial Stability Oversight Board is responsible for reporting the results of the Troubled Asset Relief Program to Congress each quarter. Since TARP was authorized, Treasury has implemented a range of programs aimed at stabilizing the financial system and preserving homeownership. As of June 30, 2010, it had disbursed $385 billion for TARP loans and equity investments, and Treasury has already recouped some of these disbursements. As of June 30, 2010,

Treasury had received almost $25 billion in dividend and interest payments and warrant repurchases and more than $198 billion in repayments.

Table 18-1
TARP Program Disbursements, Repayments, and Additional Proceeds, as of June 30, 2014, (dollars in billions)

Program	Total Cash Disbursed	Repayments	Additional Proceeds
Capital Purchase Program (CPP)	$204.9	$146.9	$17.3
Targeted Investment Program	40.0	40.0	4.3
Automotive Industry Financing Program	79.7	11.2	2.4
American International Group Investments	47.5	0.0	0.0
Home Affordable Modification Program	0.3	N/A	N/A
SBA 7(a) Securities Purchase Program	0.1	<0.1	<0.1
Term Asset-Backed Securities Loan Facility	0.1	0.0	0.0
Public Private Investment Program	12.4	0.4	0.1
Asset Guarantee Program (AGP)2	0.0	0.0	0.6
Totals	$385.0	$198.5	$24.7

The Department of the Treasury reports that as of February 28, 2014, that 98 percent of the total TARP disbursements have been repaid.

Source: Department of the Treasury Web Site: www.treasury.gov

Table 18-1 shows the TARP activity from inception through June 30, 2014. Additional proceeds include dividends from equity securities, interest income from loans and securities, proceeds from repurchases of warrants and warrant preferred stock, and proceeds from warrant auctions. Treasury has sold 2.6 billion shares of Citigroup common stock for $10.5 billion, of which $8.5 billion is included in "Repayments," and $2.0 billion, which represents gains on the sales, is included in "Additional Proceeds."

The American Recovery and Reinvestment Act of 2009

This Act was passed by the 111th Congress and signed into law by President Obama on February 17, 2009. The Act is intended to provide a stimulus to the U.S. economy in the wake of the economic downturn that began in December of 2007. The Act includes federal tax cuts, expansion of unemployment benefits and other social welfare provisions, domestic spending in education, health care, and infrastructure including the energy sector. The major categories and amounts of the Stimulus plan are listed in Table 18-2 below:

The American Recovery and Reinvestment Act of 2009 passed Congress with no Republican votes in the House and only 3 in the Senate. Many Republicans criticized the bill for not providing enough tax relief. Only 36 percent of the stimulus was for tax reductions. Some Democrats argued that the amount of stimulus was not large enough to end the recession. The Congressional Budget is often used by Congress as an authority on budget matters. A February 4, 2009, report by the (CBO) said that while the stimulus would increase economic output and employment in the short run, the gross domestic product would, by 2019, have an estimated net decrease between 0.1% and 0.3% (as compared to the CBO estimated baseline budget) The CBO estimates that enacting the bill would increase federal budget deficits by $185 billion over the remaining months of fiscal year 2009, by $399 billion in 2010, and by $134 billion in 2011.[1]

In a February 11, 2009 letter, CBO Director Douglas Elmendorf noted that there was disagreement among economists about the effectiveness of the stimulus, with some skeptical of any significant effects while others expecting very large effects. The Director said the CBO expected short term increases in gross domestic product and employment. In the long term, the CBO expects the legislation to reduce output slightly by increasing the nation's debt and crowding out private investment. The CBO also noted that other factors, such as improvements to roads and highways and increased spending for basic research and education may offset the decrease in output and that crowding out was a not an issue in the short term because private investment was already decreasing in response to decreased demand.

Table 18-2
Economic Stimulus Plan Distribution of Expenditures

Government Spending Description	$ in billions
Higher education modernization	6
Pell grants	15
Increased unemployment benefits and job training	40
Food stamps	15
Temporary increase in Medicaid matching rate	88
COBRA	39
Preventive care	4
State fiscal relief	79
Local school districts	40
Public housing and energy efficiency	15
Transform energy systems	30
Clearwater, flood control and environmental restoration	19
Modernize federal and other public infrastructure	30
Highway construction	30
Science facilities, research and instruments	10
Weatherize modest-income	6
Law enforcement	4
Healthcare IT	20
Broadband internet access	6
Transit and rail	10
Tax credits and Incentives	281
Total Stimulus Plan Spending	787

THE ELECTIONS OF 2010

November 2, 2010 was not a good day for many Democrats. Record number of voters including seniors cast their votes against Democrats in the Senate, the House of Representatives and Governors across the country. When the dust settled, Republicans had won enough seats to take control of the House, gained six seats in the Senate and nine governorships. The changes are listed below:

Description	Republican	Democratic	Republican Gain
Senate	47	53	6
House	241	193	62
Governors	29	20	9

Note: Two Senators are independents and caucus with the Democrats

Michael Baronet writing in Townhall Magazine offers an historical analysis of what happened in the November elections. According to Barone: The 2010 elections produced results that are unprecedented in the lifetimes of most readers. In nine of the 10 congressional election cycles between 1986 and 2004, no party gained or lost more than 10 seats in the House of Representatives, the one exception being 1994, when Republicans gained 54. Otherwise, the numbers were pretty static. Not so in the three most recent cycles. Democrats gained 31 seats in 2006 and another 23 seats in 2008. Now Republicans have won significantly more than the 39 seats they needed to regain the House majority they lost four years ago.[4]

THE 2012 ELECTION

The election campaign for the President and member of Congress was a grueling one. The contest was between President Obama and businessman and former Governor of Massachusetts W. Mitt Romney. On November 7, 2012, most of the results were in and Barack Obama was elected to serve a second term as President. Also, the Democrats picked up 2 seats in the Senate. The count was 53 Democrats, 45 Republicans and 2 Independents which are expected to caucus with the Democrats. The House of Representatives remained in firm control of the Republicans with 233 seats to the Democrats 193 seats with 9 contests still undecided as of November 8th.

Linda Feldman a staff writer for the Christian Science Monitor offers some suggestions about the Election results in her article: "Does Obama's historic victory give him a mandate?

An outcome that maintains the status quo in Washington guarantees Obama some important advantages. But the 2012 election results also foretell more gridlock, and the president, by not offering a path out of debt and deficit lacks a clear mandate for action.

President Obama burnished his historic legacy by winning a decisive electoral victory – sweeping most of the battleground states – despite high unemployment, sluggish economic growth, and a bitterly partisan atmosphere. The reelection of America's first black president shows that Mr. Obama's triumph four years ago was not a fluke. Not only did Obama emerge the undisputed victor on November 7th over Republican challenger Mitt Romney, albeit with a smaller popular-vote margin than in 2008, he also appears to have pulled along with him a larger majority in the Senate.

Despite predictions of diminished turnout by Obama's core constituencies – blacks, Hispanics, young voters, and women – they delivered again for both the president and the Democratic Party.

Still, 2012 was a markedly different election. Gone is the optimistic tone of 2008. The road ahead is paved with tough choices, amid worsening fiscal conditions. And the scorched-earth quality of the campaign, fueled by unprecedented spending by the campaigns, the parties, and outside groups, has left many Americans gasping for air.

The continuation of the status quo – Democratic president, Democratic Senate, Republican House – foretells more gridlock. And by not offering a detailed prescription for addressing the nation's unsustainable deficits, particularly on entitlement programs, Obama enters a second term without a clear mandate for action.

In his victory speech, Obama sought to provide a moment of lift at the end of a grueling campaign. "The task of perfecting our Union moves forward," the president told his supporters at McCormick Place in Chicago. "It moves forward because of you. It moves forward because you reaffirmed the spirit that has triumphed over war and depression, the spirit that has lifted this country from the depths of despair to the great heights of hope."4

THE ELECTIONS OF NOVEMBER 2014

On November 4, the American voters went to the polls. Before the elections, Democrats held a 55-45 (two Independents caucus with the Democrats) seat advantage in the Senate while Republicans held a 234-201 advantage in the House. With only the Senate runoff election in Louisiana in doubt, Republicans have taken control of the Senate with a gain of 8 seats. Republicans also remained the majority in the House of Representatives and increased their majority by 13 seats. Thus, Senate Republicans will now move into the chairmanship of all Senate committees and thus control the legislative agendas and priorities for those committees. House Republicans will continue to control the chairmanships of their committees. The results of the elections are summarized in the table below:

Republican Controlled Seats	Before Election Seats Controlled	Election Gaines	After Election Seats Controlled
Republican Senate Seats	45	9	54
Republican House Seats	231	16	247

Political commentator Michael Barone provided some observations about the election results.

(1) This was a wave, folks. It will be a benchmark for judging waves, for either party, for years.

(2) In seriously contested races, Republican candidates were generally younger, more vigorous, more sunny and optimistic than Democrats. The contrast was sharpest in Colorado and Iowa, which voted twice for President Obama. Cory Gardner and Joni Ernst seemed to be looking forward to the future. Their opponents grimly championed the stale causes of feminists and trial lawyers of the past.

Democrats see themselves as the party of the future. But their policies are antique. The federal minimum wage dates to 1938, equal pay for women to 1963, access to contraceptives to 1965. Raising these issues now is campaign gimmickry, not serious policymaking.

Democratic leading lights have been around a long time. The party's two congressional leaders are in their 70s. The governors of the two largest Democratic states are sons of former governors who won their first statewide elections in 1950 and 1978.

(3) The combination of Obama's low job approval and Harry Reid's virtual shutdown of the Senate insured a Republican Senate majority.

That left Democrats running for re-election stuck with 95-plus percent Obama voting records. It left them with no independent votes or initiatives to point to. Reid kept Democratic candidates well-stocked with money. But they were not with winning issues.

In summary, this was a repudiation of the big government policies of the Obama Democrats. It was not so much an endorsement of Republicans as it was an invitation to them to come up with better alternative policies.[5]

THE 2017 FEDERAL BUDGET

In May of 2017 Congress passed and President Trump signed the 2017 Omnibus Budget Act funding the Federal government for the remainder of the fiscal year ending September 30, 2017. Congress is continuing to work on the budget for fiscal year 2018. Table 26-3 summarizes the President's 2018 budget outlays and receipts. The budget called for large increases in expenditures and budget deficits in every year through 2022.

Table 18-3

Proposed Federal Budget for 2018 through 2022, Outlays and Receipts. Fiscal Year 2016 is actual data and 2017 is the current budget projection. (Dollars in billions)

Outlays	2016	2017	2018	2019	2020	2021	2022
Defense Spending	585	594	643	665	670	667	663
Other Programs	600	619	601	567	537	506	485
Total Discretionary	1,185	1,213	1,244	1,232	1,207	1,173	1,148
Social Security	910	946	1,005	1,070	1,137	1,205	1,279
Medicare	588	593	582	646	700	756	851
Medicaid	368	378	404	423	439	460	467
Other Programs	561	656	544	597	559	542	559
Total Mandated	2,427	2,573	2,535	2,736	2,835	2,963	3,156
Interest Costs	241	277	315	372	428	481	528
Total Outlays	3,853	4,063	4,094	4,340	4,470	4,617	4,832
Receipts							
Individual Income Taxes	1,546	1,660	1,836	1,935	2,044	2,167	2,293
Corporate Income Taxes	300	324	355	375	401	400	414
Social Security Receipts	810	857	892	931	972	1,027	1,081
Medicare Payroll Taxes	247	258	270	283	297	315	332
Other Insurance and Retirement	58	59	62	63	66	71	75
Other Receipts	307	302	239	227	202	181	195
Total Receipts	3,268	3,460	3,654	3,814	3,982	4,161	4,390
Deficit	585	603	440	526	488	456	442

Source: President Trump's 2018 Proposed Budget – Table S-4

Analysis of the Proposed Federal Budget 2018 through 2022

Defense Spending: From 2016 actual data through 2022 defense spending will increase by $78 billion. These expenditures will include some modernization of military equipment and will peak at $670 billion in 2020.

Other Discretionary Spending: This is mainly the cost of running the agencies of the U.S. Government. From 2016 through 2022 the budget shows a decrease of $115 Billion. This is a start but additional expense cutting is needed to balance the Federal budget in the future.

Social Security Receipts and Outlays: total receipts are budgeted to increase by $5,760 billion from 2017 through 2022. However, Social Security Outlays are budgeted to increase by $6,642 billion for the same period. For the five-year period, Social Security outlays will exceed receipts by $ 882 billion. This is an indication that the government must use the Social Security Trust Funds from 2017 through 2022 to fund Social Security payments. Another option would be to raise the payroll cap on earnings subject to social security tax.

Medicare and Medicaid: The budget shows an increase of $99 billion from 2016 through 2022 for Medicaid payments. President Trump is proposing to eliminate direct federal government payments for Medicaid and instead block granting payments directly to the states. This should slow the growth of Medicaid. Medicare shows and increase of $263 billion over the same period. Some of the Medicare deficit will be mitigated by the premiums seniors pay on their policies, but it will not be nearly enough. Medicare payroll taxes must be increased to keep this program funded for the long-term future.

Other Mandated Programs: These include Federal Employee Retirement and Disability, Unemployment Compensation, Housing Assistance, Veterans Benefits and Other Federal Benefits. One way to reduce spending in these programs is to eliminate retirement benefits for government employees and increase the cap on government contributions to the Thrift Savings Accounts. This would eliminate paying government employees for not working.

Government Deficit Spending and Debt Held by the Public: The deficit is projected to increase by $2,955 billion from 2017 projected expenditures through budgeted year 2022. Total Federal Debt Held by the Public will increase by $2,693 billion from 2017 through 2022. Total debt held by the public is projected to be $17,517 by the end of fiscal year 2022. The increase will result in debt held by the public to be 72.2 percent of the projected Gross Domestic Product versus 77.4 percent in 2017. This is a step in the right direction, but more must be done to balance the federal budget.

Interest on the Gross Federal Debt: Will reach $528 billion by 2022. This will make interest owed on the Federal Debt larger than all other government outlays except for National Defense, Social Security and Medicare. If net interest on the debt were eliminated from the 2022 budget, there would be a budget surplus of $86 billion.

Individual Income Taxes: The budget projects and increase in individual taxes of $747 billion from 2016 through 2022. This includes a tax rate increase on those individuals making over $400 thousand per year that was approved by Congress and signed into law in 2013. Also, corporate income taxes are planned to increase by $114 for the same period. For fiscal year 2022 government receipts are planned to reach $4,390 and still there is a planned deficit of $442 billion. The problem is not the need for additional taxes, the problem is out of control government spending.

THE ELECTIONS OF NOVEMBER 2016

On November 8, the American voters went to the polls to elect a new president. The candidates were Hillary Clinton a Democrat and the wife of Bill Clinton who was president during the 1990's. The Republican candidate was Donald J. Trump a successful Real Estate developer and a television personality for his long running show "The Apprentice." Most of the main street media did not give Mr. Trump a chance to win the election. But he pulled out a convincing victory in the Electoral College Vote. While all the votes had not been counted by mid-November the best guess is that the final tally will be 306 for Donald Trump and 232 for Hillary Clinton.

Republican also held on to their lead in both the House and Senate. Before the elections, Republicans held a 54-46 (two Independents caucus with the Democrats) seat advantage in the Senate while Republicans held a 247-188 advantage in the House. Republicans lost two seats in the Senate but remained in control. Republicans also remained the majority in the House of

Representatives. As a result, Republicans will now control both houses of Congress and the Presidency.

Republican Controlled Seats	Before Election Seats Controlled	Election Gaines	After Election Seats Controlled
Republican Senate Seats	54	(2)	52
Republican House Seats	247	(7)	240

ANALYSIS OF THE 2016 ELECTION RESULTS

Michael Barone a well know political commentator commented on Donald Trump's victory in an article in Townhall.com. Astounding. That's the best word to describe the tumultuous election night and the (to most people) surprise victory of Donald Trump. Hillary Clinton hoped to win with votes of Northeasterners, including those who have moved south along Interstate 95 to North Carolina and Florida (44 electoral votes). Instead, Trump won with votes along the I-94 and I-80 corridors, from Pennsylvania through Ohio and Michigan to Wisconsin and Iowa (70 electoral votes).

This approach was foreseen by Real Clear Politics analyst Sean Trende in his "Case of the Missing White Voters" article series in 2013. Non-college-educated whites in this northern tier, once strong for Ross Perot, gave Barack Obama relatively high percentages in 2008 and 2012. Many grew up in Democratic union households and were willing to vote for the first black president.

Now they seem to have sloughed off their ancestral Democratic allegiance, much as white Southerners did in 1980s presidential and 1990s congressional elections. National Democrats no longer had anything to offer them then. Hillary Clinton didn't have anything to offer northern-tier non-college-educated whites this year.

It didn't help that Clinton called half of Trump supporters "irredeemable" and "deplorable" and infected with "implicit racism." They may have been shy in responding to telephone or exit polls, but they voted in unanticipatedly large numbers, at a time when turnout generally sagged.

At the same time, Clinton was unable to reassemble Obama's 2012 51 percent coalition. Turnout fell in heavily black Philadelphia, Cleveland, Detroit and Milwaukee. Millennial generation turnout was tepid, and Trump carried white millennials by 5 points. Unexpectedly, Trump won higher percentages of Hispanics and Asians than Mitt Romney did in 2012.

Trump's surprise victory, owing much too differential turnout, resembles the surprise defeats, defying most polls, of establishment positions in 2016 a referendum in Britain. In June, 52 percent of Britons voted to leave the European Union -- the so-called Brexit, opposed by most major-party leaders and financial elites.

Something like that seems to have happened here. If you take the pro-establishment coasts -- the Northeast except Pennsylvania, the West Coast -- the vote as currently tabulated was 58-38 percent for Clinton. That's similar to Obama's 60-38 percent margin in these states in 2012.

But the heartland -- roughly the area from the Appalachian ridges to the Rocky Mountains, with about two-thirds of the national vote -- went 52-44 percent for Trump. Trump didn't do much better than Romney, who got 51 percent there. But Clinton got only 44 percent of heartland votes, down from Obama's 47 percent. The Republican margin doubled, from 4 to 8 percent.

British elites responded to Brexit with scorn for their heartland's voters. Those voting for Brexit were "poorly educated, nativist, unsophisticated, racist and unfashionable." You can hear similar invective hurled by American coastal elites (though not, to their credit, Clinton and Obama) at their fellow citizens beyond the Hudson River and the Capital Beltway. "Deplorable" is the least of their insults.

They take glee in noting that Trump ran behind previous Republican nominees among (4 year) college graduates but well ahead among non-college-educated whites. The people who complain about less educated whites voting as a bloc have no complaints about the even larger percentages received by the candidates they favor from black voters. The better approach is to show respect for each voter's decision, however unenlightened you may consider it.

Basic Economics   247

It would be a mistake also to suppose that Trump's Electoral College victory means that Democrats are doomed to defeat because they lost their hold on non-college-educated whites this year. That depends on decisions and events that have not yet occurred.[6]

How Will the Economy Perform under President Trump?

Veteran financial guru Larry Kudlow, who served as the Donald Trump campaign's senior economic adviser, tells Newsmax TV that Donald Trump will live up to his campaign vows to restore prosperity to all Americans and the nation we all love.

"Donald Trump has a very strong economic growth message which is going to be great for the economy and for profits and for businesses large and small," Kudlow, a CNBC senior contributor, said the billionaire real-estate tycoon, who beat Democratic rival Hillary Clinton Tuesday, was successful because he understands the dissatisfaction of "ordinary middle-class folk." Kudlow said Trump's economic message temporarily got lost causing an hours-long market collapse as election results were tallied. "Don't ask me why but it did. It was kind of like Brexit. The markets collapsed and then they started coming back very strong when they realized that that was a good idea," said Kudlow, who under President Ronald Reagan was the associate director for economics and planning, Office of Management and Budget, Executive Office of the President, where he was engaged in the development of the administration's economic and budget policy.

"With Mr. Trump, you're going to have across the board tax cuts, you're going to end Obamacare, which is a prosperity killer and a healthcare killer, you're going to take the handcuffs off energy, you're going to walk back all these regulations and you're going to stop the government from taking over the economy. That's a powerful message," Kudlow said.

Trump "understood that they were angry and that the establishment in Washington and elsewhere was not delivering. He understood that they wanted change and he understood that they wanted to drain the swamp, get rid of the corruption, stop the corporate cronyism," Kudlow said.

"He understood that instinctively and he knew that people were not willing to give up the American dream. I think it was effective and I think he hit it exactly right. He just understood the American people in a way that no other political figure has understood it."

Kudlow said he believes the global stock markets are ripe for investment. "I would be buying all these markets right now. I'm not a trader, Lord knows, but I would be buying it because again, fundamentally, Trump has a very strong pro-growth message and the world needs growth," he said.

"If the United States goes the wrong way, as I think it has in recent years, the rest of the world tends to follow. But if the U.S. goes the right way, the incentive way, the tax cut way, then the world will follow," Kudlow said. "With things like trade disputes and the latest arguments, I think those can be worked out in a very cooperative and positive manner,"[7]

THE FUTURE, THE ECONOMY AND THE PEOPLE

Will the combination of low interest rates, the troubled asset relief plan and the fiscal stimulus plan get the economy growing again? With interest rates lower than any time since the Kennedy administration and fiscal stimulus including tax cuts and increased government spending, the economy did, as predicted by the Federal Reserve, start to grow by the end of 2010 and throughout 2011 and 2012. In 2013 the economy continued to grow but only at 1.9 percent for Real GDP. However, there may be a new threat, inflation. Total federal government outlays according to the President's 2018 Budget is planned to increase by $1,192 billion from 2015 through 2020, the Treasury will find it more difficult to sell government bonds. This could weaken the value of the dollar, lead to higher interest rates and the crowding out of some private sector investment.

America is strong; its manufacturing ability is still second to none. All the fundamentals are still their including the financial markets, which have recovered from the recession of 2008. The war on terrorism will probably not end any time soon, but their threat to the average American should be substantially reduced as the terrorists are hunted down and brought to justice. In Iraq, there is a real chance of a lasting Democratic form of Government. By the end of December 2011 America had removed all troops from Iraq. Is the American trained Iraq military ready to take over the security of that country? Only time will tell, but they are off to a good start. Also, the U.S. is committed to leaving Afghanistan by 2014 leaving only a small contingency of armed forces behind to train that county's army.

Tables 28-4 A shows that real Gross Domestic Product for the last three quarter of 2016 and the first quarters of 2017. During this time, real GDP increased by only 1.6 percent versus the 2nd quarter of 2016. Personal consumption expenditures increased by only 1.7 percent. Gross private investment increased by 3.9 percent. The increase in investment spending will most likely result in an increase of Real GDP during the remaining three quarters of 2017.

Table 18-4 B shows real GDP as expenditures on an annual basis. real GDP was $16,349 for 2016 compared to $15,962 million for 2015 and increase of 2.4 percent. This indicates a slow but steady growth during 2016. With the steady improvement of 2016 over 2015 a most likely forecast for all of 2016 is a moderate growth rate of real GDP of between 2.0 and 2.5 percent. This could improve during 2017 as the pro-growth policies of the new administration are put into place. The key to improved growth in 2017 is the enactment of President Trump's tax reduction plan. For President Trump's 2018 budget proposal defense spending is planned to increase by $49 billion over 2017. Also, other discretionary programs will see a budget reduction of $18 billion.

Table 18-4 A
Real Gross Domestic Product for 2015 by Quarter
($ in Billions)

Description	2nd quarter 2016	3rd quarter 2016	4th quarter 2016	1st Quarter 2017	% change 2nd 2016 vs, 1st 2017
Personal Consumption expenditures	11,485	11,569	11,670	11,680	1.7
Gross Private Domestic Investment	2,784	2,804	2,868	2,894	3.9
Net Exports	-559	-522	-605	-603	7.9
Government Consumption Expenditures	2,873	2,876	2,880	2,871	-.1
Real Gross Domestic Product	16,583	16,727	16,813	16,842	1.6

Source: BEA National Income and Product Accounts April 2017 Table 1.1.6

Note: BEA Table 1.1.6 contains a residual line which is the difference between total real GDP and the sum of the detailed lines. The residual amounts are small and have been added in this table to the Government Consumption Expenditures line.

Table 18-4 B

Real Gross Domestic Product 2016 vs. 2015 ($ in Billions)

Description: GDP as Expense	Year 2015	Year 2016	% Increase 2016 vs. 2015
Personal Consumption expenditures	11,215	11,522	2.7
Gross Private Domestic Investment	2,869	2,825	-1.5
Net Exports	(540)	(563)	4.3
Government Consumption Expenditures	2,853	2,878	.9
Real Gross Domestic Product	16,397	16,662	1.6

Source: BEA National Income and Product Accounts April 2017, Table 1.1.6

SUMMARY AND CONCLUSION

Even with the current slow growth of Real GDP of 1.6 percent, we are still a great nation and we will prevail. America will continue to be the economic leader of the free world in the twenty-first century, not because of its buildings and equipment or government, but because of the will of its people to live and prosper in a free society. Today even with the 4.4 percent unemployment rate reported by the Department of Labor in April 2017, America is an economic colossus, more competitive, more innovative, and more technologically advanced than Japan and Europe.

An indication of the dynamic growth of American is the recent boom in U.S. crude oil supply. This is the result of an American invention called hydraulic fracturing that is a practice among companies that drill underground for oil and natural gas. In hydraulic fracturing, drillers inject millions of gallons of water, sand, salts and chemicals into shale deposits or other sub-surface rock formations at extremely high pressure, to fracture the rock and extract the raw fuel. The fracturing process is used to boost production at 90 percent of all oil and gas wells in the United States, according to the Interstate Oil and Gas Compact Commission. The election of successful business executive Donald Trump in 2016 may even encourage more growth over the next four years.

Ronald Reagan knew why America was so prosperous. Aids close to Reagan have said that whenever Reagan was asked whether he was responsible for the American resurgence, he would reply, "Oh no, it wasn't me. The American people did it. They deserve the credit."

NOTES:

Chapter 18
Economics in the Twenty-First Century – the Barack Obama Administration

1. Congressional Budget Office, <u>Official CBO Report to the Senate Budget Committee</u>, February 4, 2016.
2. Obama, Barack, <u>Proposed 2017 Budget</u>, March 5, 2016
3. House speaker Paul Ryan's response to the President's 2017 budget proposal, January, 2017
4. Baronet, Michael, <u>Voters Reject Obama's Big-Government Ambitions</u>, Townhall.com, November 4, 2010.
5. Baronet, Michael, <u>The Shrinkage of the Obama Majority</u>, Townhall.com November 7, 2014

www.ingramcontent.com/pod-product-compliance
Lightning Source LLC
Chambersburg PA
CBHW082323220526
45470CB00008B/2384